They Also Served

A PICTORIAL ANTHOLOGY OF CAMP FOLLOWERS THROUGH THE AGES

THEY ALSO SERVED

George and Anne Forty

MIDAS BOOKS, SPELDHURST, KENT

First published in 1979 by
Midas Books
12 Dene Way, Speldhurst,
Tunbridge Wells, Kent TN3 0NX

ISBN 0 85936 101 2

Designed and produced by
Mechanick Exercises, London

Set in Monotype Garamond by
South Bucks Typesetters Ltd
Beaconsfield

Printed in Great Britain
by Tonbridge Printers Ltd
Peach Hall Works
Tonbridge Kent

Bound by
Mansell, Witham

This book is dedicated to the thousands of unremembered and unsung camp followers who have steadfastly followed armies throughout history, bringing a little comfort and companionship to the soldiers of every nation.

Contents

Illustrations

Tents occupied by Soldiers' wives
and families, Rifle Brigade, Aldershot
31 July 1856. (From a drawing by
G H Thomas in the Royal Collection
Windsor Castle)

The Marquess of Granby aiding a sick soldier. (Edward Penny RA 1714-1791)

The Recruiting Sergeant and his
contented mates, 1780

Foreword

I have a confession to make, a secret to reveal, and this book gives me an opportunity to get it off my chest. Thirty five years ago in a small Tunisian town called Medjez-el-Bab, I fell in love with a camp follower. I tried to resist her, but her big brown eyes and her sweet affectionate nature were too much for me.

She shared my rations and, I must admit, my bed, which at that time consisted of a few blankets and a ground sheet in the back of a 15 cwt. army truck. Liaisons of this kind were forbidden by army regulations and I had to go to great lengths to conceal our relationship. We were blissfully happy for several weeks, Fifi and I, until one unforgettable day when a sergeant from the Lancashire Fusiliers took her from me. It happened when I was away collecting our rations. This hulking cook sergeant, I was told later, saw Fifi sitting near the truck and chatted her up. Moments later she went off with him and I saw her no more. Admittedly, the mess tin full of meat and vegetable stew which I brought back was not as appetising as the juicy ham bone the sergeant had been carrying, but I shall never trust a black and white mongrel bitch again.

There were countless Fifis and Fidos to be found with army units wherever I served during the war, and many orphaned youngsters, wearing cut-down uniforms and boots many sizes too big for them, found jobs for themselves in the big British and American Army depots which sprang up all over Italy in wartime. Adopted and made a fuss of and then abandoned, albeit regretfully, as units packed up and moved on, we must have left behind a legacy of hatred amongst some of those kids.

Many of the other kinds of camp followers mentioned in this vastly entertaining book crossed my path during my army days. I remember hot buttered scones and home-made jam in a Church of Scotland canteen in Dunblane, mugs of hot tea from a mobile Church Army canteen near Campobasso in Southern Italy, and egg and chips and a pint of vermouth – yes, a *pint* – in the Royal Palace in Naples, where the NAAFI had established itself. I can still remember the sound of my army boots clattering up and down the magnificent marble staircases and the uneasy feeling of vandalism they inspired in me.

I have also, in my role as an entertainer, been a camp follower myself and still enjoy doing the odd tour of Service Units whenever possible. Whether I enjoy it just because I'm reliving vicariously my own seven years as a soldier I'm not quite sure, but there is something in me, as there must have been in all the other camp followers in history, which reponds to the beating of a drum, the jingle of harness, the clatter of mess tins in the cookhouse and forms the tear in my eye when the Last Post is sounded.

HARRY SECOMBE

Introduction

There have been camp followers of one type or another ever since there have been soldiers, although over the years the reasons for their presence with the troops have in some instances changed considerably.

Webster's International Dictionary defines a camp follower as: 'a civilian that follows or takes up lodging near a military unit for the purpose of attending or exploiting military personnel'. That definition covers a very wide range of professions, from wife and mother to war reporter and war artist; from prostitute to psalm singing evangelist; from culinary expert to camp entertainer. They have provided soldiers with anything and everything from cups of tea to carnal delights, although it is the colourful image of the latter which is usually taken to represent the whole gamut.

If one uses the term 'Camp Follower' then eyebrows are raised and the average listener, with a knowing look on his face, expects to hear a risqué story. Of course there were, are still and presumably always will be, *that* type of camp follower. And please do not think too badly of them either, because in their own special way they have provided comfort of the most basic kind just when it was most needed.

In Roman times the harsh discipline of the legions made out of camp attractions all the more alluring, and as a result, small villages grew up outside the walls of their forts. These villages were inhabited by soldiers' wives (both official and unofficial) their families, veterans and retired soldiers, and by civilian entrepreneurs who provided food and drink in shops, bars, and brothels, thereby catering for the basic needs of the 'universal soldier'. Examine any overseas garrison of the present day, belonging to any nation's military forces, and you will find that the situation is remarkably similar.

We shall look first at camp followers en masse, that is to say, as members of baggage trains, where the followers and the troops they accompanied were mobile; and then at the more static conditions of camps and settlements. Following this opening chapter, we have tried to examine each type of follower one at a time. This has been done with the liberal use of photographs and paintings collected from a wide variety of sources, and by anecdotes and stories from the vast range of military literature which contains references to these fascinating people. Space permits us to deal only with a cross section, but we hope that it is a reasonably accurate sample of the whole. No doubt some readers will disagree with the fact that we have deliberately included, as camp followers, the Red Cross, SSAFA, the YMCA, Toc H, the Church Army and the other wonderful voluntary workers who have done so much for our soldiers over the years. For their part, all these organisations have said that they are very happy to be included and the profound effect they have had in making a soldier's life not quite so 'terrible 'ard' cannot be over-emphasised.

The camp following scene, like the history of warfare, is a vast subject and we can only hope to scratch the surface in this short book. Some types of followers – such as the tailor and the army agent – are not applicable to all armies, hence our inability to give truly worldwide examples. The more prosperous and industrialised a country, then the more the state provides for its soldiers and the less work there is for private initiative. Inevitably we have had to skip great chunks of history, to alight here and there in order to give examples of a particular type of follower. In some chapters, for example, when discussing servants, we have chosen to concentrate on one army and on one period of history. But this book is designed only to be a pot-pourri and readers are recommended to delve deeply into the select bibliography, should they wish to find out more about a particular type of follower.

We have many, many people to thank for their kindness and help in producing both written and photographic material, like our good American friends Colonel and Mrs Wally Steiger and Colonel and Mrs Byron Marsh. Most of their names appear in the text or captions, but in case we have missed out any of them, may we offer our sincere thanks to everyone who has helped us. We would particularly like to thank the National Army Museum, the Imperial War Museum, the Ministry of Defence Library, Bradford Metropolitan Library and the other official and voluntary bodies, both in the UK and the USA, who have so generously provided much of our background material.

GEORGE and ANNE FORTY

Bradford, West Yorkshire
March 1979

Baggage Trains and Camps

BAGGAGE TRAINS

'Advancing on their heels strayed a ragged regiment five times the length of the military column, emitting a babel that was startling after the quietness of the soldiers. The syces came riding the officers' spare ponies and driving their gharries. The stately upper servants on their neglected hacks led the lower servants in liveried array; then followed the tent-pitchers, the cooks, the grass cutters, the sweepers and the fat and lean hangers-on, the water-carriers, the camel drivers screaming at their thousands of burdened camels. . . . the hundreds of squeaking bullock carts bearing the wives and families of the angry drivers piled high on the military baggage, the native dogs diving and snarling everywhere, an elephant here and there plodding amiably under a mountain of tents and furniture. This was not the end; behind these the licensed shopkeepers and pedlars with their families and carts scurried hopefully, eager to set up their street bazaar stalls at the end of each march.'[1]

That is how E E P Tisdall, the biographer of Fanny Duberly, wife of Henry Duberly paymaster of the 8th Royal Irish Hussars and herself a brave and determined camp follower, described the baggage train of the Rajputna column to which the regiment was attached during the latter part of the Indian Mutiny. How typical this scene must have been, because from ancient times, as the quotation from the Apocrypha at the beginning of this chapter testifies, until the 'total' war of this century, armies usually travelled with a mass of camp followers.

The Persian Army of King Xerxes, for example, in BC486, when on a regular expedition into enemy territory, took along enormous quantities of food and supplies, as well as many servants and slaves. This even included boiled water from the holy River Choaspes, which was carried in silver vessels on mule-drawn wagons for royal use only. The higher officials and the 'Immortals' – the king's select bodyguard, whose numbers were never allowed to drop below ten thousand, a substitute always being ready to replace any Immortal falling sick or being killed – were allowed to bring with them all their own food, and their servants, even their concubines, on vast numbers of wagons, camels and other baggage animals.

An exception to the rule in ancient times were the Romans. They had, of course, some camp followers, cooks and a few slaves, together with a small baggage train, but as the legions normally lived off the land when in enemy territory, they did not need to carry vast quantities of supplies, a stratagem which Napoleon also used to increase the mobility of his army many years later. In addition, the Roman soldiers themselves were their own architects, masons, engineers, road

[1] *Mrs Duberly's Campaigns* by E E P Tisdall

French troops on the march by
C C P Lawson

builders, 'hewers of wood and drawers of water'. It was only after they had conquered a territory and found it necessary to build and garrison forts, that they grew their camp following 'tail'.

As we shall see later, Roman soldiers were for many years actively discouraged from getting married by the simple expedient of declaring any issue from such marriages to be bastards. The Trajan Column, which stands amid the ruined arcades of the Basilica Ulpia in Rome, shows the Roman legions on the march during the great wars fought by Trajan's army against the people of Dacia between AD101-106. The column's outer surface takes the form of a ribbon about 3ft wide and 670ft long, twisted round in 23 spirals. The spirals cover 400 slabs which are carved with reliefs containing more than 2,500 figures among whom few true camp followers appear.

Graham Webster, in his book *The Roman Army*, gives this description of the purposeful and well ordered appearance of the Roman Army on the march: 'First went the auxiliary cavalry, advancing as a screen on the front and flanks to prevent any surprise attack. . . . Then marched the auxiliary infantry followed by the engineers and surveyors responsible for setting out the camp. Behind them were the road constructors . . . then the carts and wagons of the supply train, guarded by cavalry. Following this train came the commander with his bodyguard in front of the legionary cavalry, then the siege train and heavy artillery and finally the legions in ranks six deep behind their standards and trumpeters, with centurions marching in the rear. Straggling behind were the camp followers with the baggage, borne by mules and finally a strong rearguard of auxiliary infantry and cavalry.'

How different from the armies of Charlemagne, when a warrior had to bring enough food to last for the whole campaign, plus all his own clothing and weapons. This meant each man bringing a wagonload, because his horse alone could not carry enough for his needs.

In the Crusades, a large portion of the supplies needed for the journey to the Holy Land had to be carried in scores of wagons, which were accompanied by a mass of people. A royal army of the time on the march represented a complete household removal, as the king would have to take his treasure with him and perhaps even his archives.

The scene at a halt on the way was like an episode from the almost contemporary Bayeux Tapestry, finished fifteen years earlier: 'Open-air kitchens were organised, where great cooking pots, slung from poles resting on tripods, bubbled over the fires; other dishes simmered gently over the heat of braziers. Oxen, sheep and pigs were killed to provide joints for the long wooden spits. While the cooks were busy in the background, tables were being laid for the gentry. These would be trestle tables, similar to those used in the houses of the time. The table as a fixture was unknown in the Middle Ages, and before a meal could be served it was necessary first to "set the table". Cloths were spread on which bowls and knives were laid. But most people had to eat as best they could, squatting or kneeling, and dipping bread or biscuits into their bowls of soup. They had to drink water from the streams and only occasionally for some celebration got a mug or two of wine from the casks carried along with the barrels of oil and salted fish in the baggage wagons.'[1]

Campaigning in India in the 18th century was performed in even greater comfort if the size of the baggage trains is any yardstick, when there were roughly ten followers to every fighting soldier. An army on the plains of India resembled a moving city, so great were the numbers of camp followers. For example, the baggage train of the column which took Seringapatan in 1799 advanced for over 100 miles in a hollow square which had a frontage of three miles and a depth of seven! Within the square were 200,000 bullocks, to say nothing of elephants, camels, horses and asses.

[1] *The Crusaders* by Regine Pernoud

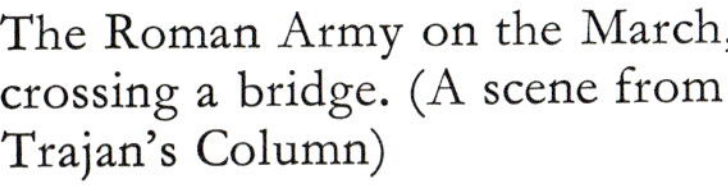

The Roman Army on the March, crossing a bridge. (A scene from Trajan's Column)

Baggage Wagon The British Army on the move in the Peninsular. Two soldiers' wives and a sick private travel on a baggage wagon, note also the dog under the wagon. (From an etching by J A Atkinson, published in 1807)

'We need an extraordinary assemblage of men, women and children, ponies, mules, asses and bullocks and carts laden with all sorts and kinds of conceivable and inconceivable things: grain, cloth, sweetmeats, shawls, slippers, tools for the turners, the carpenter and blacksmiths, goods for the tailors and cobblers, the perfumers, armourers, milk-girls and grass cutters: mooches must work the leather, puckulias carry our water, while nagurchees will supervise the travelling canteen. What a sea of camels! What guttural gurgling groanings in the long throats of salacious and pugnacious animals! What a resounding of sticks, as some throw away their loads and run away, tired servants often getting slain or miserably leaving the column, thousands of camels dying, not only from fatigue but from ill-usage and being always overloaded. Such is the picture of an army in India; Smithfield market alone can rival it.'[1]

A REGIMENT ON THE MOVE A British regiment on the move between home stations in the late 18th and early 19th centuries must still have presented quite a spectacle, despite the absence of colourful Indian servants. Here is how Mrs Fitzmaurice, wife of an officer in the Rifle Brigade, described a normal everyday move in Ireland in 1827, in her book _Recollections of a Rifleman's Wife_: 'It was on a clear frosty morning in March that I first saw a regimental move. The men assembled in marching order in the barrack-square; the baggage, which always comprises women and children, moved off first. The common Irish car, a sort of platform without any sides, and knocked together in the rudest manner imaginable, is very different to any vehicle we have in England; a raw-boned ragged horse is tackled to this with ropes, and the costume of the man or boy who runs by the side completes the picture. On these cars are packed, one above another, all the chests, boxes, and casks belonging to the regiment; and in every interstice is perched a woman with two or three children, and sometimes an invalid soldier who is unable to walk. These poor creatures sometimes fall off in the course of a long day's march, from cold or weariness; but if a child drops, the carman, as a matter of course, picks him up and hands him to his mother at the top of a pile of boxes, observing, "Sure, and isn't he a hard little chap that, ma'am?" Then follow the non-commissioned officers' wives and children, a degree better accommodated, as their cars do not carry baggage; and then the soldiers in companies, with their officers either walking or riding by them, and preceded by the band.

[1] _Mooltan_ by J Dunlop, MD

26

The Relief of Lucknow by G Jones (1786-1869). On 17 November 1857, Sir Colin Campbell relieved the Residency at Lucknow, it then took three days to move the sick and women out under constant fire from the mutineers. 'Overhearing some malcontents criticise the inadequate transport, Sir Colin, turning in his saddle, rebuffed them. "Ladies – women, I mean – you ought to be thankful that you have got out with your lives for I do not know how it might have been in two hours more with you!" ' (From *The Indian Mutiny* by Richard Collier)

I watched them slowly passing under the old archway of the castle, and winding up the hill, through which they defiled. In an hour after we were ourselves in motion, and from that time to this I have never wished to revisit Clare Castle.

'We passed the regiment, as they were halting on the road, about half-way to Limerick, and very picturesque the green jackets looked: some were sitting, others leaning on their arms, all ready to start at the sound of the bugle. While they occupied one side of a rising ground, the 99th, who were to relieve us at Clare, came up the other, with a similar train of baggage etc. It is, perhaps, unfair to compare men who were near the end of a long march to those who were but beginning, but I could not help contrasting the clean, soldier-like appearance and regular movement of the Rifle men, with the soiled uniforms and tarnished ornaments of the straggling parties of Her Majesty's 99th.'

Things in India, however, had changed little 30 years later, when the Officers' Mess of the 8th Hussars still needed 70 camels to carry its mess gear alone! But it must not be imagined that all British armies were so well endowed. In 1854, when the 1st Battalion Coldstream Guards, left London en route for the Crimea, each soldier carried on his person all the equipment with which he would live and fight on the field of battle. There were no tents, no proper stores and no medical

Cawnpore: The Passage of the Ganges by G Jones (1786-1869). The column from Lucknow, about six miles long, reached the bridge of boats across the Ganges about 5.30pm on 29 November 1857, 'the dust so thick about the heads of horses and riders that those who made part of it could not see a man a yard away . . . Indian servants, impressive beneath turbans of scarlet and gold, curvetting Arabs, lances dipping in the evening light, oxen, soldiers limping as if they walked on nails, palanquins, camels, children in bullock carts wailing lustily, litters bearing the wounded, red-curtained as always, raw stumps hanging over the sides, like torn butcher's meat, ammunition tumbrils, elephants. . . .' (From *The Indian Mutiny* by Richard Collier)

supplies. 'Following the wagons, also in the decent obscurity of the back streets, a sparse but miscellaneous collection of camp followers shambled along – decrepit old pensioners whose ostensible purpose was to remove the wounded from the battlefield, but who were more likely to be in need of assistance themselves long before they got there. There were some women too, of not particularly prepossessing appearance. They also had an ostensibly administrative purpose but in practice their part in the campaign was unlikely to be confined to cooking and washing.'[1]

The 20th century has seen a return to the ordered efficiency and organisation of the Roman Army, with the soldiers themselves entirely responsible for their own administrative services and supplies whilst on operations. Gone are the colourful crowds of hangers on, in modern war they would be blasted to pieces and would impede rather than assist the fast moving, thoroughly professional and highly trained soldiers of today. Camp followers and baggage trains are gone forever – or have they? Both world wars this century have seen some delightful exceptions to the rule, like the irrepressible Red Cross mobiles, or the NAAFI and YMCA canteen wagons, which doggedly followed the troops everywhere, even serving tea to the enemy on some occasions! Or the perfumed and highly unwarlike mobile brothels which accompanied the Italian Army in North Africa in 1940. Some of the scenes from the battlefields of the Yom Kippur war of October 1973 could perhaps qualify, when the Israeli Army, undoubtedly one of the most efficient in the world today, used taxis and civilian buses to get their soldiers up to the front line and one infantry unit even drove across Sinai on a milk float!

[1] *Crimean Blunder* by Peter Gibbs

Oxen drawn carts of supplies are seen here in the market square, Johannesburg, circa 1890. (how it has altered!)

'As Israel drove to war through the gathering dusk that Saturday afternoon, it looked like some "transport through the ages" tableau: commandeered private cars; aging buses; bread vans; removal trucks; the large open vans known as Tnuva trucks, after the dairy organisation that runs them. Men drove themselves to the front. One of the *Sunday Times* reporters on Golan later saw an abandoned Dormobile with a cello in the back – its owner had been playing in a symphony concert away from home and drove straight to his unit. The roads began to jam with traffic. The Arab Service Stations in east Jerusalem – open as usual on Yom Kippur – did a roaring trade. By the roadside soldiers were thumbing lifts, the more devout still wearing their prayer caps and shawls and clutching packets of sandwiches to eat when the fast of Yom Kippur ended – though the rabbis had hastily blessed food and transport for the war effort.'[1]

To be fair, that scene cannot really be likened to a normal baggage train of camp followers, for when a nation fights for its very existence, then every man, woman and child must give their all and every means of transport be used to the full.

[1] *The Yom Kippur War* by the Insight Team of the *Sunday Times*

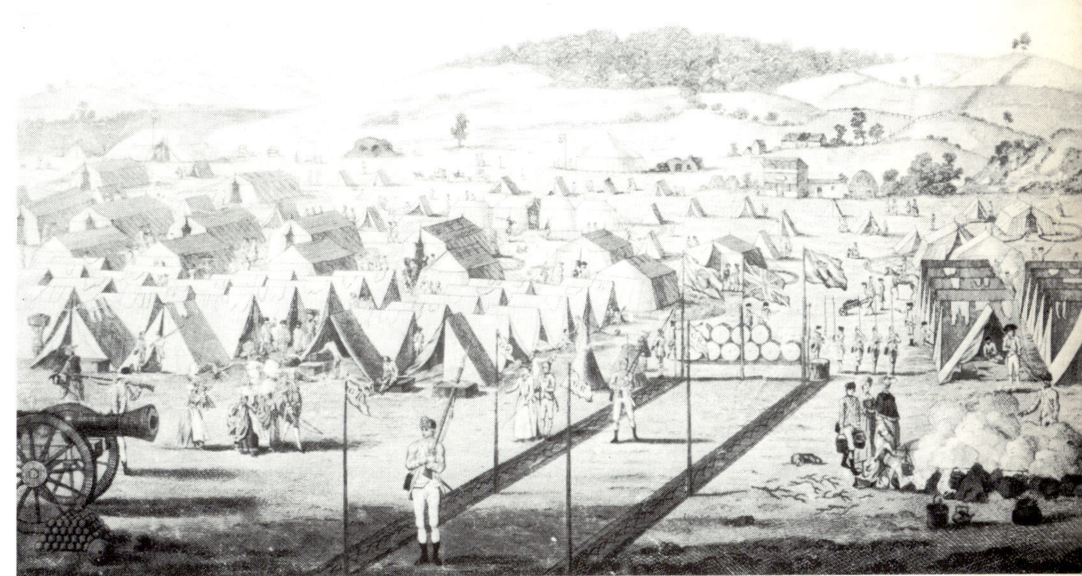

A view of the camp at Cox Heath, near Maidstone, Kent, 1778, showing soldiers on and off duty, sutling houses, kitchens etc.

SETTLEMENTS, CAMPS AND TOWNS

When the Roman Army halted for the night whilst on the march through enemy territory, they would put up their leather tents, usually carried on the pack-horses of the baggage train, one for each section of eight men which was called a 'contubernium' or tent party. They would dig a ditch and a turf rampart around the closely packed encampment with the camp followers well inside the defences. But when a more permanent camp had to be established and a fort built, then outside its walls would grow up a 'vicus' or village of camp followers, who went by the collective name of 'cannabae', literally 'the assembly of Roman citizens who live in the camp huts'. The settlement might become an important administrative centre and thus obtain the status of a 'Colonia', where the prosperous inhabitants would live in luxurious town houses, and there would be temples, baths and market halls. Not all lived outside the fort, however. The legate (the commander of a legion), auxiliary commanders, legionary tribunes and other fairly senior officers, were allocated houses of considerable size within the military establishment, if it were large enough to warrant such senior officers' presence. Centurions and equivalent officers only got single quarters for themselves alone, so their families, when they accompanied them on a posting, must have lived outside the walls.

A typical, small vicus is at Vindolanda, which lies just to the south of Hadrian's Wall, on the Stanegate road which ran from modern Carlisle to Corbridge and was, circa AD95, the frontier line some 30 years before the Wall itself was built further to the north.

The archaeologist Robin Birley has devoted a great amount of his working life to the Vindolanda site and has made some fascinating discoveries. Until his work at Vindolanda there was a popular misconception that the north of England was little more than an armed camp throughout the period of the Roman occupation of Britain. As he explains in the introduction to his book *Civilians on the Roman Frontier*, it was thought to be 'a grim military zone, where the hills and moors, windswept and foggy, were guarded by lonely legionaries against the ever present threat of Pictish invasion'. He goes on to explain how the present day tourist can see only what remains of Roman military engineering in the shape of 'knee-high walls projecting from well-tended lawns of the Department of the Environment. In the sad little Museums along the wall, the tombstones, altars and dedication slabs of the men who built and garrisoned the frontier stare impassively at the visitors. The might of Rome appears to have been blunted in these northern hills, and the sympathy of the tourist is all on the side of the invader'. However, this is not really the true situation. The Roman army arrived in the Brigantian hills of what are now the northern counties of England in the AD70s, and within 10 years the first permanent forts with turf ramparts and timber buildings had been constructed at key points, such as the river crossings at Carlisle and Corbridge. 300 years later Roman Army units were still in occupation of the land. As Robin Birley explains: 'Our knowledge of armies, ancient and modern, has taught us that whenever a military force has to settle down in a foreign land for a long spell of duty, however hostile the native inhabitants might be, they have soon attracted a considerable following of civilians. Before long

Soldiers eating in camp, circa 1803, note the scavenging dog under the serving table

A camp kitchen, Chobham Camp, 1853, by E M Ward

Votadinian and Brigantian tribesmen and tribeswomen must have been rubbing shoulders with their foreign invaders, drawn together by the spell of the "pax Romana" and the lure of Roman army pay and equipment.'

And how different is Vindolanda from the sites and museums which he mentions. A visit there would surely convince anyone that here had existed a thriving little community. One need only stand in the middle of the painstakingly excavated village with its shops, taverns and even a tourist 'hotel', or under the shadow of a recently constructed section of wall and turret built as faithfully as the Romans built the original Wall; or, inside the splendid museum among the everyday objects which Robin Birley and his helpers have found there (such as women's hair pins found in the drain holes of the soldiers' bath house inside the fort – the mind boggles with thoughts of how they got there!), to be able to imagine oneself back in those early days.

Moving thousands of miles westwards across the Atlantic and most of the American continent and advancing in time to the 19th century, one finds another frontier army with not too dissimilar problems and living conditions to those which faced the Roman legions. The 'battered cavaliers of the Indian wars' as they have been described, also built hundreds of forts to guard the frontier, tented camps initially, followed by wooden and in some cases brick structures, which have been the birthplaces of many now famous American cities and towns. Here is how one young recruit described his first fort: 'The locality was all that could be desired; the Post everything undesirable. Huts of logs and round stones, with flat dirt roofs that in summer leaked, and brought rivulets of liquid mud: in winter the hiding place of the tarantula and the centipede, with ceilings of "condemned" canvas; windows of four and six panes, swinging on doorlike hinges (the walls were not high enough to allow them to slide upward); low, dark and uncomfortable. Six hundred miles from the railroad . . . with nothing to eat but the government rations – beef, bacon, coffee, sugar, rice, pepper, salt and vinegar – together with a few cans of vegetables divided pro rata, old Fort Bayard was the

Bivouac of Cossacks near Amsterdam, 1815 by J Van Ravensway

"final jumping off place" sure enough, I thought, as I rode into it in the summer of 1871.'[1]

Into these spartan, harsh and dismal surroundings came, as well as the soldiers, the inevitable camp followers, the wives and children of the officers and some of the enlisted men, the sutlers, the Indian scouts, the whores, the gamblers and all the rest, drawn together for the very same reasons that drew the ancient Britons to Vindolanda. The wives were perhaps the ones who had the most profound effect upon the life of the military community with their 'feminine touch'. We will be examining the lives of some of these brave and determined women later, such as the daintily bred New York belle who, having put her beautiful new Oriental carpets on the hard packed dirt floor of her log cabin and hung white curtains at the windows, had everything ruined a few days later when a rainstorm swept a tide of mud through her doors, leaving the cabin in filthy disarray.

The end of WW2 has seen probably the largest movement of groups of camp followers into other countries that has ever taken place in history. When Germany was divided between the victorious Allies, each was required to occupy its zone with adequate forces who, certainly in the West anyway, were soon accompanied by their families. The emergence of West Germany and the NATO Alliance has not greatly altered the situation, there are still large numbers of dependants in Germany, for example, from the United States and Great Britain. And these families need all the normal day to day living requirements of shops where they

[1] 'A Soldier's Memoirs' by Frederick E Phelps, as quoted in *Bluecoats and Redskins* by Robert M Utley

The Officers' Lines of the Eleventh
Hussars, Eshowe, Zululand, circa
1890

can buy their own national foods, schools for their children, hospitals and so on.

Of course some would say that the 'palmy' days are over, no longer are the families able to get cheap servants who would clean and scrub for a few cigarettes, bars of soap or chocolate. The German economy is now one of the strongest in the world and so the camp followers have their own monetary problems, but it is still a good life. Certainly the majority of army wives, school teachers, or the managers of the military shops belonging to the British NAAFI (Navy, Army, Air Force Institutes) or the American AAFES (Army and Air Force Exchange Service) would not change it for a home posting.

For soldiers of the British Army in Germany – the British Army of the Rhine or just 'BAOR' as it is called – there is now the strange anomaly of living abroad and yet coming back home to a part of the British Isles, in order to serve on active service *without* their families, namely in Northern Ireland. Of course some of the troops in Northern Ireland do have their families with them, living in protected camps, with barbed wire and sentries, their lives constantly at risk from the bombs and bullets of the IRA terrorists. A similar situation must have applied to US families in Saigon during the war in Vietnam, when the Viet Cong brought the conflict right into the city. The French families in Algeria faced not only similar dangers from terrorist bombs and bullets, but also from the indiscriminate actions of their fellow countrymen of the OAS in their struggle to keep Algeria French. However, for it to happen 'right on one's own doorstep' is profoundly disturbing.

Despite these problems, the majority of camp followers, whatever their race, creed or colour are a brave and determined breed, who stick by their menfolk through thick and thin, making light of their difficulties. And as we shall see there are also many others who are prepared to put up with the dangers and difficulties in order to 'follow the drum'. It is nice to think that despite all that has happened in this century, there are still Pakistani 'char wallahs' in Northern Ireland today serving tea to the soldiers of the British regiments, which their fathers and grandfathers served before them in sunnier climes and in happier times.

These modern collections of camp followers normally remain in small foreign 'Islands' in the middle of the local population, be they friendly or unfriendly. The days of complete integration are no more, so we shall not see any new cities, like York and Chester, being founded by the camp followers of a foreign army. Those days, like the days of the baggage trains, are gone, until perhaps we send space age 'armies' onto other planets, to be accompanied as always by ubiquitous space travelling camp followers.

2

Food, glorious food!

FEEDING THE SOLDIER

'The soldier who saves a nation free should have a ration savoury.' These sentiments – expressed in an 1855 copy of *Punch* magazine – were, sad to say, not often followed by those responsible for feeding the armies of past eras. Looking back to Roman times we find that a soldier usually carried with him three days' rations, consisting mainly of wheat or – if on punishments – barley, as for the most part they were vegetarians. The pairs of millstones for grinding the corn were carried on the packhorses with the leather tents.

They would cook their own food and pay for it too – about a fifth of their pay was spent in this way. No doubt the officers had servants to prepare and serve their meals, but the legionaries fed themselves, albeit in an orderly manner: 'They live together by companies with quietness and decency, as are all their other affairs managed by good order and security. Each company hath also their wood and their corn and their water, brought them when they stand in need of them; for they neither sup nor dine as they please themselves singly, but all together . . .'[1]

Such ordered frugality was not the case in 17th- and 18th-century European armies, where supplying the food was the job of the Commissariat, not always the most honest of camp followers, many of whom made fat profits at the expense of the soldiers' empty bellies.

A typical daily ration for Wellington's Army in the Peninsular was supposed to be 1lb of meat on the bone, 1½lbs of bread, or 1lb of ship's biscuit, and either ⅓rd of a pint of rum or a pint of wine. However, the regular arrival of these supplies depended upon many factors, such as the distance of the troops from their base,

[1] *The Roman Army* by Graham Webster (the quote is from the Roman historian Josephus)

Living off the land, a forage party of Roman legionaries collect grain. (A scene from Trajan's column)

A camp kitchen in Hyde Park

the amount of transport available, enemy action, etc. When not on active service, back home in England, the soldiers fared no better.

In 1815 the daily ration was 1lb of bread and ¾lb of meat, for which 6d a day was stopped from pay. The cooking utensils for each company were just two large coppers, one for vegetables or potatoes (bought separately from local traders) and the other for meat, which was always beef and always boiled, as there was no means of roasting or baking it. In barracks the soldier had two meals a day, breakfast at 7.30 and dinner at 12.30, after which he had to go for 19 hours without food. With his eternal diet of beef broth and boiled beef, interspersed with long hours of complete starvation, the only refuge open to him was in the drink which the sutlers were always happy to supply.

There were of course exceptions to the general disinterest in soldiers' diet, a notable one being the general to whom the famous saying at the beginning of this chapter is attributed, namely Napoleon Bonaparte. When, as First Consul, he re-organised the French Army, he separated the administrative functions from the direction of military operations, establishing in 1802 a Department of War Administration. The commissariat officers remained civilians, but now they worked under the head of this new department who was a general of division. This meant more supervision and thus better food in barracks. However, once in the field, Napoleon's armies lived off the land, each man fending for himself as best he could. By this method Napoleon was able to dispense with long supply columns, thus increasing the mobility of his army over those of his enemies – the Prussian Army of the same period for instance, would halt until six days' rations of bread had been baked and loaded onto an enormous wagon train, they

A camp scene, published in May 1803, drawn and etched by W H Pyne

would then be able to march until the wagons were empty, when another six days' halt for baking was necessary!

The situation in the British Army had changed little by the mid-19th century, when the ration was still as it had last been fixed 45 years previously. The meat was still boiled and when boned and cooked seldom weighed as much as 7ozs. 'For these meagre supplies the Commissariat stoppage was, in 1854, 4½ pence out of a trooper's pay of a shilling and 3 pence per day, which included one penny beer money. It was not until 1873 that this daily ration was issued free. All other food including vegetables and potatoes still had to be bought by the men and it was virtually compulsory that a further 3 pence should be paid for it.'[1]

Things were no better on the other side of the Atlantic, where under field conditions on the frontier, food deteriorated from bad to appalling. Supply wagons supporting a column on the move would be loaded with barrels of greasy salt pork, hardtack biscuits, dried beans, coffee and sugar. In addition, each man was supposed to carry a further 10lbs of salt pork and hardtack with him, to last, in theory anyway, for at least five days. It was fortunate that fishing and hunting were normally permitted, so that the soldiers were able to augment their monotonous diet. As there were no company cooks the men cooked for themselves on the trail, doing the best they could to make their meals appetising.

In barracks the food was if anything even worse, without the fresh game to augment it; 'a standing joke among enlisted men was that the cooks killed more soldiers than the Indians did. Moreover, even if a man developed culinary talents, the food that the company cooks had to deal with was maddeningly monotonous . . . one sergeant gave this description of a typical day's meals: "For breakfast we had beef hash, dry sliced bread (no butter) and coffee (no milk): for dinner, sliced beef, dry bread and coffee, for supper, coffee straight – just dry bread and coffee." He summed it all up with simple accuracy "The food was very poor." '[2]

[1] *The History of British Cavalry* by the Marquis of Anglesey

[2] *The Soldiers* by the Editors of *Time-Life*

The cattle pier Balaclava harbour photographed by Roger Fenton. The whole of Great Britain's Crimean war effort was to be poured into this tiny harbour. (Science Museum, London)

The Barrack Hospital kitchen, Scutari. Alexis Soyer performed miracles here, improving the hospital food out of all recognition and earning himself 'three times three' cheers from the patients when he went around the wards with his tureens of soup

With food so bad and rations so meagre one can imagine the situation which faced the ill-equipped and badly administered British Army in the Crimea. When it set out from the landing beaches making towards Sebastopol, each man had only three days' rations – almost entirely salt pork – and few had full water-bottles. Without water, or a balanced diet, many suffered already from severe dysentry and were as liable to scurvy as any sailor on the high seas. They died like flies.

A CULINARY CAMPAIGN

Into this world of appalling, monotonous and badly cooked food there stepped a most intriguing camp follower, one Alexis Soyer, a famous chef from the Reform Club in London. He was so anxious to get to grips with the problems of feeding soldiers properly that he paid his own passage to the Crimea, arriving there in 1855 attended by a 'gentleman of colour' as his secretary.

First he set about improving the food for the patients in the Barrack Hospital at Scutari where, as we shall see later, Florence Nightingale worked her own special brand of miracles. He composed recipes which, by using only army rations, made excellent soups and stews. He put an end to the highly unimaginative and dreadful system of over-boiling everything and insisted on having soldiers permanently allocated to the kitchens who could then be properly trained as cooks.

He invented all manner of new equipment for the cookhouse in the field – the Scutari teapot, which made and kept tea hot for 50 men; a revolutionary new baking and stewing pan; simple ovens in which to bake bread and biscuits and his *piece de resistance* a new field stove, which was still in use in the British Army in WW2!

Although the authorities initially received him rather coolly the patients in

The flyleaf drawing at the beginning of Alexis Soyer's book on the Crimean War

the wards were soon cheering him 'three times three' when he went round the hospital with his steaming tureens of soup. Florence Nightingale had this to say of him: 'None but he have studied cooking for the purpose of cooking large quantities of food in the most nutritive and economical manner for great quantities of people.'[1]

As well as the great work he did for the hospital patients, his inventions soon transformed the feeding of the army beseiging Sebastopol, some of whom had never tasted cooked food since they landed, because of the acute shortage of fuel. His field stove reduced the amount of fuel needed to cook for 1,000 men from 3,500lbs to a mere 300.

Lt Colonel F C Eveleigh, commanding officer of the 20th Regiment, Fourth Division, said of the Soyer stove: '... I have the honour to state I consider Monsieur Soyer's stove cooks the men's rations infinitely better than the ordinary way. The saving of fuel, also, to Government is a very important consideration; and moreover I am informed by Monsieur Soyer that the men's rations can easily be baked in his stove which I consider very desirable, so as to enable the men to have a change in the way of cooking their dinner.'

On Soyer's return to England he wrote *A Culinary Campaign* with illustrations by H G Hine. The book contains many simple, yet effective recipes for example: '*No 23 – Cheap Plain Rice Pudding, for campaigning* (In which no eggs or milk are required: important in the Crimea or the field). Put on the fire, in a moderate sized saucepan, 12 pints of water; when boiling add to it 1lb of rice or 16 tablespoonsful, 4ozs brown sugar or 4 tablespoonsful, 1 large teaspoonful of salt and the rind of a lemon thinly peeled; boil gently for half an hour, then strain all the water from the rice, keeping it as dry as possible. The rice-water is then ready for drinking, either warm or cold. The juice of a lemon can be introduced, which will make it more palatable and refreshing. *The Pudding*. Add to the rice 3ozs sugar, 4 tablespoonsful of flour, half a teaspoonful of pounded cinnamon; stir it on the fire carefully for five minutes; put it in a tin or a pie-dish and bake. By boiling the rice a quarter of an hour longer, it will be very good to eat without baking. Cinnamon may be omitted.'

[1] *Florence Nightingale* by Cecil Woodham Smith

Soyer held a 'field banquet' to open his kitchen before Sebastopol

Life in a Burma Regiment. A British officer checking the weights of rations from the Commissary — very essential in order to prevent fiddling!

Or perhaps, if you prefer it, how to cook for the extra large family:

'*No 6 – To cook for a Regiment of a Thousand Men* (Headquarters, Crimea, 20th June 1855). Place twenty stoves in a row, in the open air or under cover. Put 30 quarts of water in each boiler, 50lbs of ration meat, 4 squares from a cake of dried vegetables – or, if fresh mixed vegetables are issued, 12lbs weight – 10 small teaspoonsful of salt, 1 ditto of pepper, light the fire, simmer gently from two hours to two hours and a half, skim the fat from the top, and serve.'

THE BILL OF FARE FOR A FIELD DAY Alexis was so confident of his new cooking methods and new equipment that he organised a 'field day' and invited senior officers from all the Allies to come and sample his simple, well cooked fare, which consisted of the following: plain boiled salt beef and ditto with dumplings; plain boiled salt pork and ditto with peas-pudding; stewed salt pork and beef with rice; French pot-au-feu; stewed fresh beef with potatoes; mutton ditto with haricot beans; ox-cheek and ox-feet soups; Scotch mutton broth; common curry, made with fresh and salt beef. He wrote: 'At about four o'clock my reception commenced. Lord Rokeby, accompanied by several French officers in full dress, was the first to honour me with a visit. This gave me the opportunity of fully explaining to him and his friends the plan and construction of the apparatus, as well as its simplicity, cleanliness and great economy in consumption of fuel.' It goes without saying that the field day was a resounding success.

A CULINARY EMBLEM OF PEACE Despite his dedication to producing cheap, wholesome food for the mass of soldiers in the Crimea, Soyer could just as easily produce something more exotic when the occasion demanded. His 'Culinary Emblem of Peace' contained the following list of ingredients:

12 boxes preserved lobsters
2 cases preserved lampreys
2 cases preserved sardines
2 bottles preserved anchovies
1 case preserved caviar
1 case preserved sturgeon
1 case preserved thunny
2 cases preserved oysters
1 pound fresh prawns
4 pounds turbot clouté
12 Russian pickled cucumbers
4 bottles pickled olives
1 bottle mixed pickles
1 bottle Indian pickles
1 bottle pickled French beans
2 bottles pickled mushrooms
½ bottle pickled mangoes
2 bottles pickled French truffles
2 cases preserved peas
2 cases preserved mixed vegetables
4 dozen cabbage lettuces
100 eggs
2 bottles preserved cockscombs

The sauce was composed of 6 bottles of salad oil, 1 of Tarragon vinegar, ½ bottle of Chili vinegar, 2 boxes of preserved cream (whipped), 4ozs of sugar, 6 eschalots, salt, cayenne pepper, mustard, and a ¼oz of Oriental herbs which were unknown in England at the time. The monster dish was called 'The Macédoine Lüdersienne à l'Alexandre II'.

Alexis Soyer concludes his fascinating and highly entertaining little book with the words: 'The author, after his laborious campaign in bidding adieu to his readers, does not intend to remain "Soyer tranquille" as he is most anxious after having chronicled his culinary reminiscences of the late war, to put his views into action by simple practice; . . .' Sad to say, Soyer did not live to see the fruits of his labours for very long, as he died the following year in 1858.

Florence Nightingale, with whom at that time he was collaborating on the Barrack Commission – one of his last acts was to open on 28 July (he died in August) his model kitchen at Wellington Barracks in London – wrote to Douglas Galton, 'Soyer's death is a great disaster. My only comfort is that you were imbued before his death with his notions'. Alexis Soyer was undoubtedly a camp follower to whom the British Army owes an enormous debt of gratitude.

THE LANGUAGE OF THE CATERER

To close this brief excursion into the culinary arts let us look briefly at the problems which foreign contractors face with the English language. Contractors are a fairly universal type of camp follower who provide, or augment, the rations of the Officers' and Sergeants' messes of regiments serving abroad. This has been

'The Cavalry Club', Eshowe, Zululand 1890. Not quite up to the standards of its namesake in Piccadilly, but these Eleventh Hussars' officers clearly did their best!

the practice all over the world for many years. These determined salesmen did sometimes have difficulty in expressing exactly what they wanted to say when required to put pen to paper, and here are two delightful letters written by the contractors to the Eleventh Hussars Officers' and Sergeants' messes during their service in Egypt, which were published in their regimental journal in 1922:

'Dear Sargint,

Today no chicken, he no find. If you want to-morrow, chicken.

Yours truley,

IBRAHIM

Contractor 11th Hussars.'

This however, is completely overshadowed by the following estimate received by the Sergeants' Mess President. Extracts only can be published, owing to the lack of space.

'Honoured Sir,

I hev the honer to lay before yor Kind notis the following:

I am Ahmed Ali Khali Mess Contractor Abbassia wishing to hev yor Sergints mess contractor. As regard of my qualifitions I gott meny Sertificites frame a lott of Mess. I am reddy to hev every man for 3 piastre dailey over the ration and I pay your mess 10s monthly so that I will bring the cups spones and plaites and everythink and my list will be as following.

SATURDAY

Gam fire – Tea and Biscuits

Breakfast – Fish and Ships (and chips)

Lunch – Coal Meat and Salit and Piclis and pitchtable (Salad and Pickles)

Dinner – Peas soup, Ros beef, Yoksha Bodding and pitchtable

SUNDAY

Gam fire – Tea and kakes

Breakfast – Kidness, Eggs in backing, Burgu and fresh milk and tea and coffee.

Lunch – Stik Kidness bay pitchtable in sweep

Dinner – Lantin Soup, (Lentil) begin (Pigeon) Rost and pitchtable

MONDAY's Breakfast includes "Bookshops in ships Boridge" and tea, whilst "Rost Shipper and pitchtables" are to appear at dinner.

A quartet of dusky maidens who were, one presumes, an important part of the 11th Hussars echelon in Zululand, 1890!

WEDNESDAY We shall enjoy for lunch: "Heat bay and pitchtable" and for dinner there is to be "Tabbayoka Soap Rost Matin and Mentsos with pitchtables and Swetes".

THURSDAY is a quiet day so for dinner we shall have "pitch-bull soap and meat cuttles" and on Friday we are on "Livery beaking and onions" for breakfast and "Stick and onnions" for dinner.

Achmed finished his tender Menu by informing us that "If it will be enny trouble you must not give me enny money. If the kindley Sir help me for this contractors I will ask God to save you".

It is stated that some mess members are cutting down their present diet in order that they may take well to the new Menu.'

Despite their sometimes quaint language, contractors have continued to be a normal part of the military scene wherever the British Army has served since WW2 – for example, in Palestine, Malaya, Aden, Cyprus and Borneo. Some of the more well established contractors, such as Roshan Din, have followed the troops from operational area to operational area, but in general they have been locally based merchants or entrepreneurs who saw the chance to make money – and who can blame them!

Now that the British army is, alas, more confined to soldiering in Europe, these colourful characters will eventually die out, which is a pity. I remember our potential squadron contractor in the Persian Gulf ending his request for employment with the protestation that he would 'shed his blood for us'. No doubt he would have had to do so, had his wares proved to be uneatable, but like the majority of his ilk, he produced the goods cheaply, efficiently and with a winning smile – what more could we have asked for!

3

The Servants

SERVANTS VARIOUS

For thousands of years some more fortunate men and women have had others working for them as their servants. Those with power, influence or wealth have invariably employed others to do the more mundane, yet vital, tasks which have to be done in any ordered household or community. And armies have been no exception. Officers, warrant officers, non-commissioned officers, and even in some cases private soldiers, have all employed various types of servants, who are all truly camp followers, because they provided a service to the troops they followed.

Of course they have varied enormously in status, sex, race, colour and type of employment. The body slave, for example, whose very life might be forfeit at his master's slightest whim; the knight's loyal young squire, perhaps destined to become a knight himself one day; the hired soldier servants, known as 'strikers' on the American frontier, who were employed by officers because the servant girls brought out from the east were promptly lost in marriage to other soldiers, be they pretty or plain such was the shortage of females; the devoted civilian batmen at such institutions as the Royal Military Academy, Sandhurst, who have looked after generations of gentlemen cadets – the list is endless and a detailed catalogue would be both boring and repetitive. Therefore, we have chosen to concentrate on servants from one particular country, namely India, during the period when it was ruled by the British Raj.

REGIMENTAL SERVANTS

Probably the most famous camp follower of all time was a regimental servant, namely the regimental water carrier (the bhisti or bheesti) immortalised in Rudyard Kipling's poem 'Gunga Din'. The poem is now a little hackneyed after being quoted so often, but it still remains a firm favourite. It was one of Kipling's original thirteen *Barrack-room Ballads* which appeared in 1890 in a literary weekly called the *Scots Observer*.

Kipling who had come to London in October 1889 to seek his fortune, found immediate success with the verse and prose which he had written during his apprenticeship with an Indian newspaper.

> '. . . Of all them blackfaced crew
> The finest man I knew
> Was our regimental bhisti, Gunga Din. . . .'[1]

The poetic saga of Gunga Din's bravery in rescuing a wounded soldier under fire, carrying him back to the ambulance wagon (a dooli) and then receiving a

---

[1] *The Complete Barrack-Room Ballads* by Rudyard Kipling

Indian Camp Followers

mortal wound, is well known, but not so well known is the fact that it was based on a true incident, being the story of Juma a water-carrier of the Frontier Force regiment of the Guides at the siege of Delhi in July 1857, during the Indian Mutiny, when he was selected by his comrades as the bravest man in the regiment.

As to other types of regimental servants, the following are extracts from an article, by a Captain Claude Bray, which appeared in the *Navy and Army Illustrated* in 1898, under the title 'Indian Camp Followers': '. . . From time immemorial it has been the reproach of Oriental armies that they needed at least five followers to every fighting man. For many years after the arrival of our forefathers in India, the same reproach attached to them in an almost equal degree; and though we may nowadays fairly claim to have purged ourselves of our errors so far as troops on active service are concerned, and to have brought the numbers of our following in times of peace within reasonable bounds, to this day an astonishing quantity of natives live on and by our Indian Army. The luxury of having at one's elbow a dusky attendant to perform all sorts of services is rendered possible by the cheapness of labour, while it might almost be said to be rendered necessary by the enervating nature of the climate against which our soldiers have to contend. Nor is it without the compensating advantage of expediency from the military standpoint, for it should not be forgotten that the Indian Army enjoys one solid advantage over our Army at home, in that every fighting man is kept free for the duties of his profession, the necessary services and most of the fatigues being undertaken by civilian followers, who have themselves become by right of long use and habit almost a part of the great military machine . . .

'. . . Of the lines of every regiment there is set apart a portion for the special accommodation of the followers, and this portion is known as the regimental bazaar. . . . Within the narrow limits of any one of them are to be found representatives of all the many arts and crafts which have played their part in the creation of that other Indian anomaly, the caste system, and it is not too much to say that pretty well every trade that can make a living out of the soldier will be represented in force. To attempt to detail them all would be a matter of time, but it is possible to run over a few of the more salient features of this queer community.

'The most important person in the bazaar is the *Kotwal*. He is the mayor of the bazaar, the head of the police, the mouthpiece of the commanding officer on the one side, and the representative of the followers on the other. If anything is

A Good Samaritan One of the regimental Bhisties (water carriers) giving a drink from his goatskin water bag to another thirsty camp servant

wanted, it is the *Kotwal* who is sent to arrange the matter. His principal assistants are the various *chuprassis*, maintained as part of the regimental establishment – "Wearers of the badge", as the name signifies – who are to be found in every branch of official life, and who are anything in reason from mere messengers to a sort of police.

'Next in importance to the *Kotwal* ranks the *Munshi*, . . . This official has to perform the double office of interpreter and teacher of Hindustani to the soldiers. In many regiments, especially if he happens to have a spice of the native taste for intrigue, he is a good deal more, and in virtue of the opportunities created by his intercourse with the officers who are his pupils, he manages to become a great power in the bazaar.

Next in order come the men appointed to look after the regimental establishment of camp equipage, whose distinctive uniform of blue with red facings is a feature of Indian barrack life. Their duties are nominally to keep the tents free from the ravages of the white ants and generally in repair, but in practice their services are many and varied.

'. . . The most numerous (as they are the most important) classes of Government followers in an Indian barrack are those which perform the twin services of scavenging and carrying water. The *mehter* and the *bheesti* are ubiquitous, for it has to be remembered that in India there is neither water laid on nor drainage in the fashion usual at home. For both those essential services the country has to depend on manual labour, with the result that the sweeper with his broom and the *bheesti* with his *mussick*, which is simply a goat's skin sewn up so as to form a bag, are to be met at every turn. . . . The *bheesti* is a very important man among the troops, accompanying them on the line of march and even under fire. It is on record that one of the greatest disasters that has ever befallen our arms in the

Punkah Wallah Before air conditioning the punkah wallah had to pull for 10 to 12 hours a day without a stop. (The comment on the back of this photo reads 'must be the most monotonous job in existence')

Grass Cutters With so many riding ponies, chargers and pack animals to feed, grass cutters were needed to keep the stables properly supplied

Sweeper The lowest of the low, he got all the dirty jobs but was invariably one of the most cheerful and hard working servants

country was in no small measure brought about by the failure of the *bheesties* to find water for the native troops in the fighting line. Thirst proved a deadly assistant to our enemies on that occasion.

'The above about exhausts the list of those who are maintained as part of the Government servants of a regiment on the Indian establishments, but it is among the less regularly appointed followers that the most curious variety exists. First among the unofficial following of a company come the cooks, for all the cooking in India is done by the natives under the nominal supervision of a soldier told off as the cookhouse orderly. The ration stand of a regiment in India is very different indeed from the similar institution at home. But the meat is good enough in its way, and the native cooks, according to their lights, are skilful to contrive a steak for their master's breakfast and yet leave enough to serve up a savoury dinner, and doubtless reserve sufficient for the hungry mouths in their own homes as well. Each man of the company contributes a small sum each month to pay these worthy servants, among whom, in true native fashion, the head man does as little as he can, and draws the lion's share of the pay.

'Next in importance among the company's servants is the barber, who not only cuts hair as required, but shaves as well. By some means only known to themselves these barbers can shave fifty or sixty of their clients between reveille and the seven o'clock parade, for there is seldom more than one of them to each company, and Indian companies are strong. They are so skilful, however, that they can shave a man while he is half asleep, and it is possible owing to their starting before the bugle sounds that so few men appear on parade unshaved. Next may be taken that most useful and often most unjustly abused public servant, the punkah-coolie. . . . When every other soul is recruiting exhausted nature with sleep, he has to manage somehow to keep awake.'

It has not been easy to find contemporary photographs of all these servants; however, the selection which accompany this chapter gives a reasonable cross section. With this formidable array of camp followers all falling over each other to work for the men of the regiment as well as for the officers and sergeants, the average British private soldier found that he enjoyed considerable status in India. He was the 'soldier sahib' and thus a person of importance. One clearly visible effect of having so many hands beside his own to clean, polish and launder his uniform and accoutrements, was that he was able to achieve and maintain a very high standard of turnout.

The majority of regimental camp followers were intensely loyal to 'their regiment', proudly wearing its badge and taking great pride in their service. Their bravery on the field of battle was not confined to the old days in India as the Regimental History of the 13th Frontier Force Rifles testifies.

They were, in December 1943, occupying the Villa Grande position in Italy, very exposed to enemy shellfire and to a particular nasty type of multiple six barrelled mortar called a 'Nebelwerfer'. The weather was appalling and the troops were continually drenched by snow and rain: '. . . Throughout this period the conduct of the followers, who took up hot food to the officers and men in the front line regardless of danger, was beyond praise, nor is this all that is due to the gallant followers of the 6th Royal Battalion. At the earlier battle of the Sangro, when ammunition at the front was running short, they carried forward

The 'Peon' or Orderly Room orderly
of the 2nd/4th Border Regiment, a
very quaint old chap who spoke fine
English in his own style!

boxes of ammunition and grenades through heavy shelling and mortaring right into the foward companies' position. Out of one such party of five followers only one man reached the forward company, the rest having become casualties en route. This man, Sweeper Mehr Din, was awarded the IDSM, and it is believed was the first sweeper of the Indian Army in the Second World War to win an award for gallantry. After this, the followers of the battalion were given the privilege of wearing on their right shoulders the Royal Red Lanyard like the fighting ranks. The spirit of Kipling's Gunga Din was alive indeed in the Second World War . . .'

MESS SERVANTS

Before dealing with those employed inside the mess itself we must first cover the servants which each officer could expect to have to employ to look after himself alone – and this could easily amount to at least ten, as Major General Sir Francis

A trio of bearers of the 2nd/4th
Border Regt September 1917

A 'boy' called Lachu, who served
RSM Harrison 2nd/4th Border Regt,
Abbottabad, October 1917

Howard recalled in his autobiography *Reminiscences 1848–1890*: 'I reached Umballa on 26 November 1874, and was met at the station by most of the officers of the battalion, which was in camp owing to an outbreak of irruptive fever. They had secured a very nice bungalow for me, and before many days were over, I had purchased a couple of good ponies and engaged the necessary number of servants, amounting to ten in all. This sounds a large number, but owing to the custom of the country it was impossible to do with fewer and, as their total pay in those days only amounted to about £5 a month, it was not ruinous.

'. . . The Bearer, who is your mainstay, valets you and fetches your pay in rupees every month from the paymaster. Any money you leave in his charge is as safe as if you had put it in a bank, but what you do not hand over to him will probably disappear. He settles all your ready-money bills and accounts to you once a month. I had the same one for fourteen years, and parted from him with great regret when I left India for good.

. . . The *Kitmutgar* waits on you at table whether at home or at mess. He is usually a good cook who provides you when in camp, never mind what the weather is, excellent food though his kitchen range consists of three stones with a wood fire burning between them.

'. . . The *Bhisti*, or water-carrier, is a Mussulman, and almost invariably a plucky, reliable and devoted servant.

48

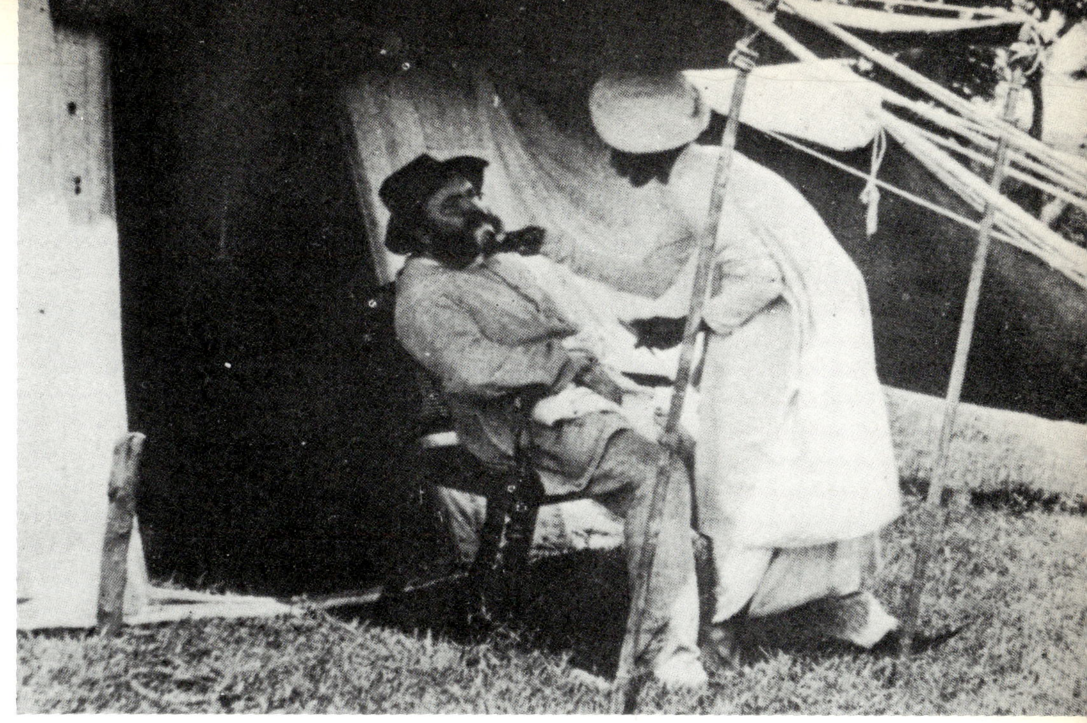

A very old photograph of a native barber (a hajam) shaving an officer in camp. The photo was taken before 1860 and is one of the oldest extant photographs of European life in India

'. . . The *Sais* (groom), a Hindoo, looks after one pony. As you never walk and invariably canter when riding, if you are going any distance you send him ahead and, being a good runner, by taking short-cuts he generally reaches your destination before you do. It says much for him that he can be trusted to march a pony from Peshawar to Calcutta, eg over 1,000 miles in what is to him an unknown country, and yet hand the animal over in good condition.

'. . . To every pony there must be a grass-cutter, who often has to walk long distances every day in search of doob grass, and returns every evening carrying the load on his head. He is generally a Hindoo and an industrious servant.

'. . . The *Mehter* does the scavenging and sanitary work connected with the

A travelling Palanquin with native porters, another very old photograph taken before 1860

Earl David Airlie with two of his servants, poses at a well after polo practice, circa 1895. (Note the 10th Hussar cap badges on their turbans)

bungalow, which is important in a country where everything in that line is very primitive. He belongs to the lowest caste, will therefore eat anything you give him, and is generally a good and willing servant, but is as regards the other servants practically an outcaste.

'. . . The *Chokedar* is supposed to guard your bungalow at night. As a matter of fact, as soon as you turn in he does likewise, but coughs loudly in his waking moments in order to impress you with his vigilance. He generally belongs to the thief caste, and his wages practically amount to blackmail levied on you by the caste, whose members do not rob if you keep a *chokedar*, but who loot you to a moral if you do not.

'. . . Taking it all round, the virtues of the mass of Indian servants are many, their faults few and trifling though somewhat irritating, and if you treat them well they will serve you with devotion . . .'

Devotion to their master was a feature of the majority of these servants, Field Marshal Lord Roberts of Kandahar told a story about an old Mahommedan servant he employed who, in the middle of a battle when the fighting was at its hottest, was wont to come up and whisper in his ear that his bath was ready! 'He was quite unmoved by the din and shots', wrote Lord Roberts in his autobiography, ' and was carrying on his ordinary duties as if nothing at all unusual was occurring.'

THE MESS Undoubtedly at the very centre of regimental life in India, lay the Officers' Mess. Here the unmarried officers spent a great deal of their time and ate their meals. Normally there was no living accommodation for them in the mess building and unmarried officers lived chiefly in unwanted surplus married officers' quarters. 'Occasionally there was a bungalow specially built for half a dozen officers where the wilder types were liable to gravitate – the sort who were too lazy if they were in bed to put out the ceiling light by using the switch at the door but would shoot out the bulb with their revolvers. Such bungalows were commonly known as "Cad's Alley" and it was quite an honour to be chosen to join this select (?) band when a vacancy arose.'[1]

[1] *Officers' Mess – Life and Customs in the Regiments* by Lt Col R J Dickinson

In addition to the serving soldiers employed in the mess – for example the mess sergeant – there were the native staff. At their head was the *Abdar* or head *Khitmagar* (waiter) who was: 'monarch of the nether regions of the mess compound and Keeper of Custom in the ante-room. Exercising control on behalf of the PMC (President of the Mess Committee) and mess sergeant over a host of *Khidmutgars, Khansamahs, Bhisties*, Sweepers and Officers' Bearers (and all their families) his knowledge of informed gossip was a little short of miraculous.'[1]

Major General P Gleadell, CB, CBE, DSO, late of the Devonshire Regiment tells of one of these formidable characters: 'Barefoot, rotund yet deft of movement, Abdul Rahman would appear silently from nowhere at the clap of a hand at any time of the day or night – whether at the behest of the orderly officer from late night "rounds", or to satisfy the needs at dawn of officers returning from manoeuvres. Unruffled, always impeccably rigged in regimental cummerbund and pugaree, the unforeseen bore him no problems. . . . A tactful recipient of telephone messages, he was ever a discreet reminder of dates, perhaps overlooked in the dinner Warning-out Book. Young officers accorded him the sort of deference they did the RSM or the bandmaster and the affection they might feel for a kindly but rather critical uncle. He spoke no English – but understood every word of it. He knew without reference to the inventory every detail about the mess silver, and he would almost genuflect when he uncased the Colours in the mess before a guest night . . .'[2]

In a separate building behind the mess was the mess cookhouse, anything up to 250yds away, so food had to be carried to a 'hot-box' at the rear of the mess where it was kept warm, in theory anyway, by a small charcoal fire. The cookhouse was the preserve of the *Khansamah* (Cook) and the *Masalchi* (washer up). The other mess servants might include a mess *Shikari* (gamekeeper), *Malis* (gardeners),

[1], [2] *Officers Mess – Life and Customs in the Regiments* by Lt Col R J Dickinson

Even when eating 'al fresco' during pig-sticking the servants were always at hand, December 1897

Abdar Sant Ram of the Punjab Frontier Force Mess. Son of Gopi Ram he was affectionately known by all as 'Santu'. He served as a band boy and sepoy with 54th Sikhs from 1903-06. He then commenced service with the 54th Sikh Officers' Mess, retiring in 1929. Within one month he had joined the Punjab Frontier Force Mess ('Piffer' Mess as it was called) in Kohat and served them until May 1944. He finally joined the Officers' Mess in the Regimental Centre – over 43 years of loyal service.

Santu could regale one with many stories of officers under whom he has served. At Haiderkash Camp on the North West Frontier on account of the danger from tribesmen snipers, no naked light was allowed after dark. When officers after dinner had called for drinks, Santu would appear with a tray of whiskeys and sodas and a lighted lantern. 'Put that light out', someone would say. Santu in gentle voice would retort, 'No buttee, no whiskeys, Sahib'

Bhisties (Water carriers), *Dhobis* (Washermen), and the *Chokedar* (night watchman) who was supposed to guard the mess during the night, but seldom managed to stay awake after the officers had all gone to bed!

MARRIED FAMILIES SERVANTS

As can readily be seen from the photographs, married officers required even more servants than single ones, particularly because the poor *memsahib* was hardly ever allowed to lift a finger in her own house. We say 'poor memsahib' deliberately, because although it is very nice to be waited on hand and foot it does make for a very boring and idle existence.

If we look at the family servants from the memsahib's point of view, then the three or four most important were her senior servant; her husband's bearer; her cook; and her children's nurse. The first two might well be one and the same person, although in most reasonably sized households there was a *khitmagar* – a butler or major-domo, who was in charge of all the other servants.

She would certainly have to learn to live at peace with her husband's bearer especially if she was a newly married, and newly arrived from England, wife. He would have been her husband's bearer probably all his service, used to the life of the gay bachelor over whom he had a considerable amount of influence. He might be the sort who would not take kindly to sharing his master with the new bride and there would be plenty of skirmishing before both sides settled down to an uneasy truce.

The *bobajee* (cook) was another powerful figure and it was normally not the custom for the memsahib to enter the *bobajeekhana* – the cookhouse, which was attached to the servants' quarters anyway, and not part of the bungalow. Instead, cook and memsahib would meet each morning when he brought her his account book. The cook also bought all the food and if a zealous wife tried to do her own shopping she would find herself paying at least 25% more for it. However, it was the custom that the cook was allowed to add on just a little to the order – his *dastur* – literally his 'bribe or perk'. He cooked all the meals, usually with the help of an unpaid apprentice called a cook's matey.

Although, as we have explained, it was not the custom for the memsahib to enter the bobajee's domain, John Masters, in his marvellous book on the Gurkhas, *Bugles and a Tiger*, tells of how two wives in India between the wars had an argument about the relative cleanliness of their cooks, one of whom was an Indian whilst the other was Chinese. They decided that the only way to settle the argument was to pay a visit to each cookhouse unannounced and this they did. As might have been expected the Indian bobajee's kitchen was filthy, inches deep in dirt and swarming with flies. The Chinese cook's kitchen was immaculate, everything spotless, but outside on the step the Chinese cook was washing his feet in the soup tureen!.

The figure of the native nurse dominated the nursery, dressed usually in a sari and blouse, with nose rings and lots of bangles on her wrists and ankles, so that when she was moving about she 'could be heard a mile away'. Ayahs were usually very sweet natured women with lovely hands, very gentle and beautiful in their movements. They had their own hierachy, at the top being the Madrassi

A splendid family group with their indoor and outdoor servants, pose outside their bungalow in Lucknow, 1883. On the left are the sweeper, gardener and tailor, next the cooks and bearers with the syce (groom) holding his master's horse on the right. In the centre the ayah (nurse) guards one of her 'treasures' whilst Mama nurses the other

ayah, the cream of ayahs, mission educated and thus given 'a good many civilised ideas'.

The virtues of a trained ayah were considerable. 'They had this capacity to completely identify with the children they looked after,' explains Vere Birdwood in *Plain Tales from the Raj*, 'and it seemed as if they could switch on love in an extraordinary way. They were so dedicated to their work, in a sense so possessive of their children that it was almost impossible for a good ayah to yield up her charge even for a few hours'.

One such paragon was Lewis Le Marchand's ayah in South India: 'She was

Lt Col and Mrs E B Powell pose in their garden with their servants. Lt Col 'Turkey' Powell, DSO, was commanding 1st Battalion, the Rifle Brigade at Roberts Barracks, Peshawar, in 1927, when this photograph was taken. The servants are listed as (from left to right): Bearer – Motor Driver – Chowkidar (with dog) – Cook (on ground) – Head Khitmagar-Mali (gardener) – Syce (on ground) – Khitmagar – Dhoby and sweeper

very fat and Madrassi and very, very oily about the hair. Her toes were quite enormous and cracked like dirty wickets that had had the sun on them for a few days . . . I didn't know her name; I called her ayah. Sometimes, being a fairly naughty boy I would anger her, but she'd never show it. She'd turn her back and go and sit cross-legged on the floor of the verandah and take out her knitting and the more I called her or the more I was naughty or rude, the more she ignored me, until finally I would come along and say "Ayah, I'm sorry," and then all would be well.

'Ayah ministered after me during the day and very often during the evening, but it was my mother's privilege – heavens knows why – to bath me and put me to bed. Ayah used to wait and, if necessary, sleep outside the doors of her children's room, laying down outside on the mat until such time as my mother would come along and say, "You can go, ayah, little master's asleep." '[1]

It was normal for the servants who worked indoors to wear white uniforms, with the regimental colours on their turbans and cummerbunds. Inside the house they went barefoot. They lived in the servant's quarters which were inside the same compound as the bungalow and its garden. The rising costs of wages and some slight easings of caste barriers reduced the normal two dozen servants employed by an average sized household before the Great War to a round dozen between the wars. Average salaries in the 1930s ranged from about 25 rupees a month (about £2) for a bearer, to 15 rupees for the sweeper, but the latter also had his *dastur*, as all the food which had been cooked and not eaten was never used again but went out to the sweeper and his family.

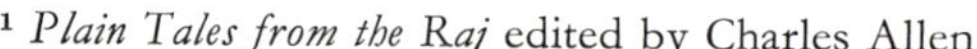

[1] *Plain Tales from the Raj* edited by Charles Allen

A more modern family group taken in Burao, British Somaliland in 1959. From left to right the servants are: Syce, Ayah, Bearer, Cook and second Syce

THE LAST OF THE ARMY WASHERWOMEN

Having said at the beginning of this chapter that we would deal only with Indian servants we felt it would be a pity not to include such an intriguing character as the last washerwoman of the British Army, who died just over 50 years ago at the grand old age of 90. It was the custom of many armies to allow some of the small number of soldiers' wives, who accompanied their husbands overseas, or who lived with them in barracks, to earn a few coppers by acting as regimental washerwomen. For example, in the American frontier army each company was allowed four laundresses who received rations and compensation – at Fort Boise a laundress got 5 dollars a month for an officer's laundry and 2 dollars for an enlisted man. In 1875 there were 1,316 of them, mostly wives of enlisted men. The 1878 Congress, however, considered that they caused more harm than good – a view held by many soldiers as well – and struck them off the rolls. In England there were primitive wash houses in most barracks in the 18th and 19th centuries, where the wives washed the soldiers' body linen. They were fitted with boilers, to which in most cases the water had to be carried by hand. The only means of drying were outdoor posts and lines, so wet linen was sneaked into barrack rooms – strictly against orders – and ironing was done on the barrack room tables.

Some regiments took great pains to spell out the duties and remunerations of their washerwomen, like these extracts from *Regulations for the Rifle Corps* published in 1801:

'. . . Serjeants' wives must learn to wash sufficiently well for the Officers, for they alone are to be their washer-women, and those of the Serjeants when their work for Officers is not sufficient. The Colonel requests that the Officers will never give their linen to wash out of the regiment, and also that they will distribute it nearly equally among the Serjeants' wives.

A very pretty Somali ayah called Dudi and her equally delightful 'Chota Sahib' (sahib's son) getting a free ride!

A baby palanquin for another 'Chota sahib' or 'Missy baba'

'The washing of all soldiers is to be distributed in equal proportions among the other women of the companies. The number of shirts and socks which are to be washed for each soldier per week, is two of each, and at least two turnovers; one of each is to be delivered to the Soldier by the washer-woman every Wednesday and Saturday afternoon, on the delivery of these on Wednesday afternoon, the shirt and socks to be washed are then to be returned to the washer-woman, and on Saturday evening after inspection, she is to receive the others. She will on that evening receive from the Pay Serjeant of the company 5d for the week's washing, or 2½d for the two periods, and if she does not take the payment at the time from the Serjeant, as no soldier is to pay for his own washing, she will have no right to complain afterwards. . . .'

The British Army's last washerwoman was a Mrs Mary Ann Jones of Welshpool, in Wales. She was a remarkable little woman, who had started work at the age of 10, marched to war with her soldier husband when she was a mere slip of a girl and later came home to live to the age of 90. Her husband was a sergeant in the Montgomeryshire Militia and when she was interviewed in 1923 by a local reporter she told of her life with her husband in the Crimean War when the Militia had been mobilised and had marched to Shrewsbury, about 20 miles away, en route for Pembroke Dock: 'I remember the day we set off from Welshpool,' she said, 'it was in 1855 and a wonderful day it was. We marched from the Armoury and hundreds and hundreds of people lined the streets to watch our departure. Some of the folks came a good part of the way with us, and Mrs Jenny Gilmour marched all the way to Shrewsbury in front of the regiment with a nanny-goat. When she got to Shrewsbury she had to walk all the way back again, but I don't think she minded much.' During the march to Shrewsbury Mrs Jones said that she was lucky enough to get a ride in a wagon. At Shrewsbury they had entrained, and subsequently moved to Pembroke to take up quarters in the barracks. 'I enjoyed the journey splendidly,' Mrs Jones went on, 'and some of us who had not seen much before thought that we must be getting pretty near to the end of the world.

'. . . We women had plenty of work to do. Each of us had to wash for 27 men, and we got 3½ pence a man. For that we had to wash two shirts, a towel, haversacks, holdalls, and other things. There were 37 washerwomen in the same place as myself; the Welshpool Town Hall was nothing to the size of the wash-house. When asked by the reporter if she was glad when the war ended and she was able to go home, she replied: '. . . Well no, I can't say altogether that I was, you see we hadn't done so badly. I went from Welshpool with a sovereign in my pocket and I came back with seven, not to mention silver.'[1]

[1] Taken from *The County Times*, Saturday 17 March 1923, paper supplied by Mrs M Stephens, granddaughter of Mary Ann Jones

Service to the Services

EARLY SUTLERS

The word 'Sutler' comes originally from the Dutch *Soeteler* which is in turn derived from the verb *Soetelen* meaning 'to befoul' – a fair indication of the status and reputation of this class of early camp follower!

Sutlers were in fact little more than private adventurers who accompanied the soldiers, selling them foodstuffs and liquor for as large a profit as possible. They were, however, a very necessary evil, because as we have seen already, the Commissariat supplied only the barest minimum of basic essential rations to the soldiers, namely bread and meat or sometimes cheese.

On occasions, as when Marlborough began his great campaigns in Flanders in 1702, bread only was issued, so everything else had to be purchased from the sutlers. The food was often bad as well as sparse, the bread being alive with weevils and the meat rotten and stinking, however, the sutler normally found it more profitable to sell liquor than food, as his customers were more inclined to drown their sorrows with drink, rather than to fill their empty bellies.

Some of these beverages were lethal, for example, American sutlers during the Revolutionary War sold a mixture of raw spirits and fusel oil (a nauseous oil of spirits distilled from potatoes, grain etc), which cost the sutler about 90 cents a gallon and he then sold to the soldiers for 25 cents a drink!

Attempts were made to control sutlers, to limit their charges and to ensure that their merchandise was of a reasonable quality. Both King Gustavus Adolphus of Sweden and King James II of England caused articles of war to be enacted for the control of sutlers in the 17th century, with punishments such as confiscation of goods and the wearing of an iron collar, whilst Cromwell's 'Lawes and Ordinances of Warre, Established for the better Conduct of the Army' warned of 'pain of Imprisonment and further Arbitrary punishment' for those caught selling 'naughty victuals' or for any victualler who 'entertained souldiers in his House, Tent or Hut, after the warning piece at night, or before the beating of the Ravalee in the morning'.[1]

FAMOUS SUTLERS

It was common practice for old soldiers to become sutlers as is evidenced in Shakespeare's *Henry V*, when the Ancient (Ensign) Pistol says that he will forswear soldiering for the more lucrative calling of a sutler: 'I shall sutler be, unto the Camp, and profits shall accrue . . .' However, although it was a dangerous and chancy profession, many sutlers were in fact female, indeed, those whose bizarre stories have been recorded are mainly women.

[1] *Cromwell's Army* by C H Firth

Space permits only a small selection of these fascinating tales, so we have chosen three examples viz: 'Mother Ross', the great British sutleress of Marlborough's wars, who was fortunate enough to have had Daniel Defoe as her ghost writer; 'The Great Western', a rough, tough American laundress, who became a legendary figure along the Mexican border in the 1840s; and finally, a creole from Kingston, Jamaica, rejoicing in the name of 'Mother Seacole', who ran an hotel and restaurant in a shack she had built on the road from Balaclava harbour, during the Crimean war.

'Mother Ross' was born Christina Davies in Dublin in 1667, daughter of a brewer; she married a man named Welch. One unlucky day in 1693, he got very drunk and woke up to find himself, with the King's shilling in his hand, an enlisted private of infantry on his way to fight in Flanders.

Christina did not sit at home and weep for her lost love, instead she donned one of his suits – 'quilting the waistcoat so as to protect her breasts from hurt', put on a wig, bought a silver hilted sword and managed to enlist as Christopher Welsh, in Captain Tichbourn's company of foot; in the regiment commanded by the Marquis de Pisare.

She proved an excellent, gallant soldier, and was both wounded and taken prisoner at the battle of Landen. She was subsequently exchanged and again saw action in the assault on the Schellenburg. Here she was wounded for a second time, so seriously that her sex was discovered and she had to be discharged.

A lesser mortal might have gone home to the brewery, but not Christina, she re-enlisted as a trooper in the Royal Regiment of North British Dragoons (The Royal Scots Greys) and fought with them until the French cracked her skull at the battle of Ramillies. Discharged once again she at last caught up with her missing husband and was reconciled to him – he had been living with a Dutch woman, whose nose Christina was reputed to have hacked off when they first met!

He then launched her as a sutleress, in charge of a canteen, so she remained in the thick of the fighting and was wounded three times at Malplaquet, whilst serving beer to soldiers in the firing line. Her husband was killed shortly afterwards and Christina came under the protection of a Captain Ross, whom she subsequently married.

She was by now catering as much for the officers as for the common soldiers. After a long march she would have dinner ready prepared for a general and his staff, stealing all the pigs and poultry she needed. This would have meant the gallows had she ever been caught, because Marlborough was very strict about plundering. She is said to have been a regular 'virago' with a rich command of bad language and quite strong enough to do her own chucking out!

Eventually her colourful career came to an end and in 1717 she was awarded a pension of 5 pence a day for her service as a soldier in Flanders. Three years later this was raised to one shilling a day at the insistence of the Lord Justices. Her third and last husband was an In Pensioner at the Royal Hospital, Chelsea and she died there on 7 July 1739 at the ripe old age of 72. She was buried with full military honours in the churchyard of St Margaret's, Westminster.

Our second sutleress flashed across the pages of history in the late summer of 1845, in a military camp which General Zachary Taylor was establishing at Corpus Christi in Texas. One morning, a group of soldiers lounging in the sun,

A typical sutling booth in the military encampment, Hyde Park, circa 1780

were amazed to see a giant of a woman striding along a street in the lines of the 7th Infantry Regiment. One of them was foolish enough to mutter something rude about this strange figure as she passed by. Before he knew what was happening she had turned around and hoisted him effortlessly, high in the air against the side of a wooden building. 'I didn't mean no harm ma'am,' he stammered 'it won't happen again.'[1] The Amazon said nothing but merely released her hold and the unfortunate soldier crashed to the ground; she turned abruptly and stalked away.

This was the Army's first meeting with Sarah Borginnis, who had been born in Clay County, Missouri in 1812. Her first husband was a trooper in the 7th Infantry Regiment and she began her military life as a laundress which enabled her to accompany him while on campaigns.

The Great Western by Henry N Ferguson published in *Armor* magazine (January–February 1975 issue)

The Post Trader, where American servicemen obtained their personal needs before the establishment of the Post Exchange on 25th July 1895

A British sutleress circa 1700. This is how the famous 'Mother Ross' must have been dressed during Marlborough's campaigns

A French vivandiere (sutler woman) of the 19th century. They were dressed in uniform similar to that worn by the soldiers of the regiment they supported. This woman probably served with an artillery or engineer unit. The cap she wears is the same as the one still worn today by the Polytechnique School in France

She was a lusty woman, well over 6ft tall who could reputedly 'lick any man of her size and weight in the Army'. She soon became known throughout the ranks as 'The Great Western', the nickname probably coming from a huge steamer – the world's largest in the 1830s – which had crossed the Atlantic without the aid of sails.

She accompanied her husband southwards towards the Rio Grande and, after he had fallen sick and been shipped home with the other casualties and all the wives save his own, she obtained a mule cart, cooking gear and supplies and went on with the marching troops across the desolate sand wastes of South Texas.

From then on she remained in the firing line, calmly serving meals or steaming mugs of coffee amid exploding shells and gunfire. Her husband was later killed in action, so she attached herself to a cavalry squadron, marrying, without the benefit of clergy, one of the dragoons.

This she did so that she could accompany them to California; however, she never made it, falling ill en route, when the troops reached Chihuahua City. There she was abandoned but, after much hardship and suffering, managed to reach El Paso and opened an hotel. She catered mainly for the 'Forty-Niners', on their way to the rich gold fields of the West Coast.

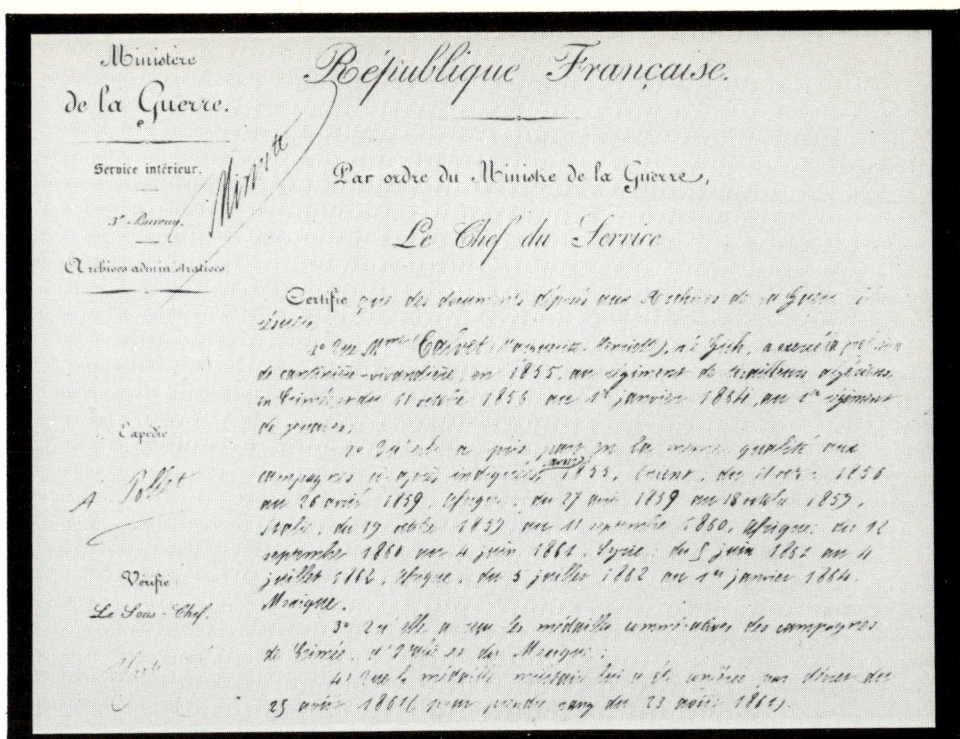

Eventually she went on to Yuma where she opened a restaurant which she ran until her death on 22 December 1866. She was buried with full military honours at Fort Yuma, the only woman to be interred in the post cemetery.

Following the Mexican War she had been brevetted a colonel for her services and made a pensioner of the government. Later all the bodies in the Fort Yuma cemetery were moved to the National Cemetery in the Presidio in San Francisco, where she rests today, under a headstone bearing the name 'Sarah A Bowman'.

The last of our intrepid trio was 'Mother Mary Seacole', who was born in Kingston, Jamaica; her mother was a creole and her father a Scottish soldier. She learnt all about the catering trade in her mother's boarding house and all about soldiers from the men of the British garrison.

She was always rather coy about her true age and colour, liking to describe herself as having been born 'sometime in the present century' and of being 'only a little brown'. As a girl she led an adventurous life in Panama and the '49 gold rush in California, but eventually turned up in London in the autumn of 1854.

As well as her interest in catering she had a burning ambition to become a nurse and, hearing about the Crimea and the work of Florence Nightingale, resolved to go there to help. But alas, she could not find anyone in London in authority who would agree, although she did manage to obtain a letter of introduction to the great 'FN'.

Fortunately she also met a Mr Day who was just about to leave for the Crimea on shipping business. Mr Day was very enthusiastic when 'Mother Seacole' told him about a proposal she had dreamed up to open an hotel and general store near the camps in the war zone. They went into partnership and sailed together for the Crimea aboard the steamer *Hollander* on 25 January 1855. En route, she not only collected suitable supplies and arranged for further regular consignments from

A Sutler's licence belonging to Marguerite Heneriette Calvet born in Gilh, who was 'cantiniere-vivandiere' with The Algerian Light Infantry Regiment (Tirailleurs). She took part in various campaigns including the Crimean War

Tulia, chief vivandiere and water carrier with Gaunt's Brigade in Samoa. She was a Taupo village belle who supported the British and even captured a German flag during one battle! Her photograph appeared in a copy of the *Navy & Army Illustrated Magazine* published on 8th July 1899. (Note that she carries a coconut instead of the usual brandy barrel!)

Three o'clock Sundays, 1870. The regiments featured in this expressive cartoon are (from left to right) 15th Hussars, Royal Horse Artillery, Gordon Highlanders and 16th Lancers

Constantinople, but also met many old army friends from her early days in Jamaica.

Thus by the time she reached the Crimea, she was well known and was consequently welcomed with open arms by all save 'FN', who must have decided that the hospital at Scutari just wasn't big enough for two such dominant females and therefore 'regretted that she had a full quota of nursing sisters'. So Mary Seacole set about arranging for the building of her hotel and restaurant, using wreckage from Balaclava harbour as building materials. She had engaged two sailors, called 'Big Chips' and 'Little Chips' plus some Turkish labourers to do the building and until all was ready, she slept each night on board the *Medora*, a gunpowder ship which was moored in the harbour.

A typical early regimental canteen
bar at the Halifax Barracks in 1908.
(Note the 'Civilians cannot be
served in this Canteen' notice over
the bar)

An early WW1 Division Canteen set
up in a partly damaged building just
behind the front line

A splendid old WW1 mobile canteen
marked 'Expeditionary Force
Canteen'. Note the solid rubber
tyres, they must have made stirring
the tea quite unnecessary!

A French Red Cross canteen near
Vitry le Francois, WW1

Newspaper Reading Room in a
German Soldiers' Club, WW1

An American Field Exchange in the front line, WWI

By early summer the British Hotel, as it was called, was completed at a cost of about £800. She opened each day before daybreak, so that she could serve hot coffee to soldiers returning from night duty in the lines, and remained crowded all day long until 8pm when she closed. She did not allow Sunday opening, nor dice, nor card playing.

In addition to providing a haven where the officers and soldiers (her 'children' as she called them) could relax in a sort of 'tuck shop' atmosphere, she also blended herbal medicines which were soon much preferred to those given out at the hospital. She charged fair prices, gave real value for money, and also spent a good deal of her profits caring for the sick and wounded as they passed her hotel on the way to the hospital ships in the harbour. She sat by them, cheering them up, she tended the delirious and the dying. 'Many a man was later to confess that his most abiding memory of the war was that of Mother Seacole seated by the deathbed of a young soldier, who was comforted by the illusion that the black breast pillowing his head was really that of his mother'.[1]

She was one of the last to leave the Crimea once the war was over. Almost bankrupt, with a great pile of stock to dispose of and many outstanding bills, she still managed one final visit to London to see her beloved 'children' before returning to Jamaica, proudly wearing her Crimean War medal.

[1] *Colonel's Lady and Camp Follower* by Piers Compton

'*Right Dress!*' NAAFI female staff being drilled by an RASC (EFI) Sergeant. Both male and female NAAFI staff became military once war was declared in 1939. The women's uniform is as worn in North Africa (Algeria/Tunisia) in 1942/43

REGIMENTAL CANTEENS

Despite such colourful characters, the soldiers were not on the whole well served by either the sutlers nor the commissariat, the low standard of both being an indication of the lack of public concern for the way in which they were treated. However, the increased publicity given to the dreadful conditions of the Crimean campaign slowly began to stir public conscience in the latter half of the 19th century. Better living accommodation, better food and medical care followed and, in the British Army in 1863, new regulations were published making the running of canteens a regimental responsibility. But they were still only as good as the canteen steward was industrious and honest.

Some enlightened officers, foremost amongst them being Captain Lionel Fortescue of the 17th Lancers, started a campaign for honest canteen stewards and later, with two friends, formed the Canteen & Mess Co-operative Society, which was the real fore-runner of the NAAFI (Navy, Army & Air Force Institutes).

In America too, a similar progression took place. The sutler system was abolished by Act of Congress in 1866 and a system of 'post traders' established in its

A typical NAAFI mobile canteen Men of the RAF Regiment queue for a 'cuppa' at a NAAFI refreshment van at RAF Station Biggin Hill, 1942

A typical American Post Exchange
('PX' for short) during WW2. (Note
the cigarette prices!)

The World's End coffee trailer in
the Heliopolis suburb of Cairo,
circa 1947-50. It was built onto the
chassis of an old Italian mobile
cookhouse captured in the Western
Desert in WW2

A small selection from the wide range of NAAFI brand name goods on sale to the families of HM Forces in NAAFI supermarkets all over the world

A NAAFI mobile canteen is always a welcome sight, especially to soldiers on anti-terrorist duty in Belfast

place. These suffered from similar problems to their British counterparts, particularly in sparsely populated areas, and soldier co-operatives known as 'Canteens' began to appear. Recognising their success, the War Department issued an order on 1 February 1889, establishing a canteen for enlisted personnel. When the Post Exchange came into being six years later, the best of the Post Canteen features were retained. As with its British equivalent, the AAFES (Army & Air Force Exchange Service) no longer serves just the one Service.

GROWTH THIS CENTURY

The growth of both NAAFI and the AAFES during the two world wars has been meteoric and today they are very large organisations, catering for servicemen and their families all over the world.

For instance, during WW2, NAAFI grew from a small distributive organisation with a trade of about £10 million, and a staff of 5,000, into a canteen colossus with a trade of £200 million, a staff of 120,000, and 10,000 establishments in over 40 countries, serving 5 million customers!

For hundreds of thousands of men and women the amenities provided by the NAAFI and the AAFES, helped to soften the transition from civilian to service routine, filling the gap in the daily life of the new sailor, soldier and airman that was formerly occupied by his 'local', his corner drugstore, his billiard saloon, his favourite restaurant, his snack bar, his cinema and even his music hall.

An amusing example of the lengths this 'Service to the Services' is taken can be illustrated by the good ship *Menestheus*, NAAFI's floating brewery – the only one of its kind ever built in the world. It had a short life, alas, but a gay one, when just after WW2, it completed a world-wide cruise. In addition to the Davy Jones Brewery, it operated a cafeteria, a revue company, concert and dance orchestras, a cinema, clothes and shoe repairers, a voice recording studio and many other features!

Today the NAAFI and the AAFES must still be ready to expand their activities to meet the requirements of war, or to provide services and facilities for what are termed 'brush-fire' operations – the current garrison in Belize, formerly British Honduras, is a perfect example. NAAFI supply arrangements must include the maintenance of reserve stocks in strategic locations to meet any emergency.

5

The Entertainers

EARLY ENTERTAINERS

As one might expect, an army as efficiently organised and run as the Roman legions, did not neglect any aspect of the morale of their troops. And so, even in those early days, there were entertainers who gave shows to Roman garrisons all over their empire. It is doubtful if this was centrally controlled and more often than not the artistes would be fairly local. Whether some of the 'actresses' performed other services is not recorded, but it is probably very likely! Gladiatorial contests and like entertainments were put on for the troops in larger garrisons. However, it was not until the 20th century, that forces entertainment, both live and recorded, became a regular part of the camp following scene, with radio and now television, playing an even larger part than live entertainment.

FORCES BROADCASTING

WW2 was well under way before the British could begin Forces Broadcasting on a wide and effective scale. The Germans and Russians had already tackled the problem with great success, particularly the Germans, who used radio on a mass scale for propaganda purposes. They planned their Forces broadcasts with typical Teutonic thoroughness, sending out news, fiery political messages, sports bulletins, martial music and entertainment. Four chains of transmitters broadcast to the German forces in Norway, Western, Eastern and South-eastern Europe.

The Cardigan Minstrels The regimental concert party of the Eleventh Hussars, Maritsburg, Natal, circa 1890

A car load of amateur performers who entertained the troops on a voluntary basis in WW1, returning from the front in 1918 in a magnificent car

By 1942 the Russians were also broadcasting regularly to and from the front line. A feature called 'Letter from the Front' was transmitted three times a day with family messages, liberally spiced with political and patriotic slogans.

The Americans, too, had accurately assessed the vital importance of direct broadcasts to their troops. Their mobile transmitters, with plenty of staff and equipment, were regarded as an essential part of the US fighting machine. They were, for example, in operation within hours of their troops' arrival in Tunisia.

The growth of British Forces Broadcasting Services was, as one might expect with anything British, mainly unplanned, depending to a great extent on trial and error. Their first 'do-it-yourself' Army Broadcasting Station had been captured from the Germans in Tunisia! Of course the original Army broadcasters were soldiers, so this is one type of 'camp follower' who began in wartime in uniform and has ended up by being completely civilian run for the benefit of our forces all over the world. The original main contributions used in Army sponsored programmes were provided by an organisation known as 'ORBS' – the Overseas Recorded Broadcasting Service. They recorded complete programmes at the ENSA theatre in Drury Lane, which were then flown out week by week to the

Mai Bason (centre) and her 'Happy Landings' ENSA concert party in France, 1940. Her son was one of the first RAF pilots killed in the war

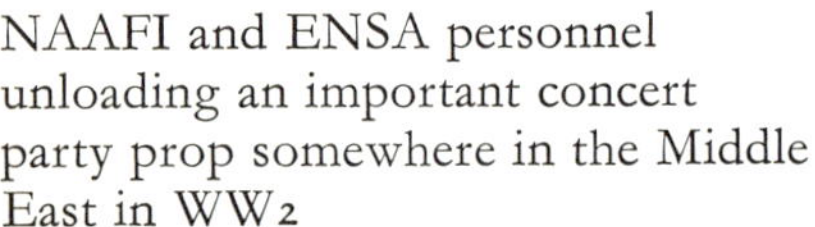

NAAFI and ENSA personnel unloading an important concert party prop somewhere in the Middle East in WW2

various stations. The broadcasters had to learn the hard way: 'they took to the microphone as kittens take to milk. They learned to operate the controls, to write scripts, to announce programmes and to take a smart cue in plays and features. It wasn't enough just to be an announcer. They became engineers, authors, interviewers, actors, "presenters" of request programmes and taught themselves the skill of balance and control.'

By April 1944 a specially designed mobile station was operating within earshot of the battle of Cassino; other mobile field transmitters followed fast on the heels of 21st Army Group when they landed in Europe; whilst Radio SEAC, a powerful transmitter in Ceylon, broadcast to the troops all over South East Asia. To many soldiers, serving thousands of miles away from their loved ones, the broadcasts gave a much needed morale booster and 'Calling Blighty' was a favourite programme with both troops and families back home. The direct radio link back to UK also had its other uses; for example, a soldier facing the Japanese in a forward battle area was whisked out, driven to the nearest airfield by staff car, flown to Calcutta and recorded a message of comfort for his sick wife. The disc was then flown to the beam station and five hours later was in London, ready for transmission to the hospital. Next day a War Office signal arrived saying: 'Inform Private . . . wife now out of danger thanks to message.' In these days of satellite communications that may seem a very trivial story, but in 1945 it was not far short of a miracle.

As one might have expected, Army Broadcasting did great work entertaining the troops of the occupation forces in Germany – 'BFN – The British Forces Network', was soon familiar to listeners at home as well as to the men and women on active service in Europe. From the end of the war until 1957, Forces Broadcasting continued to operate but without the active support that it had received towards the end of the war. In the background was the thought that the BBC

might take over, but this never happened. Instead 'BFBS – The British Forces Broadcasting Service', was born and now has its own headquarters near the Thames Embankment at Westminster. The thousands of British troops and their families in Germany enjoy their own specially organised radio programmes, controlled from a major studio centre in Cologne. They are also making great strides in television, working with the Services Kinema Corporation, who supply the TV sets.

BFBS have had stations all over the world, wherever British troops have been

A German concert party
(Fronttheater) in Russia July/August
1943

An early BFBS radio station in
Gibraltar, Barbara Garner making an
announcement

Mary Martin, 'washing that man
right out of her hair', on stage
during an USO Show

General George S Patton, Jnr,
shakes hands with Bob Hope during
the comedian's tour of US forces in
Sicily. Bob Hope was accompanied
by Frances Langford, Jack Pepper
and Tony Romano. Palermo,
2 November 1943

required to serve. The spread of these stations is, of course, much reduced nowadays, but the efficiency, devotion to duty and inventiveness of the BFBS staff is
just as high as it has ever been. Their studios and recording equipment at their
headquarters is among the most modern in the country; their Gurkha programmes
were a fascinating and challenging task which they successfully took on some
years ago. Their motto could well be summed up in these words from the Bible,
which appeared on a notice displayed in the studio of the Forces Broadcasting
Station attached to the Eighth Army: 'Except ye utter by the tongue words easy
to be understood, how shall it be known what is spoken? For ye shall speak into
the air. . . .' (1 Corinthians, xiv, 9)

ENSA

In WW1 the troops had to organise their own entertainment, with the help of such
professionals in their midst as Mr Basil Dean, a pioneer army entertainments
officer, who was destined to become the director of ENSA (The Entertainments
National Service Association) in the Second World War. Despite this lack of
outside support, long before the 1918 armistice, every division, corps and army
had its own concert party. 'With a few sheets of canvas, lengths of timber, corrugated iron and unlimited enthusiasm, a stage could be improvised in a few hours
or an auditorium fixed up for a show by the Expeditionary Force Canteen film
unit.'[1]

[1] *Services to the Services* by Harry Miller

Bing Crosby and Fred Astaire entertaining some lucky nurses during one of their tours in WW2

When war loomed in 1938 Mr Basil Dean mobilised a team of volunteers from among his show business friends, to co-operate with NAAFI in organising entertainment for the Forces. Thus ENSA was formed. Eight days after the declaration of war, the Theatre Royal, Drury Lane, was taken over by NAAFI for its entertainments branch and ENSA headquarters. By Christmas 1939 ENSA was giving a thousand shows every week in the United Kingdom alone. By April 1940 its total audience had grown to 3 million. ENSA went everywhere – Gibraltar, Malta, Italy, the Western Desert and the Middle East, to East and West Africa, to Aden, India and Ceylon, to the Faroes and Iceland and to remote outposts such as the Cocos Islands. 'They suffered bombing and shelling with the troops, but in good theatrical tradition the show went on.'[1]

To name all the famous people who gave performances for nominal fees under the ENSA banner, would fill the rest of this chapter, but they included stars like Gracie Fields, Vera Lynn, George Formby, Bea Lillie, Josephine Baker, Geraldo and many, many others. Allied troops were entertained by many of their own artistes who were also exiled from occupied Europe. By 1944 there were 4,000 artistes on the NAAFI payroll. In one month ENSA put on 13,500 stage shows and 20,000 film shows. The total wartime cost to NAAFI was about £17 million.

CSEU

In a very similar manner to BFBS, with whom they are closely associated, sharing the same headquarters building in London, Forces entertainment is now run for all three Services under the single banner of 'CSEU – The Combined Services Entertainment Unit'. Show business personalities still give much of their time to entertaining Servicemen all over the world, particularly just now, in Northern

<hr>

[1] *Services to the Services* by Harry Miller

Ireland. Harry Secombe, once in battledress himself, has long been a generous supporter of CSEU. When BFBS held their 21st Anniversary celebrations in 1964, special 'Forces Gala Night' was recorded in conjunction with the BBC, at the Victoria Palace Theatre, London on Sunday, 1 November 1964. The gala programme which was subsequently broadcast to troops all over the world, included such artistes as the Goons, Jimmy Edwards, Anne Shelton, Ted Ray, Richard Murdoch and Kenneth Horne.

CAMP SHOWS INCORPORATED

On the other side of the Atlantic the development of an adequate entertainment programme had its growing pains and, although in 1941 the military authorities had constructed 186 new camp theatres, for most of the time they were dark and empty, as no organised way had been found to supply live entertainment. Several civilian groups tried to help, but their resources were limited. One of the most successful was the 'Friends of New York Soldiers', organised to entertain the men of the 27th Division who were mainly recruited from the city of New York. They did manage to reach a number of camps east of the Rockies in the summer of 1941 and were given $500,000 by the USO to help finance this work.

Meanwhile, a Hollywood committee, backed by agents and producers gave several large shows at a few Californian camps, with the co-operation of the Screen Actors Guild. When the Hollywood group learned about the New York initiative they were very concerned. They knew that they would be asked to furnish talent and to have to work with people entirely unfamiliar with show business, no matter how well-intentioned, was bound to lead to untold problems. After discussions it was agreed by the USO that 'Camp Shows Inc' should be set up as a separate organisation, affiliated to and supported by the USO. Camp Shows came into being on 30 October 1941 and the scale of their activities was soon worldwide.

There was no standard theatre as such; in one location they might be entertaining 15,000 GIs, sitting outdoors on the ground; in another as few as 25 men in

USO Show troupes, such as this one performing aboard an aircraft carrier in the Mediterranean, continue to bring live entertainment to American service personnel isolated in remote duty stations around the world. Since 1941 USO Shows have brought song, dance and laughter into the lives of millions upon millions of servicemen and women, and today remain one of the most important and popular aspects of USO's worldwide programmes

jeeps stationed at some lonely outpost: or perhaps by the bedside of a single wounded soldier in hospital.

As with ENSA there is no space to list the great number of dedicated performers who gave freely of their time and talent. However, one of the first to go overseas, one of the few to complete four overseas tours and later to set the record of 25 years of continuous service to the USO is Bob Hope. The troops loved him, he had only to walk out on a GI stage for the audience to explode into laughter. When President Johnson presented him with the USO Silver Medallion he said: 'We all know that wherever American men fight for freedom there will always be Hope. And Bob, two generations of Americans raise their glasses to you. Thanks for the Memories.'

In the weeks before D Day all available units played to the men waiting to embark for the invasion of Europe and on 28 July, only 48 days after the invasion landings, several Camp Show units landed on Utah Beach. Joe and Jane McKenna, a comedy team, followed the Normandy landing. Their assignment was to visit small gun emplacement locations. They drove their own jeep and were always told to 'be home by dark'. One time they didn't make it and were captured by a platoon of German soldiers, who could not speak English. Somehow by pantomine and their showmanship the McKennas convinced their captors that they were unarmed entertainers; however, they remained captive for 12 days – until advancing Americans freed them.

Stars and Stripes, official War Department newspaper in Europe, commented in an editorial in August 1944: 'The Army Special Services Section called them "Soldiers in Greasepaint" – the girls and men of the USO Camp Shows in Normandy are proving their right to that name by entertaining thousands of GIs daily within sound of the front line guns . . . these American troupers are living in Army tents, washing in their helmets, spending long hours at night in their slit trenches to escape flak and tracer bullets and eating Army chow. And when the Army moves forward they move too, in order to play to the men in the rest camps near the front. . . .

'To the troupers who are bringing joy and relaxation to the front line GIs, the *Stars and Stripes* extends a grateful tribute straight from the heart of the Army.'

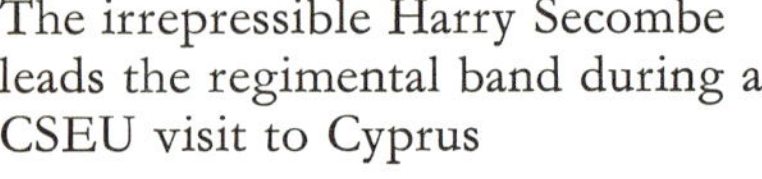

The irrepressible Harry Secombe leads the regimental band during a CSEU visit to Cyprus

Two lucky soldiers with their arms full of Julie Ege and Lois Lane during a CSEU Show in Cyprus

'Throughout the war, Camp Shows entertained wounded in hospitals in Europe, the Pacific and the United States. There were touching reactions to their performances. In one hospital in Italy while an actress sang to a group of wounded, a soldier called her to his bedside and asked if she would sing "Abide With Me". Of course she would, "But not now," he whispered in pain, "at my funeral," She tried to josh him out of the thought but he grabbed her hand pleading. Two days later she sang "Abide With Me", tears mingling with the sloshing rain, as they buried him on an Italian hillside.

'A comedienne singing in a ward of injured men, wondered why a doctor and a nurse were crying and laughing at the same time. They pointed to a boy who had applauded vigorously. He was suffering from a nervous paralysis. This was the first time since he had entered hospital that he had used his arms – for any purpose.

'A quiet activity suitable for use in hospital wards was sketching. More than 170 artists were recruited to tour stateside and overseas hospitals, sketching portraits of wounded men and mailing copies home. Sometimes the results were dramatic. A young Navy veteran at the Brooklyn Naval Hospital whose hands had been severely burned had become convinced that they were useless. The medical officers knew it was a psychological block. He spent each day doing nothing but gazing at his bandaged hands. A woman sketch artist asked if he wouldn't like a picture of himself. He turned away refusing to answer. She went to another bed and worked on a sketch. By the time she finished, the boy with the burned hands had got out of bed for the first time, walked to the washroom, shaved himself and combed his hair and was now striking poses waiting his turn to be sketched.

'One badly wounded infantryman said to a visiting artist: "Don't make me the way I am. Make me look nice and handsome for my mother. It may be the last she'll see of me." He was right.'[1]

From inception to 31 December 1947, Camp Show Inc had given 428,521 performances to a total audience of 212,974,401. At the height of production immediately following VE Day its curtains rose 700 times a day. A total of 7,336 entertainers were sent overseas and several times this number performed in the USA. Camp Shows enlisted and co-ordinated the greatest number of entertainers, performing to the largest audience, playing the most locations and travelling the greatest number of miles in the history of show business.

Since WW2 Camp Shows Inc have still had plenty to do, for example, during the Korean war they gave over 5,000 performances to battle-weary servicemen in Korea and the wounded in hospitals in Japan. The build up of American forces in Vietnam presented yet another challenge and in 1966 their 25th anniversary year, they had 35 'Professional Units' giving shows to US military personnel all over the world. Bob Hope still topped the list of performers, going out every year during the Vietnam war to give his Christmas show under the USO banner.

[1] *USO Historical Highlights, 1966* issued by the 25th Anniversary Committee

The Proudest Badge

THE MAN IN WHITE

At dawn on Friday, 24 June 1859, the armies of Austria, France and Italy were joined in battle in northern Italy, a few miles south-east of Bresica. The Austrians who, after declaring war had already lost two major engagements, were occupying what they believed to be an impregnable position, on a 15 mile front located in a low range of hills around Solferino.

Their young Emperor Francis Joseph had about 170,000 men and 500 artillery guns which dominated the heights and covered all the major approaches. The allied armies of France and Italy, numbering some 150,000 men with 400 guns and led by Emperor Napoleon III, had advanced in the darkness towards the Austrians, neither force having any idea that their enemy was so close until the moment of first contact, so all were totally unprepared for the savage fighting that followed.

The battle lasted for over 15 hours, all through the heat of the day and on into the evening, when the weather suddenly broke and torrents of cold, numbing rain drenched the exhausted soldiers. By then the Austrians were in full retreat and Napoleon was later able to send a message to his empress telling of 'a great battle and a great victory'. During the fighting the Austrians had suffered over 21,000 casualties, the allies nearly 17,000. Thousands more would die of their wounds in the days that followed, through lack of medical attention. A deliberate spectator of this carnage was a young Swiss industrialist, named Jean Henri Dunant.

Anxious to secure the patronage of the Emperor Napoleon for some ambitious business ventures in Algeria, he had left his home in Geneva earlier in the month, arriving at the Apennine village of Pontremoli on 20 June. Here he obtained a letter of recommendation to one of Napoleon's marshals from a friend, General

A Roman legionary receives first aid treatment (on the left) during the Dacian Wars (a scene from Trajan's Column)

Jean Henri Dunant (1828-1910)
founder of the Red Cross

Members of the International
Ambulance Organisation tending
wounded on the battefield during
the Franco Prussian War of 1870-71

de Beaufort. De Beaufort had also said to him 'if you want to see a first class battle you should cross the Apennines at once'. Dunant, immaculately dressed in a white tropical suit, hurried on, reaching the small town of Castiglione, near the battlefield, on 24 June.

He was horrified by the terrible scenes all around him and by the mass of wounded who poured into the town, filling all available shelter to overflowing. There was little skilled medical assistance although there were plenty of untrained volunteers and adequate supplies of lint and bandages. Dunant took it upon himself to organise the townsfolk, the women to take water around for the wounded to drink and to wash their wounds; the children to refill the pails of water and to bring the soldiers jugs of soup. He also took over the Church of San Maggiore where the wounded lay in closely packed rows in the nave, the side chapels, and even on the altar steps.

He made a point of treating friend and foe exactly the same, 'Tutti fratelli – all men are brothers', he remonstrated to a crowd, who were in the act of throwing two wounded Austrian prisoners out of the church. This phrase became a password throughout the town, as all laboured to help in the impossible task of dealing with so many dreadful injuries.

A merchant from Neufchatel who, like other volunteers just happened to be in the vicinity of the battle, devoted himself for two days, writing letters to families of the dying, as well as dressing wounds. After three more horrendous days and nights most of the wounded were moved to Bresica and other nearby large towns, where they could receive better care and attention, whilst Henri Dunant set off in his carriage to the French headquarters, where he was able to arrange for the release of all the captured Austrian doctors so that they too could help with the wounded. He then returned to Castiglione, moving on to Bresica to continue his selfless work.

Two ambulances sent out by the English National Society (The Red Cross) for service during the Turco-Servian War, pictured in Belgrade, 1876

An early Red Cross volunteer helper, Mr T E Smith, a storekeeper at Saarbrucken during the Franco-Prussian War of 1870-71

'The man in white' as he was called by the wounded, was profoundly affected by all that he had seen, in particular by the woeful lack of experienced volunteer nurses and medical orderlies. Two years later he wrote a short, but extraordinary book called: *Un Souvenir de Solferino*, in which he told of the battle and the terrible scenes that followed, graphically describing the rough surgery performed without drugs or anaesthetics. He ended the book by asking the question as to whether or not it would be possible to form, in peacetime, relief societies based on international agreements which had been sanctioned by a congress of nations.

The book was first published in the autumn of 1862, printed in Geneva, an edition *de luxe* of 1,600 copies. Dunant sent it to all the crowned heads and princes of Europe, to ministers of war and foreign affairs and to everyone he thought might help. It created a sensation and letters of congratulation poured in from all quarters. However, despite the stir the book caused at the time, it could well have been forgotten had it not been for the drive and initiative of Gustave Moynier, one of Geneva's leading lawyers, who bustled the unpractical, visionary Dunant into positive action. He got the Geneva Public Welfare Society, of which he was chairman, to appoint a committee to prepare a memorandum on the proposed relief society. From this small beginning they went from strength to strength and finally an assembly was called of the representatives from as many sovereign states as would respond.

This first international conference was held in Geneva in October 1863, when the delegates of 14 states met to consider the proposals which 'the man in white' had made in his book. It was a momentous and unforgettable occasion, which led directly to the signing of the 'Convention of Geneva for the amelioration of the condition of the wounded in armies in the field'. The chief delegate from Great Britain was Surgeon-General Sir Thomas Longmore who had come there to explain how our military hospitals were run and to put over the comments of Florence Nightingale, to whom Dunant had sent a copy of his book. 'The Lady of the Lamp', whilst commending the spirit of Dunant's proposals, felt that it was up to individual governments to take action and not to have their responsibilities removed from them by private relief societies. However, Longmore did sign the draft convention although, as he had explained, he came without full authority. But the chairman General Dufour, General-in-Chief of the Swiss Republic, had the answer to that problem and, taking out his penknife, cut a button from Longmore's jacket saying: 'There your Excellency, you have the arms of Her Majesty.' So the seal to the British signature on the Geneva Convention is the imprint of a British Army button.

The agreement thus signed would give protection to the sick and wounded on any future battlefield, as well as those who went to help them. Field dressing stations and medical supplies would also have the same protection. National Societies would be formed to train the volunteer personnel and to prepare and keep the supplies ready in the event of war.

By 1867 all the Great Powers had ratified the Convention, except for the USA who did so in 1882. It had been decided that the emblem of the Society should be a red cross on a white field, the reversed colours of the Swiss flag, which General Dufour had also created some years earlier. And so the Red Cross Society which has for over a century meant protection, relief and comfort, to thousands

The price of an Eastern Empire
Russian suffering in the battlefields of Manchuria during the Russo-Japanese war of 1904-05

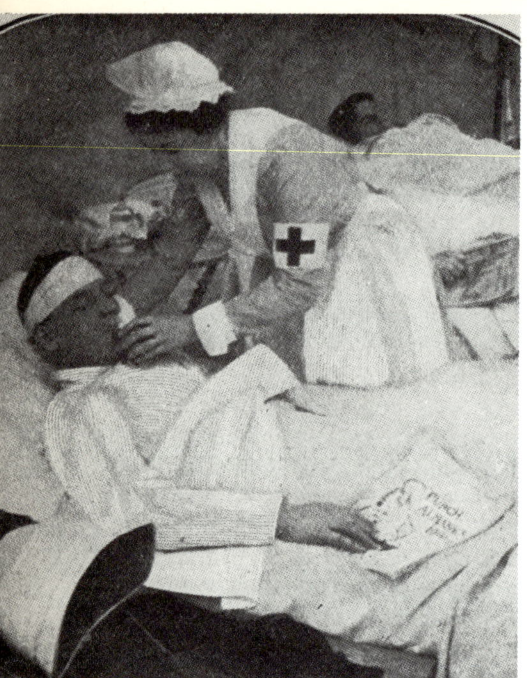
A Red Cross nurse at work in a
Field Hospital on the Tugela River
during the South African War
(1899-1902)

of soldiers, sailors and airmen, whether sick, wounded or prisoners of war, came
into existence.

But what of Henri Dunant? Sadly, his private affairs went from bad to worse,
until imminent bankruptcy forced him to move to Paris, where he lived in penury
for many years. Towards the end of his life, however, he was 're-discovered' and
from then on tributes and honours were heaped upon him. The crowning accolade
came when he was awarded the Nobel Peace Prize in 1901, which carried with it
an annuity of over 10,000 francs. He died on Sunday 30 October 1910, but the
Society which his vision had founded has gone on growing until it now spans the
entire world, with over one hundred societies, called Red Cross or Red Crescent
according to which emblem their countries use. There is, in addition, The Society
of Iran called Red Lion and Sun, and finally the Societies of the Soviet Republics,
which also use different emblems but are part of the Alliance of Red Cross and
Red Crescent Societies.

EARLY NURSING

One must of course, look further back than Solferino to find the beginnings of
military nursing. From the very earliest times some help was usually provided
for wounded soldiers. The Roman Army, for example, had a doctor of wounds, a
'Medicus Vulnerum' with each legion.

During the Crusades, civil aid was given to troops, but usually during the
Middle Ages sick or wounded soldiers were either killed by their own comrades
to prevent them being tortured by the enemy, or just abandoned.

Gradually doctors, called Surgeon-Barbers in the English Army, came to be
an integral part of most European armies. Although professional nurses and
hospital orderlies were still practically non-existent, there were a small number of
exceptions. During the Civil War in England for example, the London hospitals
of St Bartholomew, Bridewell, St Thomas and Bethlehem, supplied the only

Camp life in a high wind A nursing
sister's tent blows down in South
Africa, but she still manages a
cheerful wave

permanent provision for the cure of sick and wounded soldiers. From 1642 to
1653 they were freed from all taxes and assessments because 'great numbers of
sick, wounded and other soldiers have for the time of twenty months past, been
constantly kept in said hospitals at very great and extraordinary charges especially
for their diet and cure.'[1]

In November 1644, two military hospitals were created – Savoy and Ely
House. The nurses of the Savoy hospital were 'ordered to be chosen from the
widows of soldiers so far as fit ones can be found and to be paid 5 shillings a
week.[2] One woman called Hester Whyte petitioned the Parliamentarians explaining that she had taken charge of some wounded Roundheads after the battle of
Edgehill, 'who continued at her house in great misery by reason of their wounds
for three months'. She had often sat up night and day with them and in respect of
her 'tenderness to the Parliament's friends' had laid out her own money to supply
their wants.

John Hunter, writing on the campaign in Portugal in 1762-63, noted with
interest that female nurses were for the first time officially included in the expedition. The hospital matron was a Mrs Sullivan and she received half-a-crown a

[1,2] *Cromwell's Army* by Charles Firth

Indian stretcher bearers under fire in
South Africa

day. There were two head nurses – Mary Fenton and Ann Milrose and three
women cooks at one shilling per day. There were also five washerwomen at the
same rate of pay and eighteen women nurses at sixpence each, so the washerwomen
received twice as much as the nurses!

In his excellent book on life in Wellington's army, Antony Brett-James explains
how the medical machinery worked better when a battle was being fought near
a large town or city, not only because there was more accommodation to use for
the wounded, but also because the: 'energy and resources of the local population
became instantly available.

'On 22 July 1812, for instance, many inhabitants of Salamanca came out,
carrying with them tea, coffee and other refreshments, while carts laden with
fresh fruit, provisions and containers of water squeaked their way to the scene.
Women back in the city had already prepared a large quantity of lint and rags for
binding up wounds, and many Spanish girls were to be seen that evening supporting from the battlefield those among the wounded soldiers who were able to walk.
They also carried their knapsacks and muskets. The local doctors too, came out
by torchlight with jackasses laden with bandages and other stores in order to dress
the wounded – or some of them at least – on the spot'[1]

THE CRIMEA AND FLORENCE NIGHTINGALE

It is true to say that the real history of British nursing started with Florence
Nightingale who was born in 1820, in the city after which she was named. She
was born into the idle, frivolous, smooth rich life which, she wrote in later years,
'was utterly distasteful' to her, even before she had reached her teens. She grew

[1] *Life in Wellington's Army* by Antony Brett-James

into an attractive girl, slight of build and graceful, with a fair complexion and rich chestnut hair.

Her home life was secure, affectionate and comfortable but it was not peaceful, for her family lived on their emotions. Florence herself was extremely sensitive, prone to exaggeration and highly emotional, but was also clear-minded and realistic. One can discover a lot about her inner feelings as she had a habit of writing notes. And fortunately a great many of them have been preserved.

When she was not quite 17 she wrote: 'On February 7th 1837 God spoke to me and called me to His service'. Although she spent a great deal of her time in a dream world this was something quite different. The problem for her was that although she had been called, she had no idea as to the purpose. It wasn't until eight years later that she discovered it was nursing, and a further eight years before she actually became a nurse.

She had no practical knowledge of nursing; her only experience was looking after her ailing grandmother, her old nurse and some of the local villagers. When she broke the news of her plans to the family they were horror-stricken. Her mother, Fanny, had hysterics – she knew that Florence could make a brilliant marriage; she was popular, intelligent and a social success.

But Florence wrote in one of her notes that in order to be worthy to be God's servant she must resist 'the desire to shine in society'. The family had good reasons to be horror-struck. In those days hospitals were dreadful places and hospital smell, which was completely nauseating, was accepted as inevitable. There were normally 50-60 beds tightly packed into a ward and the filth was indescribable. Several years later Florence wrote in Notes on hospitals 'floors were saturated with organic matter, which when washed gave off a smell something quite other

An early pre WW1 picture of some members of the First Aid Nursing Yeomanry (FANY), founded in 1907 as a band of mounted nurses who would ride out to the actual scenes of action. The group were composed of adventurous upper-class ladies who could provide their own mounts

than soap and water. Walls and ceilings were saturated with impurity and a minute vegetation appeared.'[1]

The patients came mainly from the slum areas and had no idea of cleanliness. The nurses were no better. They were notorious for their promiscuity and drunkenness. Some of them carried on their prostitution at the same time as nursing. They were dirty, undisciplined and unsupervised. No respectable woman ever thought of nursing in a hospital.

However, after eight years of frustration, opposition and studying in secret she finally overcame family opposition and went to The Sisters of Charity in Paris. Whilst there she wrote endless questionnaires to hospitals all over Europe and their answers, together with the notes she made at first hand, gave her a clear picture of hospital administration. She took to hospital life as if made for it.

In 1853 when she came back to London, Florence heard that the Institute for the care of Sick Gentlewomen in Distressed Circumstances required an administrator. After an interview, Florence went to manage the Institute. She had started on her career at last.

Although she did a lot of practical nursing her main task was balancing the accounts and controlling the committee. Soon she could quite easily control both. By January 1854 when all was running smoothly at the Institute, Florence set about the task of reforming conditions in hospitals for the nurses.

At this time, after 40 years of peace, the British Army was mobilising for the Crimea. As the victorious Wellington's army had been allowed to run down, volunteers had to be drafted in to make up the numbers. Then, amidst flag waving and band playing, the army sailed off for the Crimea.

They landed at Varna but before they could even get to grips with the enemy they were hit by a cholera epidemic. Over 1,000 cases were sent back to the military

[1] *Florence Nightingale* by Cecil Woodham-Smith

hospital at Scutari. A few days later the British and French troops fought and won the battle of the Alma and the wounded joined the cholera victims whose numbers had already been swelled by a further 1,000 cases. The hospital at Scutari was already filled by the first cholera victims so when the wounded and the other cholera cases arrived, the huge barracks, to which the hospital was attached, had to be used as well.

The casualties lay on filthy floors in filthy blankets. There was no medicine, clothing or bedding, few doctors and not even basic commodities like cups and spoons. The sick lay in crammed rows, some without even a drink of water for hours and sometimes days. The horrors of Scutari came as a complete shock to the public at home. They had been told of the great victory at Alma, but nothing of the dreadful conditions. They were put in the picture by our first war correspondent, William Howard Russell. (*see Chapter 9*)

It was as a result of his despatches in *The Times*, that Sidney Herbert, who had been appointed Secretary at War, wrote to Florence Nightingale asking her to take charge of a group of female nurses who were to be sent over to Scutari. He wrote to her: 'There is but one person in England that I know of who would be capable of organising and superintending such a scheme.' The terms of his letter she took to be her charter. It was quite clear that she was required more for her administrative abilities than for her nursing. Her appointment was the talking point of the day.

Her family, forgetting that they had caused her 16 years of frustration, were elated. On Saturday, 21 October 1854, Florence and her party of 38 nurses (of mixed religious denominations, as she insisted that nurses had to be chosen for their fitness for the job with no regard to their religious beliefs) left London for

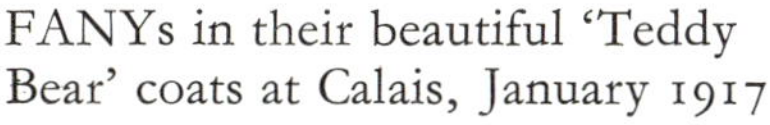

FANYs in their beautiful 'Teddy Bear' coats at Calais, January 1917

A VAD Dressing Station at Abbeville, 1917

Constantinople via Boulogne, Paris and Marseilles. They were to go straight to the hospital which was by then expecting an influx of wounded from the Battle of Balaclava.

Poor Florence. A more depressing arrival would be hard to imagine. It was pouring with rain, everywhere was a sea of mud and refuse. Scutari hospital and barracks, which had looked so magnificent from a distance, changed dramatically the nearer they approached. It was an enormous, ramshackle, filthy building. Built as a square round a courtyard, one wing was closed as it had been damaged by a fire sometime before their arrival, the rest was damp and decaying, the smell was dreadful and it was infested by rats, lice and fleas.

They found no accommodation had been arranged for them and were squeezed into five tiny rooms without beds or bedding. The Army Medical Department, most of the doctors and staff – and Dr John Hall, Chief of the Medical Staff, in

The Duchess of Sutherland with some wounded soldiers at her hospital, Calais, July 1917

particular – were determined to make life difficult for them, stating that they were 'an unwise indulgence, unfavourable to medical discipline and to the recovery of the patients'.

On 9 November, something happened to make everyone forget their differences and every available person had to help. A flood of starving, frozen sick men poured into Scutari. They were the remnants of the exhausted and demoralised British Army, suffering from scurvy, dysentry and exposure to weather, which would have been hard to bear even if well equipped. They weren't equipped at all. Most of them had merely the tattered clothes on their backs. They had been living rough with no tents, permanently wet and with little to eat. The Army was disintegrating.

The overworked and harassed officials realised gradually that there was only one person amongst them with the money for supplies and the authority to use

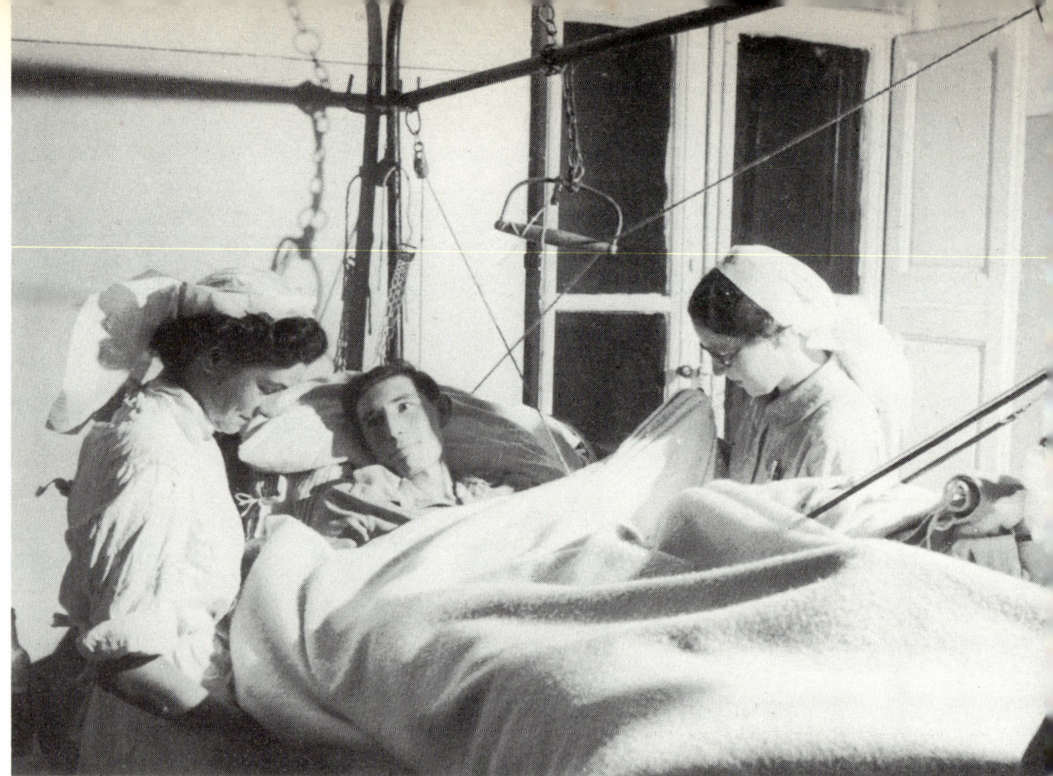

VADs in Italy, December 1944 The first 100 VADs from the UK to nurse in Military Hospitals in Italy arrived on 8 October 1944 at Naples. These girls were accompanied by a unit of Maltese VADs belonging to the Order of St John of Jerusalem who had volunteered for service overseas after the siege of Malta had been raised. All the girls were volunteers

it, and that was Miss Nightingale. Florence took things into her own capable hands.

As they needed more space she authorised and paid for the fourth wing of the barracks to be repaired. She had the wards scrubbed and equipped, supplying shirts, socks, slippers, cutlery, towels, soap, operating tables, disinfectant, scissors and bedpans. The sick continued to pour in. Often Florence was on her feet for 24 hours at a time.

The troops idolised her – content just to watch her walk by, if they couldn't speak to her. Not only did she nurse the worst cases herself, she also had to do a huge amount of administrative work. On top of all this she wrote letters for the soldiers, long detailed accounts to Sidney Herbert, also official letters and reports. It was work and hours that would have daunted strong men and Florence was a slight woman born to luxury. She did not mind the hard work or long hours, but what she did mind was the intrigue and malice of Dr John Hall and Mr David Fitzgerald, the Purveyor in Chief, and their followers.

At last some semblance of order was established, but the arguments went on. Besides being harassed and plotted against by the medical staff, Florence also had problems with the different religious groups – Catholics, Protestants and Anglicans had all sent out sisters and nurses – her orders were disobeyed, her authority to command questioned and her position constantly undermined by sectarian quarrelling.

But the general public at home had made her into a legend. There were songs and poems written about her, biographies, paintings and china ornaments of her. Queen Victoria wrote to her and sent an enamel and diamond brooch which was inscribed 'To Miss Florence Nightingale as a mark of esteem and gratitude for her devotion towards the Queen's brave soldiers from Victoria R, 1855'.

Florence was determined to reform the lot of the ordinary soldier. She was convinced that if he had something to do and somewhere to go, during his off duty hours, he would not just get drunk. She wrote to her sister: 'Give them the opportunity promptly and securely to send money home and they will use it. Give them schools and lectures and they will come to them. Give them games, books and amusements and they will leave off drinking . . . I would rather have to do with the Army generally than any other class I have attempted to serve.'

After much opposition she opened a reading room for the walking sick. In spite of the pessimism of the authorities, it was a great success. Florence started to collect money from any soldier wanting to send it home; she also sent a plan of the new method for sending money home to the authorities, and the Queen (to whom Florence had also written) sent the plan to Lord Palmerston who thought it a good idea. Lord Panmure, then Secretary of War disagreed, saying that the soldiers would rather spend their money on drink. But he was proved wrong and over £71,000 was sent home in the first few months.

More recreation rooms were opened and books, puzzles, games and writing materials were provided. Four schools were opened with professional teachers. From then onwards the British soldier lost his image of a drunken, brutish lout and became a human being.

Although she laboured unceasingly Florence still had to contend with 'malicious and scandalous libels'. Finally she wrote an official letter to the War Office complaining about John Hall's deliberate undermining of her position.

On 16 March the following despatch was published in General Orders – 'It

Inchon, Korea Mrs Jerry Crewe of the British Red Cross Society and her American counterpart, Miss Mary O Ingles, visit patients in the 121st Evacuation Hospital near Inchon, during the Korean War

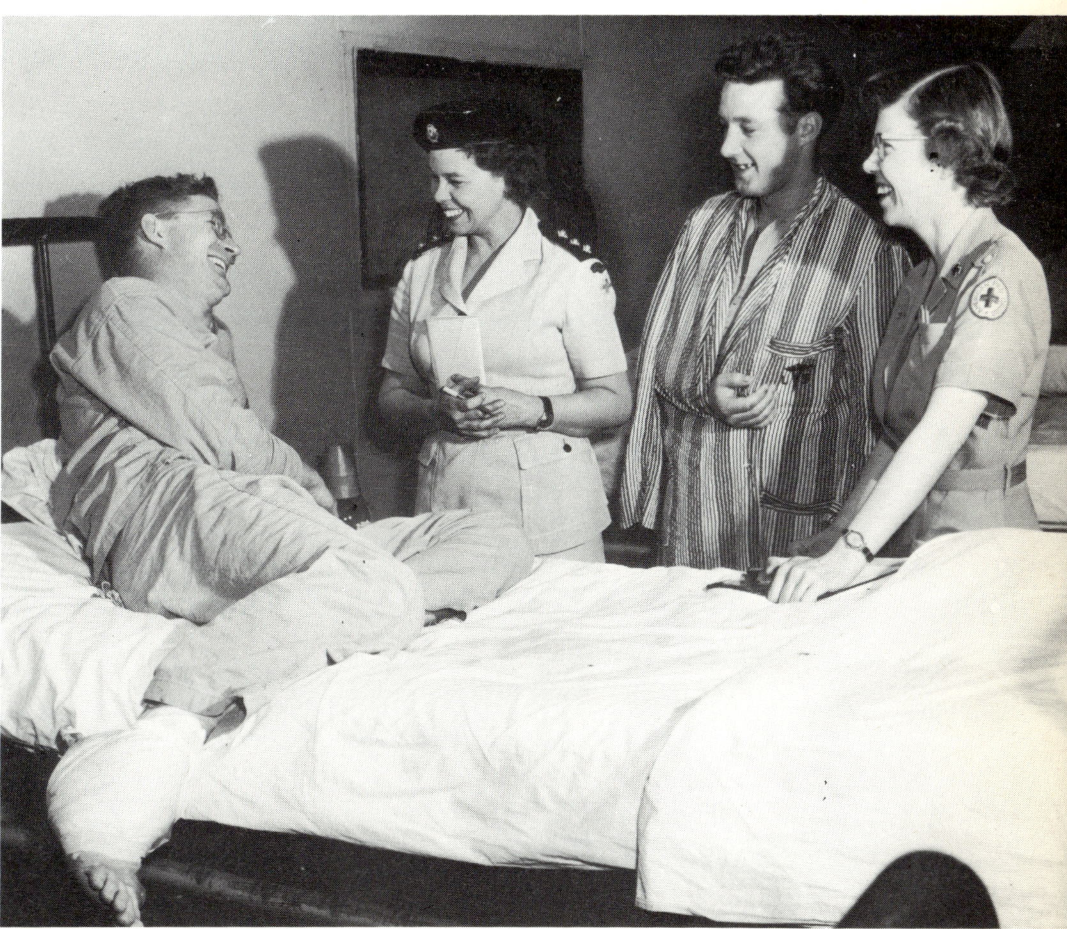

appears to me that the Medical Authorities of the Army do not correctly comprehend Miss Nightingale's position as it has been officially recognised by me. I therefore think it right to state to you briefly for their guidance as well as for the information of the Army, what the position of that excellent Lady is. Miss Nightingale is recognised by Her Majesty's Government as the General Superintendent of the Female Nursing Establishment of the Military Hospitals of the Army. No lady, or sister, or nurse, is to be transferred from one hospital to another, or introduced into any hospital without consultation with her. Her instructions, however, require to have the approval of the Principal Medical Officer in the exercise of the responsibility thus invested in her. The Principal Medical Officer will communicate with Miss Nightingale upon all subjects connected with the Female Nursing Establishment and will give his directive through that Lady.'

Florence was vindicated – it meant complete failure for Dr Hall and his associ-

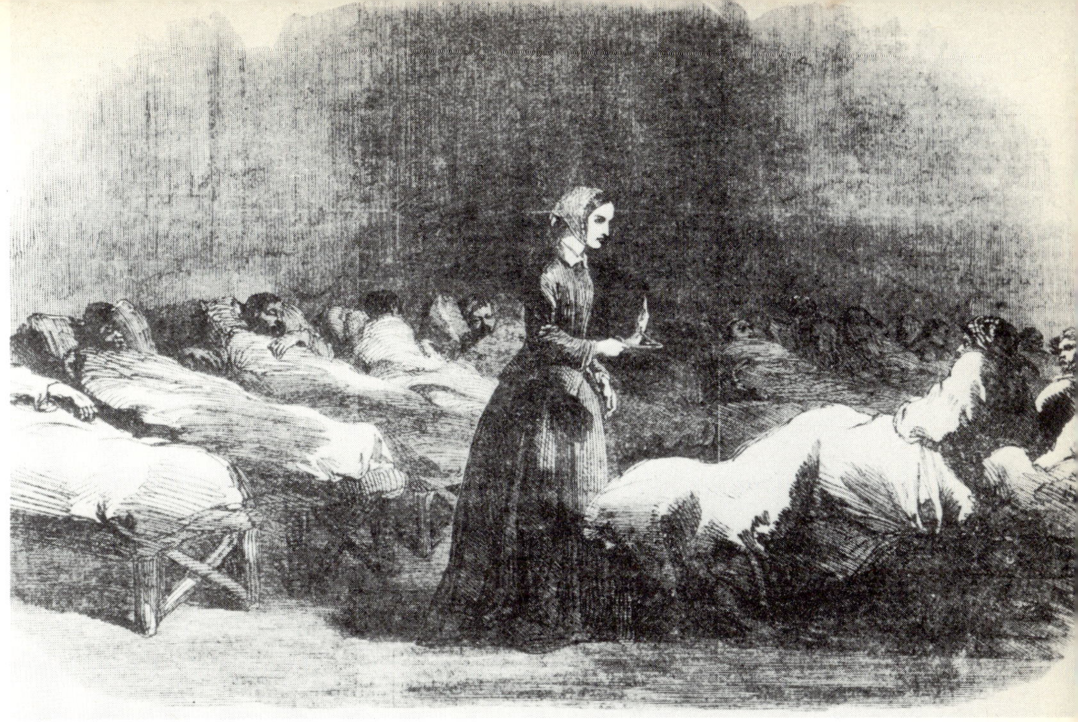

ates. Her huge task was over and the war was nearly over too. She was famous but was afraid of her fame. People wanted to fête her, but in spite of all their efforts to find out when and where she would land in England, Florence slipped in unobtrusively and went home. This, however, was not the end of her career; she was about to start on another great fight – to reform the health administration of the British Army.

CLARA BARTON – ANGEL OF THE BATTLEFIELD

America's most famous nurse, Clara Barton, was born on Christmas Day 1821 in Massachussetts and, like her English counterpart, became a household name. She was the youngest of five children but was a lonely, timid child. Many years later, when writing her autobiography she wrote: 'I had no playmates but in effect six Fathers and Mothers.'

She grew into a small (5ft), plain, sensitive woman full of nervous energy and determination. Her patience and honesty were impelling and her compassion for the sick inspired devotion.

For a short time she was a clerk in the Patents Office in Washington – possibly the first officially appointed female civil servant. But at the outbreak of Civil War she took it upon herself to console and comfort the homesick Massachussetts soldiers in Washington.

Horrified by the total lack of facilities at the Battle of Bull Run, she advertised in a local paper – the (Mass.) *Worcester Spy* – for provisions for the wounded, and using her own small lodgings as a store-room she gathered together bandages, medicines and food. Despite opposition from the War Department and Medical staff, in the summer of 1802 she and some friends packed these supplies on to a mule train and distributed them to the ill-equipped hospitals and camps on the battlefields of Virginia and Maryland.

She then nursed the wounded and dying at the battles of Cedar Mountain, Second Bull Run, Chantilly, South Mountain, Antietam and Fredericksberg.

Because she was both co-operative and persuasive, she was able to obtain army

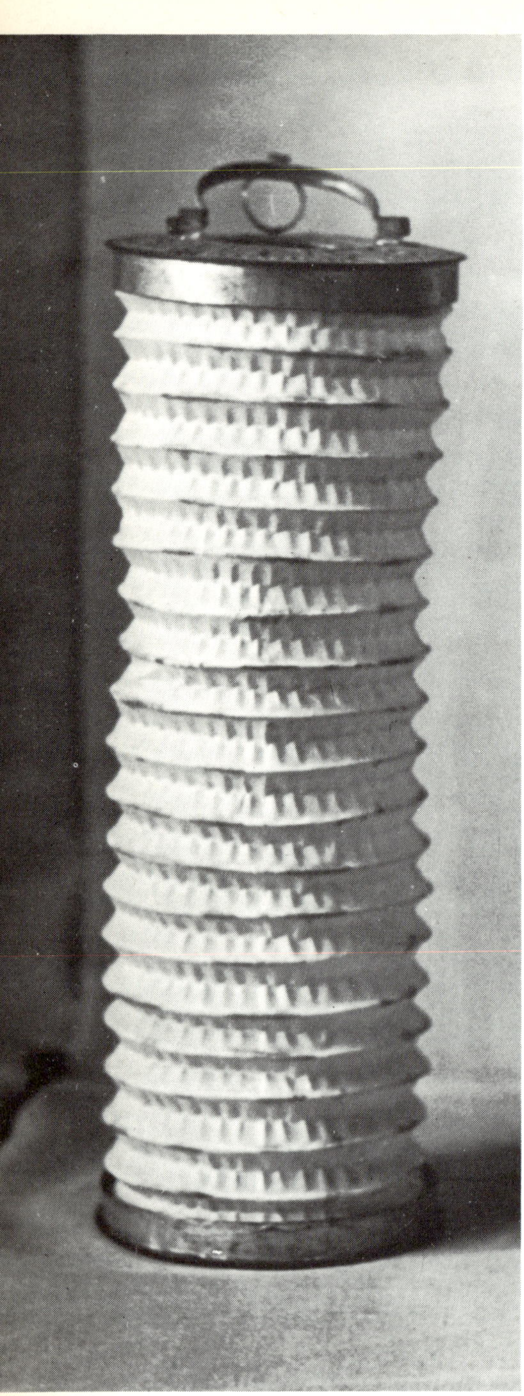

The actual lamp used by Florence Nightingale in the Crimea. It was of Turkish design

mules and wagons to transport desperately needed supplies to the battle lines. To thousands of soldiers she was the 'Angel of the Battlefields' having given first aid or prepared soup or coffee for them. One surgeon said: 'If heaven ever sent a holy angel she must be the one, her assistance was so timely.'

Realising that organisation was required if prompt action was to be taken, she allowed nothing to stand in the way of her mission. Distressed by the neglected wounded on the battlefields, she reported her findings to Senator Wilson who instituted an investigation.

The press began to write of her exploits on behalf of the soldiers, and the soldiers themselves wrote to their families about her. As a result she received an avalanche of supplies.

Eventually, as the official agencies grew more efficient, Clara had less and less to do, so she returned to Washington. In 1865, with Lincoln's approval, she set up an office in Annapolis, with a small staff, and began to piece together information about missing men, giving the results of her findings to their families.

Also, with the help of a young man who, whilst he had been a prisoner of war, had been ordered to keep a death roll, she saw to the marking of the graves of 13,000 men from the notorious Andersonville prison.

Thanks to Senator Wilson, the following year Congress appropriated 15,000 dollars to pay back Clara for all the heavy expenses she had shouldered in carrying out these tasks.

Worn out by a countrywide lecture tour describing her experiences, Clara had a breakdown and went to Europe to recuperate. Whilst in Switzerland she heard about the formation of the International Committee of the Red Cross and was invited by Dr Louis Appia to work for them in the Franco-Prussian war. She established a sewing workshop in Strasburg for war victims – needy women who were thus able to earn their own living.

After another breakdown and a year spent mainly in England, Clara returned to the USA. At the outbreak of the Russo-Turkish war her interest in the Red Cross revived and she started what turned out to be a five-year campaign for the organisation of the American Red Cross, as the State Department had steadfastly refused to ratify the treaty.

To persuade Congress, the State Department and White House she wrote pamphlets, newspaper articles and gave public speeches.

At last, on 1 March 1882, the President signed the treaty which was ratified by the Senate two weeks later.

During the Spanish-American war, at the age of 73, despite intolerable conditions, Clara took to driving mule wagons of supplies to the battlefields once again. The Red Cross distributed over 6,000 tons of provisions, valued at half a million dollars, for the incredibly low administrative cost of 11,706 dollars.

There was criticism within the organisation however, as Clara was unwilling to adapt to new conditions and was unable to delegate. In 1904, with great reluctance and pressure from her board of directors – and even President Roosevelt – Clara resigned.

Clara died in 1912, aged 91. She had been the most frequently honoured woman in America and had received medals and honours from the rulers of many foreign countries.

Florence Nightingale in old age.
Miss Nightingale is seen here at
Claydon House in 1889. She was
full of vitality and gaiety in her
closing days, the end coming on
13th August 1910. 'To be a good
nurse one must be a *good woman*, or
one is truly nothing but a tinkling
bell'

A HEROINE OF THE BATTLEFIELD

Alas, space does not permit us to go into sufficient detail to describe the wonderful
work done over the years by the nurses and nursing orderlies of the Red Cross,
the FANYs, the VADs, the St John Ambulance Brigade and their many foreign
counterparts, but the photographs accompanying this chapter show graphically
how they have toiled unceasingly on behalf of the sick and wounded.

However, it would be wrong not to include any first hand examples of the work
which these volunteer nurses undertook. We have chosen two from the Great
War, the first being a glimpse into the daily life of Florence Farmborough, a
young English girl, who had been teaching English in Moscow when war was
declared and immediately volunteered for Red Cross work.

After training in a hospital in Moscow she became a member of a medical
'Flying Column' (A Russian Red Cross Surgical Field Unit) in which she was the
only true volunteer, the rest being conscripted into the service rather like the
soldiers they treated.

The USA's most famous nurse, Clara Barton, known as 'The Angel of the Battlefield' during the American Civil War. Her relief work was comparable to what FN had achieved in the Crimea

In March 1915 she was sent to the front line, serving first in Poland and Austria, and later in Roumania. Almost straightaway she was caught up in the chaos of the great Russian retreat, attending to endless wounded soldiers under the most primitive conditions, fleeing by night, sleeping rough or in deserted houses and peasant huts, a witness to the most appalling scenes of devastation.

In 1916 the Russian Army had advanced into Austria, but was soon checked by lack of supplies. Back in Russia the murder of Rasputin was followed by the abdication of the Tsar, against a background of famine and unrest. At the Front there was panic, rumour and confusion, as contradictory orders were received and food and supplies grew more and more scarce. Mass revolt and desertion followed, leading eventually, in 1917, to all out Civil War.

The 'Flying Column' was disbanded, but Miss Farmborough managed to get back to Moscow. From there, late in 1918, she escaped across Siberia to Vladivostock and eventually reached America and safety. Here is a short extract from the diary which she kept during her service with the 'Flying Column' '. . . *Tuesday, 24th May*. The guns have been terribly active all night. It had rained heavily towards dawn and I found the outside world very wet and dirty when I set off to relieve the Sister on duty at 8am. There had been a few wounded during the night, but as the morning lengthened they came in their numbers. We were all working steadily, no time to waste in useless commiseration; compassion would prove only a hindrance; so, numbly, we worked on and on. By 2.30am most of the severest cases had been dealt with. . . .

'*Wed 25th May* . . . I felt unutterably weary; the odd hour of rest seemed to have done me more harm than good, but the wounded were still coming in and hands were badly needed. We worked all night. Several badly wounded and exhausted

Miss Florence Farmborough is seen here (on the right) in summer transport moving off to the front line

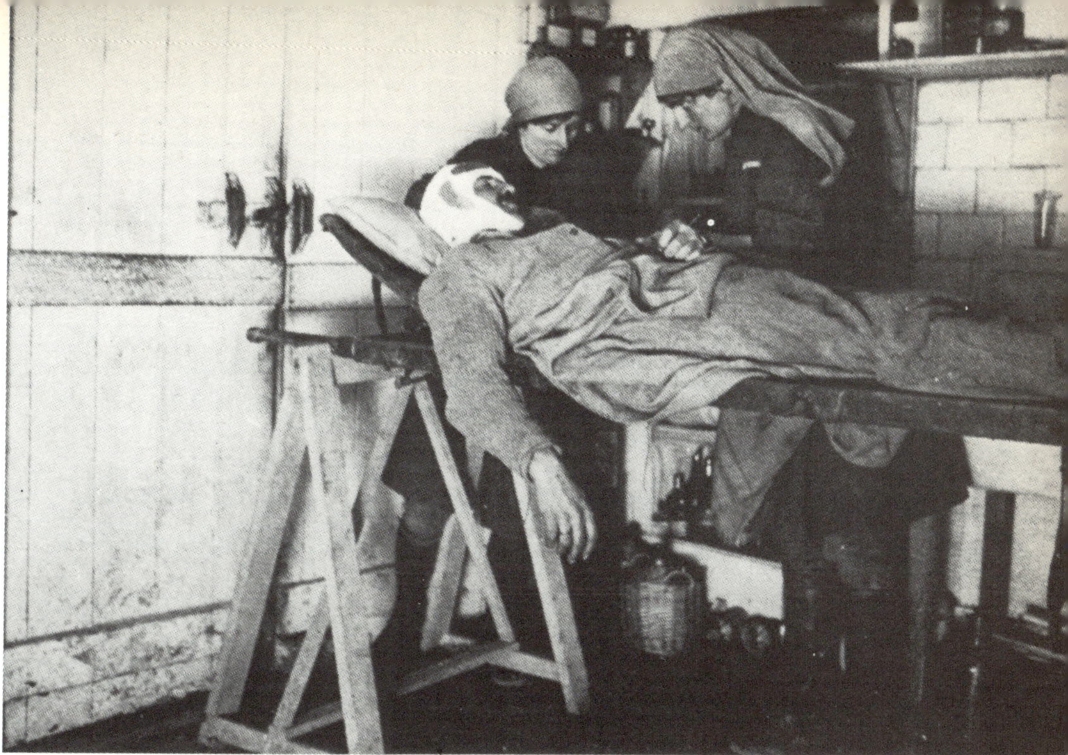

The two women of Pervyse, Baroness de T'Serclaes and Miss Mairi Chisholm, attending a wounded Belgian soldier in their advanced dressing post in Pervyse

Austrians were among our men; one young Austrian officer had a smashed skull and had died in transit; a second had received such a dreadful head-wound that his face was thickly covered with clotted black blood – he too, died before we could attempt to clean and dress his wound.

'*Thursday, 26th May* . . . It has been another hard-working night. Some of the wounds have been dreadful to look at. Several men were dead on arrival; seven died during the night. Two were so badly mauled by shell-fire that I marvelled to hear them still able to speak. Here was a man with half-a-dozen fatal wounds on his body and his strength of will is such that he can ask the time of day, the exact location of our Red Cross unit, even the latest news from his sector of the Front. And, having received the answers, he turns his face to the wall and quietly surrenders his wounded body to Death. Is there in our language no greater, more laudatory word than "hero" for a man of this calibre? I feel terribly tired today and my back aches acutely; I am afraid that there is not much of the "hero" about me – not a scratch on my body and yet I can scarcely walk! An adjutant from our divisional staff came in the evening. He affirmed that the Austrians were retreating fast before our advancing troops. . . . In the midst of our elation at the success of our fighting-men, there came a flash of bad news from England. Lord Kitchener, the great English General, had died; drowned off the northern coast of Scotland when the cruiser on which he was sailing was torpedoed . . .'[1]

THE TWO WOMEN OF PERVYSE

Only two women were allowed by the Allies to live and work in the trenches on the Western Front, an English woman Elsie Knocker (later the Baroness de T'Seracles) and a young Scots girl Mairi Chisholm, who together, for three-and-a-half years, ran a cellar first aid post just behind the front line trenches in the ruined Belgian village of Pervyse.

[1] *Nurse at the Russian Front* by Florence Farmborough

The Baroness de T'Serclaes and Miss
Mairi Chisholm in the 'garden' of
their third post in Pervyse,
9 September 1917

They were originally members of a flying ambulance service, raised in August
1914 by a Scots doctor, Hector Munro, for service with the tiny Belgian Army as
it faced the initial massive German onslaught. After two months of service with
the ambulances, Mrs Knocker decided that, because of the very real danger of
casualties dying from shock and exposure during their nightmare journeys to
hospital, the real answer was to establish a first aid post right up at the front line,
where she could deal with them as quickly as possible after they had been wounded.
She asked Mairi to join her and together they went to Pervyse, where the determined Mrs Knocker persuaded the Belgian authorities to allow them to set up
their post in the cellar of a ruined house and even to provide them with orderlies.

Her most important job was to drive the wounded back to the nearest hospital
at La Panne. Once Mrs Knocker had given them first aid, the orderlies loaded up
the primitive, rickety ambulance and Mairi began the journey: 'You drove the
three miles to the hospital in the pitch darkness. You had absolutely no protection
– no windscreen or anything like that. And you sat on a bench to drive, with the
rain coming down, possibly in torrents, and the wind blowing. Also of course,
troops and replacement guns were going up to the front. You had to listen all the
time and have your eyes out on stalks. If you got off the centre strip of cobbles,
you sank, possibly right up to the hubs, in mud.'[1]

In February 1915 the King of Belgium personally pinned the Order of Leopold
onto their tunics and later both were awarded the British Military Medal – two
of only a handful of women to receive the award in the Great War.

After a while they found it was too difficult to cope with the endless stream of

[1] *Women at War, the two heroines of Pervyse* published in *The Listener* 28 April 1977

100

wounded in their cramped cellar, so they moved to another house, but were shelled out of it, missing death by inches. Their third post was a concrete structure inside the shell of a house, with plenty of sandbags on top for added protection.

They continued to work in their new shelter despite gas attacks, as Mairi explained: 'Because of the roar of the guns, it was impossible to say a word to anybody, as they couldn't hear you. And then the odd gas-shells started to come in and we got into our gas-masks. For 48 hours, this attack raged – salvos of shells mixed with gas-shells and not a chance of the wounded getting anywhere near us. We were both really pretty well exhausted because the gas-masks of those days had wire nippers which fitted on to your nostrils and squashed them absolutely tight. They really hurt, they were so tight. We had these on and off the whole time for 48 hours and then there was a kind of respite and we both took off our masks and tried to breathe the air. Between the reception room and our pillbox was open air and into this had dropped two gas-shells, very neatly. They didn't contain mustard gas. . . . It was arsenic gas we were gassed with.'[1]

Sent home for treatment and a brief spell of recuperation, Mairi returned alone to Belgium and was gassed again. The war was by then grinding to a close and that was the end of the work of the 'Women of Pervyse', but their incredible bravery will live forever, as an inspiration to all.

MODERN NURSING

Nowadays in sophisticated modern war most armies have properly organised and uniformed medical staff, so the need for the brave volunteers of the past does not normally arise. Of course the Red Cross continues to provide world wide assistance, during any kind of emergency, to soldier and civilian alike. How many of us now living owe our lives to the vision of 'the man in white' all those years ago? 'Tutti fratelli – all men are brothers.'

---

[1] *Women at War, the two heroines of Pervyse* published in *The Listener* 28 April 1977

7

The Volunteers

A CHANGE OF PUBLIC OPINION

'The Son of Man is come to seek and to save that which was lost'
LUKE, CHAPTER 19, VERSE 10

Without doubt it was the Crimean war that began the change of attitude in public opinion towards the British Army and its place in society. What had for generations been described as the 'brutal and licentious soldiery' was transformed by the end of the 19th century into Kipling's 'thin red line of 'eroes' and hailed for the first time as the 'People's Army'. When one remembers that it did not truly become a people's army until the Great War, then it makes the dramatic change of public attitude all the more surprising.

One of the major reasons for this change was the considerable force of Christian militarism which grew with the belief that soldiers deserved to be 'saved' and that perhaps Christians made the best soldiers anyway – a view vindicated by the evidence of the Indian Mutiny and the successful defeat of the mutineers by such heroes as Henry Havelock, who died at the siege of Lucknow.

This religious revival led to the formation of innumerable societies, 'The British and Foreign Seamen's and Soldiers' Friendly Society' and 'The Soldiers' Friend and Army Scripture Readers' Society', to name but two. The majority of these well meaning organisations have long since ceased to exist but some have

The first Church Army 'Kitchen Car' waiting for an inspection by HM Queen Alexandra in March 1915. The car did excellent work at the front, often close to the firing line, providing drink and refreshments to weary soldiers from the trenches

Beds in London The Buckingham Palace Hotel was taken over by the Army Pay Dept in conjunction with the Church Army during WW1 and used to provide accommodation and refreshments to soldiers on leave from the trenches

flourished because they were prepared to adapt their ideas to the swiftly changing structures of 20th century society and, above all, because they were genuinely interested in the well being of the soldiers among whom they worked.

We believe that these 'volunteers' as we have called them, would be both proud and pleased to be counted among the ranks of camp followers, although a large number of their companions in this book share neither their high ideals nor their belief in selfless service. It is inevitable in such a short space that we cannot cover them all; however, those we have included do represent these wonderful people very adequately. By their example many soldiers, sailors and airmen, who before had held the Church in small regard, found friendship and renewed faith in the midst of battle, far from their native land.

FIGHT THE GOOD FIGHT

The Church Army made its first and lasting acquaintance with the British Army, when, at the request of the War Office and the Archbishop of Capetown, nine of

A Church Army Recreation and Rest
Tent at Marble Arch London 1915

The Buckingham Palace Hotel and
the Royal Riding School were used
by soldiers on leave from France,
nearly 600 beds were available and
both were under Church Army
management, March 1917

The Church Army 'Friends of the
wounded' entertaining parties of
convalescents from hospital to tea
and taking them for visits in this
splendid charabanc, seen here at
Hampton Court, July 1915

Anzio 1944 A Church Army mobile canteen at the Anzio beachhead serving tea, cakes and cigarettes 'in the Shadow of Death'

the Society's evangelists went to South Africa to help the army chaplains and to do all they could for the soldiers during the Boer War. 'They marched with Tommy Atkins from the Modder River to Pretoria, they sat down with him at the camp fire when he counted the living and spoke of the dead, they watched beside his hospital cot and wrote his last letter home and in the chill greyness of early dawn they stood by the open grave and read the service that spoke to bystanders who might be under fire the next hour, of "a sure and certain hope" '.[1]

During the Great War, Church Army recreation huts and tents, also huts of devotion, were erected in most camps at home and abroad. By 1917 for example, more than 800 centres had been established. To give some idea of the cost of these operations, the Church Army Blue Book for 1916-17 quoted £20,000 as the annual cost of free stationery, books and magazines for their huts alone. It went on to say: 'Our huts, tents and clubs etc are looked upon by our brave fighters as the last places where they can find the touch of home as they wend their way to battle and the first places where they can find the first sign of civilisation as they return with the marks of battle upon them.' A typical unsolicited testimonial of the Great War reads: 'I desire to place in writing my appreciation and sincere thanks for the excellent service rendered by the Church Army. Your Huts and Tents are giving the greatest satisfaction to the troops of the . . . . . Army here, in the mud and discomfort of a Flanders winter.'

In WW2 the Church Army continued to serve the troops. Here, for example, is a quotation from *The Eighth Army News* of 4 April 1944: 'Every night, after dark, a camouflaged Ghost Truck moves up the line, taking into the Cassino

[1] *Wilson Carlile and the Church Army* by Edgar Rowan

An airborne 'cuppa'! A Church Army mobile canteen driver hands a cup of tea to a helicopter pilot at RAF Andover 13 July 1945

sector tea and cakes for our battle-weary troops. Often the truck runs the gauntlet of shell-fire, for Death lurks along the road twenty four hours in the day. On black nights the journey is a nightmare for the driver who has to "feel" his way, yard by yard, along the crater-pitted highway into war-gashed Cassino. A shell screams overhead; giant guns belch forth their venom in an almost incessant roar, the red, green and orange flashes revealing for a split second the sinuous column of vehicles of war, Cassino-bound. As the Ghost Truck reaches its destination, shadowy forms emerge from the roadside. Silently, speedily, freshly baked cakes and steaming hot tea in special containers are unloaded. The Ghost Truck cloaked in the shadows of the night stands by, ready to move off at a moment's notice. Meanwhile, the tea and cakes have been passed up the line to the men who need them most. Money wouldn't buy the refreshments which, night after night, the Ghost Truck brings to grateful British infantrymen in the Fighting Line. They are the gifts of the Canteen Service of the Church Army. In this Division, the Canteen Services are under the supervision of Captain Nelson, Church Army. He and his colleagues wear British battledress, with "Church Army" flashes on each epaulette. They are doing a first class job . . .'

A DREAM COMES TRUE IN FLANDERS FIELDS

From 1914 to 1918 the whole of Belgium was occupied by the Germans except for a very small corner, the western tip of Flanders. The centre of this tiny patch was Ypres, held against everything the Germans could produce, by the guts and determination of the British Army.

The diameter of the Ypres Salient was about 15 miles, its greatest depth from Ypres less than 10. In this small space lie buried over 200,000 men of the British Commonwealth, 80 per cent of them from the United Kingdom. Of these, 90,000, lost in the mud of Flanders, have no known graves, their names being carved on the Menin Gate at Ypres and at Tyne Cot Cemetery. The casualties sustained in the defence of Ypres represented one-fifth of our total casualties on all fronts – land, sea and air – in WW1.

The Old House at Poperinge. The sign reads 'TALBOT HOUSE 1915 – EVERYMAN'S CLUB'

A group including 'Tubby' Clayton, Miss Alison Macfie, Barclay Baron, G H Nash and Major Paul Slessor, on the landing of Talbot House, 1930

On the German side, the losses were at least as heavy. The Ypres battlefield is thus the greatest graveyard in history. It was in this hellish setting that a great Christian movement was founded, which now encompasses the world.

The soldier of the Great War, marching westwards out of Ypres, would have found himself after seven miles in the market town of Poperinghe. Every building along the route was in ruins, every tree blasted by shellfire, so 'Pop' as it was affectionately called, was probably the first habitable place he had seen for weeks. It was of course bombed and shelled, but people still lived there. You could buy egg and chips or a glass of beer at the local estaminets; a makeshift cinema was in operation; and so the town became a 'rest area' for our troops, as well as being the main point of entry for the thousands of reinforcements going into battle.

It was here that the senior chaplain of the 6th Division, Nevile Talbot, and one of his chaplains, Philip (Tubby) Clayton, opened a house as a Services club. It was called 'Talbot House', in memory of Neville Talbot's brother Gilbert, a lieutenant in the Rifle Brigade, who had been killed at Ypres nearly six months earlier.

'Everyman's Club' – as the original signboard which still hangs above the entrance calls the house – was founded to meet the emergency of the moment. It is far better known as 'Toc H', which is what the troops called it, using 'tele-graphese' on the initials 'TH'.

In a little book called 'Tales of Talbot House', Tubby Clayton told of those first formative years. He explained that Toc H was not a clerical preserve, not a baited trap which offered fellowship upon conditions of reluctant worship: 'Old Talbot House was no confused conception. It knew the part God meant it to perform towards the multitudes of homeless men, wave after wave in the low Flanders plains. It spoke to them of Home, of love, of duty. It breathed the

Festival at the Royal Albert Hall. Lamps of Toc H during the Ceremony of Light

A Toc H mobile canteen serves troops six days a week at the famous Brandenburg gate which stands in a loop in the Berlin Wall and is in a 'No man's land' area

courage of Christ upon them. Here they laid up their griefs, their fears, their burdens. Hence they emerged comforted and renewed.'

Throughout the long years of war, Toc H provided a small haven of friendship, a place to relax – 'All Rank Abandon Ye Who Enter Here', read the message above Tubby's room – a place to write a letter home, to drink a cup of cocoa, to sleep in a bed, to say a prayer – 'the doors were open day and night. Men swarmed about the place from ten a.m. to eight p.m., and officers flowed in from seven p.m. till the leave trains came and went. From each officer we demanded five francs for board and lodging, on the Robin Hood principle of taking from the rich to give to the poor. For this sum the officers secured on arrival from the leave train at one a.m., cocoa and Bath Oliver biscuits, or before departure at five a.m. a cold meat breakfast.

'The bedrooms were communal, save for the dressing room which we turned ambitiously into the "General's bedroom", on account of a bed with one real sheet to speak to him of home. The field officer who was fortunate enough to secure this luxury was free to decide whether the sheet was more appropriate above or below his horizontal person. We had two sheets, but one was at the wash.

For the rest, stretcher beds and blankets provided more facilities for sleep than a leave-goer required, or than a returning officer expected. . . . The House was always what the Canadians called a "soft drink" establishment, but no one resented this, lapping up tea or cocoa or bovril with thanksgiving.'

With the coming of the Armistice the House was closed as a club in 1919, but ten years later was bought and presented by Lord Wakefield to the now firmly established and ever growing Toc H. In 1941, the night before the Germans requisitioned Talbot House, the people of Poperinghe, removed every article of furniture, book and scrap of paper, hiding them in their homes. The original lamp, that familiar symbol of Toc H, was buried in a garden for three years.

Elise Sandes (1851-1934) plays the piano at Christmas time in her Belfast Soldiers' Home

Toc H has now spread all over the world and the size and scope of its activities must far exceed its founders' wildest dreams. A Toc H Women's Association was established in 1922 by Alison Macfie, a nursing sister, who travelled the world on its behalf until her death in 1963.

Despite its wider scope nowadays, Toc H still retains permanent links with the Services and is one of the splendid voluntary organisations now forming the CVWW – the Council of Voluntary Welfare Work, which also includes both the Church and Salvation Armies, and the Church of Scotland. Their canteen service is particularly appreciated by the troops in BAOR and Northern Ireland.

THE TRUMPET CALL OBEY

'The "ping" of billiard balls against one another, the click of the cues, the thud of hard rubber quoits on wood, music from the wireless, gramophone and piano, the cheerful tinkle of cups and saucers, and the deep laughing talk of men – these are ever-present sounds in the recreation rooms of The Sandes Soldiers' Home at Ballykinler, and in similar Homes the world over. Outside there is often rain and wind, and under such conditions there could be no more dreary spot than the Ballykinler military camp, in the wilds of County Down.

'Even if it is fine – a rare occurence nowadays – there is nothing but the "sameness" of full corrugated iron huts drawn up in precise military formation, and stretching away in unrelieved lines to the waste spaces beyond. Outside, the sounds of intermittent firing of Lewis gun bursts, and of shouted commands, come from the ranges away in the waste spaces by the sandhills. Uninteresting noises you would think; and yet, in her upstairs room, with windows thrown open, and all the sounds of the Home and the camp drifting in on the light breeze, there rests

The US Christian Commission Coffee Wagon Designed by Jacob Dunton of Philadelphia to give comfort and strength to weary and wounded soldiers during the Civil War. (The US Christian Commission was organised by the YMCA in November 1861 to provide for the spiritual, intellectual, social and physical comfort of the Union forces) The coffee wagon was made of wrought iron. It had boilers in the rear heated by wood fires to prepare hot coffee, tea, chocolate or soup. The three smoke stacks baffled the soldiers because the vehicle at first glance resembled a battery caisson.
(From a painting by Robert Weaver)

HH Princess Victoria 'Motor Restaurant'. This splendid canteen did yeoman service in WW1

an old lady to whom to be without such noises would be almost to cease to exist. Frail and white-haired, she is eighty years old; her name is Elise Sandes.'[1]

Elise Sandes was a young girl, living in the little Irish town of Tralee, when the 1859 Revival swept through Ireland. She was greatly influenced by it, but it was not until 1869 that she found her true vocation, trying to improve the lot of the downtrodden British soldier.

It all started by a friend asking her to help with the welfare of army drummer boys, aged between 15 and 18, serving with the regiments in Ireland. Elise did so enthusiastically and soon a group of young soldiers, from the barracks in Tralee, would visit her and her mother in their home and Elise would try to teach them how to read and to understand more about religion.

When the regiment left Tralee a few months later, Elise was faced with the problem of making contact with the new regiment. She had many disappointments and, even when the men began coming regularly in large numbers, she was still not satisfied. It was grand to see them joining heartily in the hymns and listening to God's Word – even taking part in the informal Bible discussions – but Elise

[1] *Elise Sandes and Theodora Schofield* by Ella Potter and Winifred Matheson

110

wanted to see more lasting results. She wanted to see men's lives so changed by the power of Jesus Christ that, no matter where they went or what happened to them, they would still follow Him. While she was passing through this period of concern and uncertainty, people began to criticise her for what she was doing.

In those days it was a little unconventional, to say the least, for a young lady to have anything to do with soldiers. Conditions in the Army were bad and many of the men who found their way into the ranks were from the dregs of society. But, Elise argued, these were the very men who needed help most. Far too many of the Army chaplains did not seem to care about the spiritual welfare of their flocks. Fortunately for the Army, Elise was not discouraged either by her initial difficulties with the new regiment or by public criticism, and she vowed that she would never again doubt that this was God's work for her.

As numbers grew, Elise hired rooms in Tralee, paying for them and furnishing them out of her own pocket. Christian friends who became interested soon found themselves helping with the meetings. Then one day in 1875, six years after she had begun, Elise went to Cork to visit the men of a regiment that had been transferred from Tralee. That visit nearly broke her heart.

The Christian men were indeed standing firm and had a prayer meeting in a tiny room. But many other boys who she had thought interested in spiritual things and cured of their evil ways, had succumbed to the temptations of a big city and had sunk lower than ever. What else could be expected? 'There were many hands stretched out to pull them down and not one stretched out to help. If only she had a Home for them! A Home where there was light and gladness and warmth and love, and a welcome for all. For two years she worked and prayed and in 1877 the Cork Home was opened.'

A YMCA tea car serves tea to anti-
aircraft gun crews during an air
raid in WW2

The Belfast Home in Clifton Street followed in 1891 and 30 years later there were 30 Sandes Soldiers' Homes and many other ladies in Britain had followed Miss Sandes' example and had sought to help the soldiers. Of the Sandes Homes, 8 were in India, and 16 in Southern Ireland.

However, towards the end of 1922 the work suffered a great setback. The withdrawal of British troops from Southern Ireland meant the closing of 13 Homes. One or two were transferred to the North, but for many of them it was impossible to find a purchaser. In spite of failing health, Miss Sandes would not give up and her courageous spirit inspired her helpers to consolidate the work and to be ready to take advantage of every new opening.

When Elise Sandes died in 1934, and was buried with full military honours in Tyrella Cemetery near Ballykinler Camp, she left behind her 19 flourishing Homes. Her work was acclaimed by the leaders of the nation as well as by hundreds of ex-servicemen. Since then other permanent and temporary Homes have been established. Some have had to close, notably in India, where 8 Homes had to be given up in 1947. In recent years the work has been extended to include both the men and women of all three Armed Services, so there are Homes on airfields as well as in army camps. 'If Miss Sandes was able to come back and visit one of her Homes today she would find them run on very similar lines to that very first Home in Cork. . . . She might wonder that, instead of being in a half-pint mug with a bun (1d), the tea was in a cup and the cup was on a saucer. She would take a second look at the worker too. Miss Sandes herself always wore her famous black apron, large enough to protect ankle-length dresses. Now overalls, patterned and plain, brighten while they protect. Miss Sandes would find the Homes themselves brighter, just as private houses have now shed Victorian gloom. . . .

Table-tops are scarlet formica instead of scrubbed deal; tubular chairs, strip lighting, oil-fired heating – how she would revel in all the improvements that now benefit "her boys". She might be surprised at the smaller number of men attending the meetings ... These are days of materialism and indifference, but she would hear them singing the same hymns: "Rock of Ages", "The Lord's my Shepherd", "Stand up, stand up for Jesus", and the speakers giving out the same message that the strong Son of God can save from the power and guilt of sin. Perhaps the change Miss Sandes would find most surprising would be that the Homes are almost all run by married couples instead of single ladies. Often they undertake this demanding work with young families growing up around them. This can in a special way provide the "home" atmosphere, which, from the first has been regarded as so important.'[1]

YMCA WORK WITH THE FORCES

The first recorded instance of YMCA personnel operating with Servicemen on a national basis is that of a canteen which served both sides in the American Civil War. It was a splendid contraption, as the painting by Robert Weaver shows, with wood fired, rear heated boilers, used to prepare hot coffee, tea, chocolate and soup. Initially, the soldiers were baffled by the canteen's three high chimneys, thinking it must be some type of mobile artillery piece. However, they soon realised their mistake when approached with hot drinks and words of encouragement!

The US Christian Commission, who manned the canteen, was set up by the

[1] *The Trumpet Call Obey* by M Helen Jeffrey

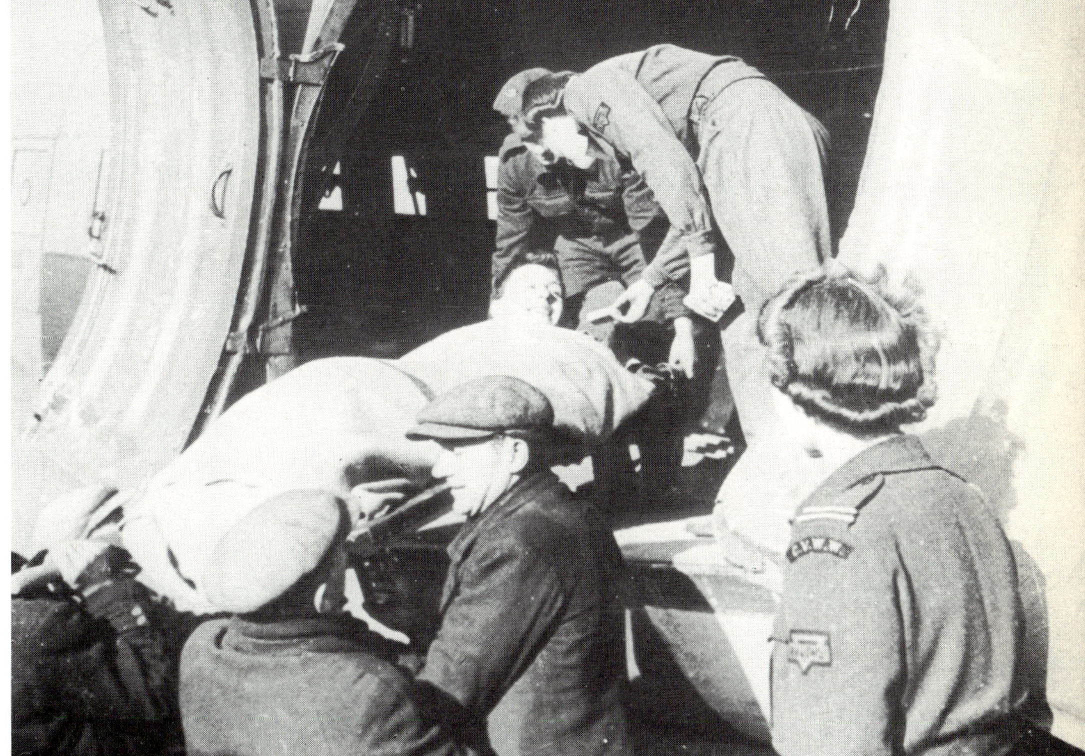

CVWW (Council of Voluntary Welfare Work) helpers give packets of cigarettes, write letters and generally look after the wounded whilst they wait for air transport from the Western Front, WW2

YMCA Bookshop in Berlin The YMCA run many such amenities for troops in the British Army of the Rhine and elsewhere.

YMCA in November 1861, to provide for the spiritual, intellectual, social and physical comfort of the Union forces. However, before the war was over Commission delegates were administering to both Union and Confederate soldiers. They became familiar sights in the frontline areas, with their mobile canteens and kitchens.

The excellent service to the soldiers eventually involved a total of 4,859 volunteers who were sent out to battlefields, hospitals and military camps. By the end of the war, 111 branches and local YMCA Army Committees were active and all subsequent volunteer sevices were modelled on the pattern they had established. They carried food as well as drink for the soldiers to 'strengthen the body', magazines and letter paper to 'strengthen the morale' and Bibles to 'strengthen the soul'.

Some YMCA activity also took place during the war between America and Spain in 1898, and in the Russo-Japanese war of 1904-5. The British YMCA operated during the South African war under the name of the 'Soldiers Christian Association', a pseudonym for the 'Military Department' of the YMCA. From the summer of 1901 the British YMCA provided tent centres at annual camps for Volunteers – a scheme tried out earlier in Canada. This experience formed a base which enabled the YMCA to be operating 250 recreation centres within ten days of the outbreak of the World War in 1914. It was at this time that the famous Red Triangle first became widely used as a symbol for YMCA work. It was not long before centres were operating in all the Base Camps in France and, indeed, even at the Forward Base at Abbeville. This developed into a group of over 100 centres in France alone and soon the YMCA was operating in all the theatres of war.

The younger members of the YMCA staff soon joined up and it is worth recording that twelve of them won the Victoria Cross. This drain of manpower, which increased as medical and age standards for the Forces were lowered, produced a situation which would have been disastrous had it not been for help from

An American Red Cross mobile canteen serves officers and men at HQ XII Corps in the European Theatre of Operations, WW2

Troops, shortly due to go overseas, are shown how to mend their own socks by the WVS, WW2

lady workers. HRH Princess Victoria became President of the Women's Work of the Association, now known as the YMCA National Women's Auxiliary. At its height there were 40,000 women working for the YMCA. Space does not allow us to detail the huge variety of ways in which the YMCA served the Forces, but one item must be mentioned. At the request of the authorities the YMCA started an educational programme and as a consequence was recognised as the agent for carrying out the Army Education Scheme in the Lines of Communication area. This was something that had never been done before and was much appreciated. In 1919 H A L Fisher, then President of the Board of Education, paid tribute to the YMCA for 'introducing and developing the largest scheme of adult education which has ever at any one time been launched from this country'. Even today the YMCA regularly receives letters of thanks for what was done between 1914 and 1918.

During the years of occupation, centres operated all over Germany, the largest being at Cologne where between two and three thousand men assembled nightly. These centres continued until the return of the Army of the Rhine in 1928. A YMCA team also accompanied the Defence Force to Shanghai in 1927. Gradually the service centres closed as the need grew less, but permanent establishments were opened at Plymouth, Tidworth, Larkhill, Cranwell and Catterick. Many Territorial camps were glad of the homely atmosphere provided by YMCA centres.

The outbreak of the second World War saw a vast expansion of YMCA work for HM Forces. Although not the only voluntary organisation operating in WW1, it was two-and-a-half times as large as all the others put together, whereas in WW2 it was equal to all the rest. Wherever the YMCA tea cars, educational programmes and other services operated they were every bit as welcome as in

A WRVS worker weighing Gurkha babies in Hong Kong 1959

A WRVS in a hospital in Singapore 1973. The WRVS do wonderful work providing entertainment for soldiers all over the world

1914-18. Among the places where they were operating was the Normandy Bridgehead only a few days after the landings, which incidentally took place on the day the YMCA celebrated its centenary. In general, YMCA activities during this war followed the previous pattern of service to the Forces, but it should also be noted that as part of its war effort canteens served those of other Services who were involved in the 'blitz' on London. The Red Triangle was once again in the forefront of the battles.

Today, with the change in Services, welfare arrangements and the vast increase in married personnel, the YMCA shows especial care for wives and families. Centres and shops are in action in Germany and Cyprus, where the mobile canteens are very welcome to small parties of troops at isolated posts such as the Troodos mountains. In the United Kingdom one new centre has been opened recently at Catterick in memory of HRH The Princess Royal – an untiring President of the YMCA National Women's Auxiliary. Eslewhere, particular care is taken for those serving in young soldier or similar units. Recently, the YMCA headquarters received a postcard which read 'I wish to make a small donation for the rebuilding of the London Tottenham Court Road YMCA in grateful thanks to the YMCA for providing me with accommodation when I was a Private in the Artists Rifles 1915-16 and hoping boys up from the country 1971 forward will be able to get treated likewise.'[1] They will.

THE USO

Early 1941 was a strange time in America. It was possible to escape thinking about the war in Europe, but not easy. The Conscription Act had been passed and the first peacetime callup in American history had begun. 'Young men were being inducted into an Army ill-equipped to receive them; to train with broomsticks for a war they had been assured they would never have to fight. Some were bitter. Some were hostile. Almost all were bewildered. All, however, were loyal. There

[1] Information taken from a YMCA Fact Sheet No 6

were no bands for them. There were no great outpourings of public sympathy, support or understanding. In fact, the reaction to them was curious. They were looked upon not as young men preparing to defend their country but rather as unfortunates who had somehow been the losers in a lottery. The communities they left hardly missed them. Many of the cities to which they were sent, the camp towns, treated them with a mixture of annoyance and disinterest.'

That is how the USO describes the background to their formation in their Silver Jubilee brochure published in 1966. It goes on to explain that the major problem was one of morale, on and off the post. The Army was doing all it could with a newly formed Morale Branch, providing the citizen-soldiers with movies, sports, libraries and the like, on the post. But something was missing, as a seasoned reporter of the *New York Sunday Times* explained: 'Off the post,' wrote Meyer Berger on 23 May 1941, 'the soldiers' needs are not so easily met because the new Army, sprung up overnight, overwhelms small communities near the camps as army ants swarm over a crust.

'Most towns near cantonments barely have accommodations for a regiment, let alone a division. Soldiers turned loose on one-night passes or on long weekends have no place to go. You see them near forts and camps spread out along the highways in dejected groups eager for sport and civilian contact, with none to be had. You find them clustered in bewildered and uncertain knots on street corners in tiny towns overrun with their kind, or lined up in patient queues outside small town movie houses.'

Of course the soldiers wanted social contacts with civilians just like they had back home, but how? It was from these needs and problems that the USO was born. In the Great War six major organisations had worked with the AEF in France: the YMCA, the YWCA, the National Catholic War Council (Knights of Columbus), the Jewish Welfare Board, the Salvation Army and the American

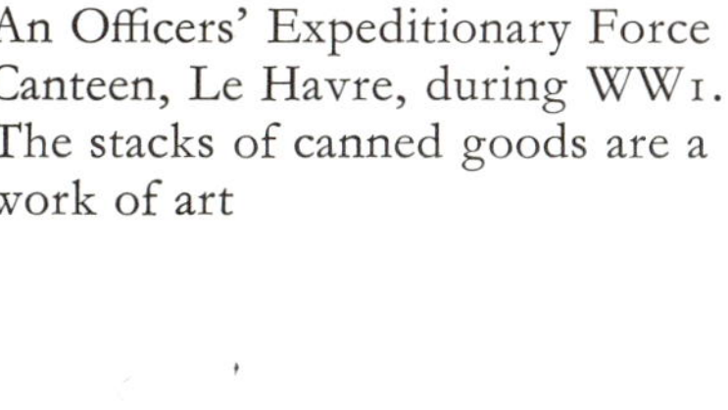

An Officers' Expeditionary Force Canteen, Le Havre, during WW1. The stacks of canned goods are a work of art

Australian troops returning from the
line are pictured here in the mud
outside an Australian Comforts Fund
Canteen, Longueval, December 1916

Library services. Although these organisations did join together during the last
months of the war in 1918 for a very successful fund-raising campaign, they had
operated as separate organisations for the rest of the time. In 1940, informal
discussions were held between these six agencies, and although no specific
commitments were made, the general feeling was that a joint organisation should
be formed. Nothing definite would have happened, however, had not President
Franklin D Roosevelt himself decided that there had been enough talk. 'This is the
way I want it done!' he said, 'I want these private organisations to handle the
on-leave recreation of the men in the Armed Forces. The government should put
up the buildings and some name common to the organisation should appear
outside.'

On 4 February 1941 the 'United Service Organisations for National Defense
Inc', later shortened to 'United Service Organisations Inc' came into being. Five
of the six member agencies were the same as those which had operated indepen-
dently in WW1, with the National Travellers Aid Association (in 1966 it changed
its name to the Travellers Aid Association of America) replacing the American
Library Association as the sixth member. The USO had its growing pains, one of
them being how to combat the desperate lack of live entertainment for the troops
and as we have already explained in an earlier chapter, 'Camp Shows Inc' was
formed to take care of this aspect.

The sheer size of the problem defies the imagination. Take, for example, the
situation which faced the small town of Sayre in Pennsylvania. The local USO
committee there had offered to feed troops in transit on trains that made a brief
stop. One day, early in the war, they were told to expect three troop trains that
night. By 4am the next morning not three but seven trains had stopped. They fed

Listen to the Band! A Whitsun concert by a Military German Band in the grounds of a soldiers' hostel in Brussels, June 1918

30,000 men and there wasn't a drop of milk, crust of bread or bottle of coke left in the entire town! Sayre went on to serve over half a million customers. There was no typical USO clubhouse, all sorts of buildings being used, including churches, a museum, a log cabin, a barn and even an old castle.

The programme for a particular club was varied to suit the needs of the servicemen in that particular location, but included such items as dances, snacks, facilities for pressing clothes, sewing on insignia, showers, shaving equipment, desks for letter writing, stationery, reading rooms, arts and crafts, religious counsel and literature, information on local points of interest and sightseeing, table tennis, checkers, juke boxes, cots or bunks, and many more. Dancing and meeting girls was rated as the most popular activity, with eating a good second. However, when GIs were asked what they did the last time they were in a USO, the list in order of frequency was: write a letter, read a magazine, listen to the radio, talk to girls, listen to records, play games, meet friends, see a movie, take a shower.

From 1948 to 1950 the USO maintained its corporate structure and a small headquarters staff, but for all intents and purposes was out of business. The outbreak of the Korean war soon changed all that and ever since then the USO has continued to serve the troops. In their silver anniversary year, for example, they were operating ten clubs in South Vietnam, with an average daily attendance of 15,000. Worldwide they had 45 overseas clubs in 14 different countries providing a 'home from home' for American servicemen and women.

Their Jubilee brochure closed with the words: 'It is not possible to know what the future holds but USO has the strength, leadership and demonstrated flexibility to continue voluntary services to the Armed Forces, wherever the need may exist. Hopefully the day will come when this troubled world will learn to live in peace – and wars and rumours of wars will no longer plague the earth. But until the last bugle blows for an American Reveille on a foreign shore, USO will be there, with our men and women in uniform, wherever they are. This is the continuing mandate of a thoughtful American people.'

THE WOMEN IN GREEN

During WW2, the Women's Voluntary Service (WVS) began running station canteens, serving refreshments to Servicemen travelling by trains; these quickly developed into centres near railway stations and in towns, around which many other forms of welfare for the Services grew up spontaneously. In 1943 the WVS was invited by the Director of Army Welfare to co-operate with the NAAFI and undertake welfare and social activities in the large Leave Clubs run by NAAFI overseas, and in March 1944 the first party of volunteers left for Algiers. Soon the WVS moved into Italy and later on into France, Belgium and Germany. In 1945 WVS members went out to Burma, and soon were serving all over South East Asia Command, in Singapore, Malaya and Japan.

As we have explained, NAAFI had accepted the sponsorship of all WVS Members overseas during war time, and it was decided at the end of hostilities that the service was too valuable to be discontinued. So, during the 1950s and 60s, WVS Service Welfare Members worked for the Army and the Air Force in unit canteens, Junior Ranks Clubs, leave centres and town clubs, still under NAAFI auspices, all over the world, wherever the forces were stationed. At the end of National Service and the gradual withdrawal of the Armed Forces from overseas, the number of WRVS[1] declined with the forces' diminishing requirements. However, at the same time costs kept steadily mounting and this, together with the changes in our society and in the Armed Services, caused the NAAFI to give notice of their intention to discontinue their sponsorship of WRVS Members as from 1 November 1975. The RAF accepted this, but the Army, anxious to preserve WRVS services, sought other means of keeping a limited number of overseas members. Discussions still continue over the financial support for the few remaining members who are serving overseas. Some of these work amongst the wives and children of Gurkha soldiers in Hong Kong, Brunei and at the Gurkha recruiting depot in Nepal.

[1] 'Royal' was added to their title in 1966 by Her Majesty the Queen

SSAFA

A silver statuette presented by the founder of SSAFA, Colonel Sir James Gildea, to the Officers' Mess of his regiment (The Royal Warwickshires) on his retirement

FOUNDATION

'The Soldiers' and Sailors' Families Association', as it was first called, was founded in 1885 by Major (later Colonel Sir James) Gildea, an officer of the Warwickshire Regiment, for the initial purpose of looking after the wives and families of British soldiers who were going overseas with the Second Egyptian Expeditionary Force. This was necessary because the army had neither the means to do so nor, to be honest, did the War Office give a 'tinker's cuss' what happened to them.

Major Gildea took a passionate interest in the welfare of Servicemen and their families and for thirty five years devoted all his energies to helping them. Indeed, he became known as the 'Soldiers' Friend'. After the original expeditionary force had returned, Gildea did not allow his Association to die, instead he and his committee widened its scope and undertook to look after the dependants of all the men in the Regular Army and Navy.

Shortly after formation, the committee decided that the only way to do their job properly was to establish a visiting service, which could go to the homes of the Servicemen's families and find out at first hand what help was needed. Voluntary representatives were therefore recruited all over Great Britain, so successfully, that by the start of the South African War, there were already 3,000 of them.

Her Royal Highness the Princess of Wales, later HM Queen Alexandra, became the first President of the Council and took a very active interest in all aspects of the Association's work – her concern is typified by an old cartoon from *Punch* magazine, which shows a soldier who is going off to the Boer War, saying goodbye to his wife and children at a railway station. Standing beside them, holding the children's hands as the wife embraces her departing husband, stands HRH who is saying: 'Do not be uneasy about your wife's comfort, Tommy, I will look after her and the children.'

The Association changed its title in 1921 after the formation of the RAF, becoming 'The Soldiers', Sailors', and Airmen's Families Association', better known by the initials SSAFA. Its title is itself unique, in that because it was founded to look after soldiers' families first, 'Soldiers' takes precedence over 'Sailors'.

In 1886, Colonel Gildea founded the Officers' Widows Branch, with the main purpose of providing rent-free accommodation for the widows and unmarried daughters of deceased officers, who had been left with inadequate means. Houses were first rented for this purpose, and in 1904 a quadrangle of sixty flats was built in Wimbledon called Queen Alexandra Court. The entire property is now named 'The Royal Homes' and has been recently completely modernised. The charter of the Officers' Widows Branch precludes it drawing on central SSAFA funds, which are used exclusively for the families of Other Ranks.

An early Alexandra Nurse SSAFA started their District Nursing service in 1892. After HRH the Princess of Wales became the first President, the Sisters were henceforth known by the honoured courtesy title of 'Alexandra' Nurses. With the passing of the National Health Act of 1946 the Alexandra Sisters at home were absorbed into the National Health Service. The cost of the 100 plus SSAFA Sisters in overseas commands is now borne by the Ministry of Defence, but they still remain under the administrative control of SSAFA

GROWTH

As well as recruiting voluntary workers at home, the Association also formed overseas branches wherever British troops were serving, and by 1887 there were working representatives in India, Hong Kong and Singapore. As the scope of their work expanded so did the Association and in 1892 it started a District Nursing Service both at home and abroad.

When HRH the Princess of Wales became the first President, the sisters were henceforth called 'Alexandra' nurses. The next development was in 1895, when a Clothing Branch was formed. Its original aims included the supply of warm clothing to such places as Bombay, Malta and Egypt, for wives, widows and children returning home. 'For women – warm petticoats, crossovers, and shawls for wrapping babies in. For girls – warm frocks, petticoats attached to bodices for preference, and capes and jackets. General – woollen socks and stockings, cuffs, mittens, gloves, caps and hoods.' At the height of WW2 the Clothing Branch was issuing a million garments a year, but has now ceased to operate.

SSAFA's first big test came with the outbreak of the Boer War, when thousands of Servicemen's dependants turned to the Association for help and such was the public's confidence in its as yet virtually untried organisation, that over £1,200,000 was subscribed to be disbursed through 12,000 voluntary workers in the relief of more than 200,000 families during the three years of war.

The Association also made strong representation to the Government that the care of widows and orphans of servicemen: 'should become, in the main, a national charge and not a charge on the rates or wholly upon charity.' But it was charity, inspired by patriotic fervour and verses such as Rudyard Kipling's which had to find the money. Verses like his 'The Absent-Minded Beggar':

'When you've shouted "Rule Britannia", when you've sung "God save
the Queen"

When you've finished killing Kruger with your mouth,
Will you kindly drop a shilling in my little tambourine
For a gentleman in khaki ordered South?'[1]

It was printed in the *Daily Mail* a few days after the outbreak of war and by giving general permission to circulate it, Kipling raised over £250,000 for family aid. Certainly the British Army had much to thank him for.

When peace came the Association managed to remain intact which was very fortunate, because the scale of the Great War took the Government completely by surprise. The machinery for paying marriage allowance broke down and SSAFA was asked to pay marriage allowance on behalf of the Government, until the official machinery could catch up. In the first five months of war SSAFA paid out over £1 million to 440,000 dependants.

They were also heavily engaged throughout the Great War, championing the cause of Service families, and in 1915, won a notable victory when the Government accepted for the first time that the state had a liability to pay out war pensions. The Government then said that SSAFA was to have strong representation on the statutory committees set up to pay out these pensions. During the Great War the Association spent over £3½ million on relief.

[1] *The Complete Barrack-Room Ballads* by Rudyard Kipling

SSAFA continued to operate between the wars, adding 'Airmen' to its title in 1921 as we have already explained, and dealing with the problems of the families of ex-Servicemen, widows and orphans. The volume of work declined gradually, until at the time of Munich, SSAFA was once again fully mobilised onto a war footing. When the Second World War started, the Government politely told SSAFA that they 'did not anticipate needing their help'. That was, of course, before Dunkirk and when the bombing started things were soon very different from the 'phoney war'. Once again SSAFA got to work. One of its first major successes was the setting up of an Air Raid Enquiry Service, to provide quick answers to Servicemen overseas about the safety of their relatives at home. This was later developed into a general Overseas Service which provided a link between the Servicemen and their homes, through SSAFA branches all over the United Kingdom and some 225 full-time SSAFA workers in overseas commands. This service became so important to the Forces, that it was soon classed as an 'operational necessity'.

Sixteen Children's Homes were opened, also as a result of the air raids. The Clothing Branch grew so large that it had to be decentralised to 400 sub-depots. Indeed, the volume of work increased in all directions, changing the Association from a charity into a fully fledged organisation undertaking general family welfare work. By the end of the war SSAFA had 29,000 voluntary workers and was administering over £1 million a year.

SSAFA TODAY

Since the end of the war, as between the two wars, the volume of work has declined slowly to a peacetime level. However, the organisation of branches at home and abroad remains in being, ready to deal with any crisis – and there have been quite a number!

The Association's aims today are fourfold: firstly, to look after the welfare of the families of both Service and ex-Servicemen. In the tradition of Colonel Gildea's words this is the 'ready help of friends to friends', and SSAFA's voluntary workers

SSAFA Clothing Branch The Clothing Branch was established in 1895. At the height of the Second World War, it was issuing over a million garments a year, but has now ceased to operate

The first SSAFA Nursing Sisters to go to BAOR after the war, 21 August 1946

The SSAFA Children's Home,
Springbok House, Great Baddow,
near Chelmsford. The matron tells
the kiddies a story, 14 April 1950

The oldest of the 70 residents at
Queen Alexandra's Court,
Wimbledon, SSAFA's Royal Home
for the widows and unmarried
daughters of officers, who had just
celebrated her 100th birthday, is
greeted by Her Majesty Queen
Elizabeth, The Queen Mother,
during her visit in 1973 on the
re-opening of the Court. Mrs Foster
is wearing Queen Alexandra's ermine
cape which was given by Queen
Alexandra and is by tradition
handed on to the oldest resident

Radio Lausanne's wedding gift to HRH Princess Elizabeth Twenty children, chosen by SSAFA, pictured on their return from one month's holiday in Switzerland, November 1947

A SSAFA nursing sister inspects a small camp follower in Cyprus

seek to act as friendly advisers with their problems and difficulties, no matter how personal or how varied they may be.

Secondly, SSAFA seeks to help them to obtain all the assistance to which they may be entitled from statutory sources as well as from Service and Regimental Funds. Over the years all regiments have established their own Benevolent Funds in order to help their comrades who have fallen on hard times. In the main these funds are disbursed only on the advice of SSAFA, and a similar situation exists with larger funds, such as the Army Benevolent Fund.

SSAFA's third aim is to help, by means of temporary grants, those who are in distress and whose need is not provided for by the State.

Finally, they represent the cause of these Service families to the appropriate Government departments whenever it is necessary. SSAFA publish both a regular magazine and a news sheet, which contain details of their work all over the world.

DISTRICT NURSING WITH SERVICE FAMILIES OVERSEAS

What is it like to be an SSAFA worker? What does her job entail? Miss Margaret Leitch, RGN, SCM, QN, HV, explained her job thus: 'When the young wife of a soldier, sailor or airman goes overseas to join her husband, she finds life very different in Germany, Singapore, Cyprus, Gibraltar or wherever it may be. If she is lucky, she may move into a quarter on a "married patch". Or she may live quite a distance from the unit in a private hiring, where the only other neighbours do not speak English and where she may be very lonely while her husband is away at work all day. If she is very young – and many of the wives of today's serving men are – and accustomed to relying on the Welfare State at home, she is quite likely to panic when anything, however small, goes wrong, with the baby, the house or the neighbours. With no mum or grandmother or trusted friends to turn to, she can quite quickly become desperate.

'To deal with that kind of situation and to care for, sustain and comfort the families of serving men overseas, are the SSAFA Nursing Sisters, members of a Service founded 85 years ago. When founded in 1892, their object was: "To provide fully qualified District Nurses to attend in their own homes the families of serving men in large garrison and seaport towns at home and abroad." In those days, a soldier had to ask permission to marry and those who married without permission were "off the strength" of the regiment and did not exist at all, as far as the Army was concerned. When Mrs Norah Diamond, the first SSAFA District Nurse, was appointed to Curragh Camp, Dublin, most of her patients lived near the camp, "in huts and hovels not fit for cattle". The wife of the GOC urged SSAFA to choose a nurse who would be "ready to make shift with the minimum of conveniences", adding "I heard a district nurse say the other day that she had to 'boil the water in a lobster tin to make a poultice!'" Mrs Diamond was obviously just such a person, since she stayed at the Curragh until her retirement in 1922.

'Today conditions are very different and members of the SSAFA Nursing Service are always part of a team working from a Family Medical Centre in liaison with the medical officer and his staff. In the particular context of Service life overseas – where the many specialist agencies of the Welfare State are not

available – they provide a comprehensive family service combining the work of the District Nurse, the Health Visitor and the Midwife at home.

'Originally our nurses were General Trained and sometimes Midwives. Today they are not only General Trained nurses with a Midwifery Certificate, but must also hold a Health Visitor's certificate. Each Sister is responsible for about 1,350 women and children. When a family arrives on her station, she visits them promptly to assess how much help or care they will need in relation to the area in which they are living. For instance in the Far East, boiling drinking water and keeping up the families' cholera inoculations, special care of the skin to prevent infections, prickly heat, blisters and sunburn, conditions with which they are not normally concerned at home.

'She visits and keeps in touch with all the pregnant mothers, advising and encouraging them as necessary, visits them again the day after they are discharged from hospital with their new baby, and regularly afterwards sees them at home or at the Infant Health Clinic. In this connection, it is of interest that the SSAFA Sister covering the area received notification in the usual way of a new baby born to the Duke and Duchess of Kent in the officers' married quarters in Hong Kong. When she visited, as she would have done any other Service wife, the Duchess of Kent opened the door, invited her in, showed great interest in the work and asked her to return regularly to discuss the Earl of St Andrew's development.

'Medical follow-ups and after care are also undertaken by the SSAFA Nursing Service for medical officers and specialists. Routine and special visits are made to all children under five and regular visits paid to schools. Liaison is established with teachers for discussions on the progress of children who are maladjusted, failing to progress or showing signs of ill-health.

'The wives of men posted from Western Europe, often for a second tour of duty in Northern Ireland, are the special care of the SSAFA Sisters, whose friendship, comfort and support are of great value to them during these times of separation and constant anxiety. Health Education is another important aspect of the work and Sisters teach as they visit, impressing on the families the principles of healthy living and the prevention of mental and physical ill health. They run mothercraft and relaxation classes, give lectures to school-children and Wives Clubs, assist at school medical examinations and carry out school health inspections.

'There are 94 SSAFA Sisters now serving. They are stationed in Western Europe, which includes Holland, Belgium and Berlin; the Near East (Cyprus); Gibraltar, and Hong Kong. Though they remain civilians, they are attached to the Services and share many of the privileges and advantages of the serving officer. On joining they hold honorary equivalent rank of Captain, may later be promoted to a Senior Sister/Group Adviser, with the equivalent rank of Major, or Deputy

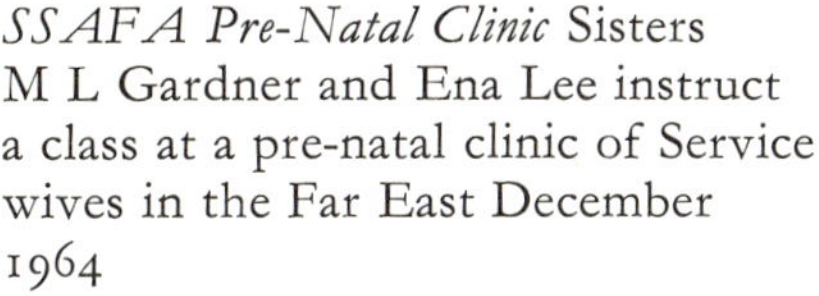

SSAFA Pre-Natal Clinic Sisters M L Gardner and Ena Lee instruct a class at a pre-natal clinic of Service wives in the Far East December 1964

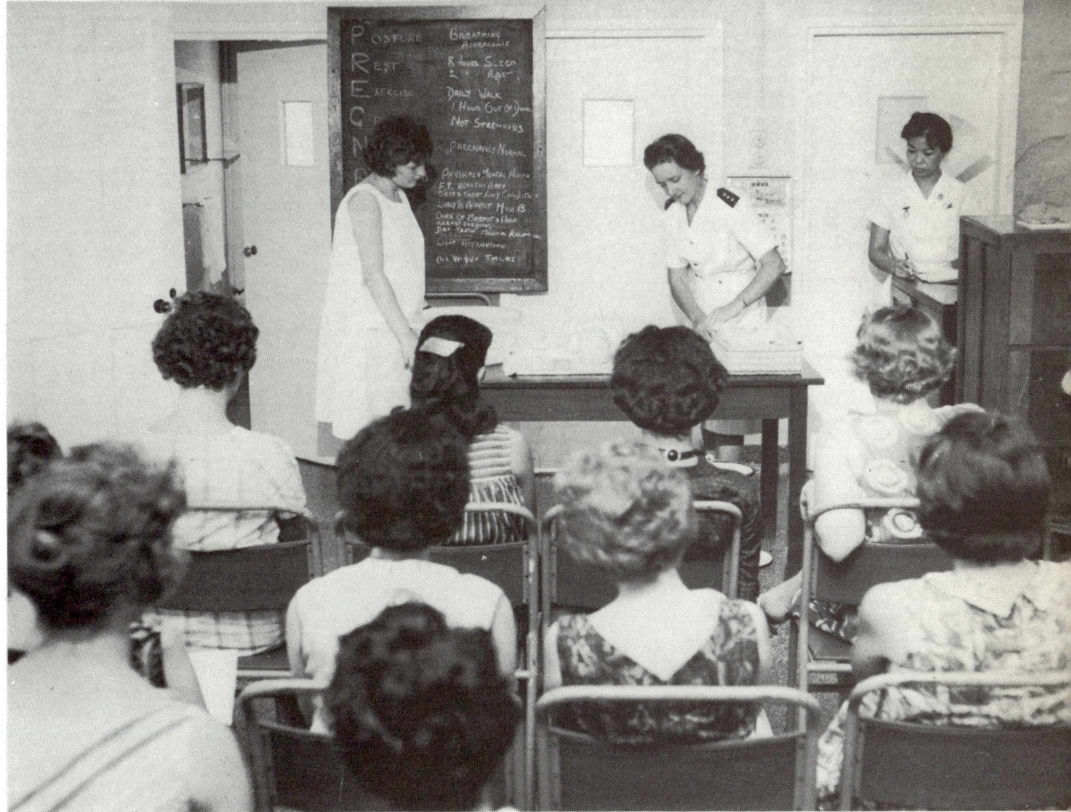

Director (Nursing and Welfare) with the equivalent rank of Lt Colonel. They live either in an officers' mess or share a flat with a colleague.

'Since the service was founded in 1892, SSAFA "Alexandra Nurses" – a courtesy title bestowed on them by Queen Alexandra, first President of the Nursing Service – have served all over the world, on garrisons and stations at home and abroad. During the Boer War one served at Pietermaritzburg and another at Mafeking. In both World Wars, while the family casework side of SSAFA increased, the Nursing Service diminished as the families were moved out of barracks and garrisons to make room for more troops. However, Sister J M P Smith was awarded the MBE for her war service in Malta and the Sisters in Cairo and Palestine went with the families when they were evacuated to South Africa. During the riots in Tripoli and Benghazi, when families were evacuated from Trieste, during the emergencies in Malaya, Aden and Cyprus the SSAFA Nursing Sisters were there. They looked after the Malayan Police and Federation Army families, as well as British ones, travelling out to the rubber plantations in constant danger of ambush. One was awarded the Perak DCM by the Sultan of Perak for gallant conduct in the jungle and another delivered a baby in Aden's notorious Grenade Alley.

'When the families were flown home from Aden and from the Far East, the Persian Gulf and Malta, SSAFA Sisters were there with the Service reception teams to care for pregnant wives and mothers with young babies or large families.

'In 1948, following the passing of the National Health Act, the duties of SSAFA Sisters in the UK were taken over by local health authorities, but those overseas continued, the cost being recovered from public funds. They now work closely with the 15 SSAFA Social Workers, also employed on an agency basis on behalf of MOD, who help Commanding Officers overseas to deal with the most complicated and deep-rooted problems of their men's families.'

The Reporters

A NEWS-HUNGRY PUBLIC

The 19th century saw a great revolution in news media, caused by ever increasing demands from a better educated public for up to the minute information on what was going on in the world about them. For the first time the man in the street began to take a real interest in the soldiers fighting his country's wars. And he soon wanted to know what was happening just as quickly as possible after a major event or battle had taken place. So new methods of passing information rapidly, such as the electric telegraph (invented 1844), had to be used.

This increased public demand for war news led to the arrival on the camp following scene of an entirely new breed of follower, namely the War Reporter. He depended upon war for his livelihood, sending back his despatches, drawings or photographs to the eager public at home. The first war reporters appear to have had unrestricted freedom of movement in the battle zones and to have been a remarkably resourceful and brave species of camp follower.

In this chapter we will look briefly at the careers of some of the more famous of the early reporters. One celebrated war correspondent, Archibald Forbes, is quoted by an equally famous early war artist, Frederick Villiers, as laying down the following rules for the war reporter to constantly bear in mind; firstly, that no matter how interesting the battle might become, the correspondent must get away before his communications are cut, because his material would then be held up and might never arrive home. Secondly, he must never be taken prisoner or get wounded as he would then become a useless expense to his paper. Finally, if he was silly enough to get himself killed, then he would be 'an infernal fool'.

'THE FIRST AND GREATEST OF WAR CORRESPONDENTS'

The above inscription appears on the memorial to Sir William Howard Russell (1821-1907) in St Paul's Cathedral. Although he was undoubtedly the most famous of the early war correspondents, Russell was not truthfully the first. That honour belongs to a Yorkshireman, John Bell, one of the original proprietors of the *Oracle and Bell's New World*, *The Weekly Messenger* and *The Morning Post* newspapers. He founded *The Oracle* with the express intention of using it to abuse his former business partner, a Captain Edward Topham. In 1793 Bell was ordered to appear in court for libelling the Foot Guards. He failed to turn up and as a consequence all his goods were seized and sold at public auction. Bell then decided that the only way he could recoup his losses was to boost the circulation of his newspaper *The Oracle* – his only remaining asset – by writing on the spot accounts of the fighting which was taking place between Britain and France in the Low Countries.

The normal practice at the time was for English newspapers to copy war news

Sir William Howard Russell (1821-1907) 'the first and greatest of war correspondents', photographed in the Crimea by Roger Fenton

out of suitable foreign papers, or to rely upon rumours or 'exclusive reports' from whichever capital city was the nearest to the fighting. 'The readers of *The Oracle* knew at first hand the true nature of the war's progress. They were able to follow Bell on what he described as his "perilous excursion through Flanders" and to read his accounts of the British victories at Le Cateau-Cambresis, Villiers-en-Cauche and Troixelles, followed by the disheartening report of a major defeat at Tournay at the hands of Marshal Pichegru.'[1]

The Times proprietors were furious at being beaten to the punch by Bell and described him as a 'bloody satellite of Robespierre and a promotor of Jacobite [sic] heresies'. John Bell died in obscurity in 1831, ten years after the birth of the man to whom history has given the accolade of 'first war correspondent'.

In fact Russell, known in America as the Father of War Correspondents, was the first to telegraph his despatches from the battlefield and his fearless reporting did much to open the eyes of the public in Britain to the deplorable way in which their soldiers were being treated in the Crimea. He also introduced Florence Nightingale and helped to make her a living legend. His highly critical reports greatly alarmed the British generals who were not used to that kind of thing happening.

His reports were couched in the type of flowing prose the Victorians adored, witness this opening paragraph of his description of the Charge of the Light Brigade, which was published in *The Times* on Tuesday, 14 November 1854: 'If the exhibition of the most brilliant valour, of the excess of courage, and of a daring which would have reflected lustre on the best days of chivalry can afford full consolation for the disaster of today, we can have no reason to regret the melancholy loss which we sustained in a contest with a savage and barbarian enemy . . .' Russell dated his despatch '25th October 1854', so it was nearly three

[1] *The Shell Book of Firsts* by Patrick Robertson

Sir Winston Leonard Spencer Churchill (1874-1965) pictured here whilst serving as war correspondent to the Morning Post during the Boer War

Roger Fenton's Photographic Van which he used during the Crimean War (1854-1856). Marcus Sparling, the driver, is seen here on the driving seat. This photo was taken on the day that Fenton and his assistants had been to photograph 'The Valley of the Shadow of Death'. The van was a frequent target for enemy artillery, the Russians probably thought it was an ammunition wagon. When Fenton left the Crimea he was able to sell the van for £35!

weeks out of date when it reached England. In fact his last despatch in that particular copy of the newspaper was dated 28 October and begins: 'The mail leaves at 9a.m. and I have barely time to say a word . . .', which reduces the transit time to about two weeks. Of course shorter despatches were telegraphed and the same edition includes one dated 12 November from St Petersburg, which gives a brief account of another battle near Sebastopol, which had taken place on 5 and 6 November.

Russell continued to send back his despatches throughout the Crimean War and was later asked by Mowbray Morris, the editor of *The Times*, to become their Indian correspondent on a salary of £600 a year plus all expenses. 'I hear that you are not entirely satisfied with your new occupation,' Morris wrote to him, 'as to regard a return to your old one with any aversion. I may say, also, that the interval that has elapsed since you left us has not produced anything like a conviction that we can do perfectly well without you. Although China goes on very well under the auspices of Wingrave Cooke, yet India is at present a blank, a blank I fear it will remain unless you will fill it. What do you say? Will you go there for a year, salary £600 to be paid to your wife or other nominee at home, and all expenses if out of pocket reimbursed. The terms renewable at our option with reasonable notice according to circumstances.'[1]

Russell's brief was more than just to report on the Mutiny. He was also to investigate the rumours of atrocities committed against the white population, and inquire into the circumstances of the failure of British rule which had led to the mutiny. The influence of his despatches was once again enormous and the policies

[1] Introduction to *My Indian Mutiny Diary* by W H Russell edited by Michael Edwards

of clemency and justice which ended the Mutiny, were undoubtedly partly the product of his fearless reporting in the face of a good deal of criticism for being too soft.

A NEW CONTENDER

Russell's place as top war reporter was taken later by a young officer of the 4th Hussars, who sent back despatches to the London newspapers in the 1890s. Commissioned in February 1895 and finding no wars in progress which involved the British Army, Winston Spencer Churchill went to Cuba with another subaltern, where insurgents were harassing the Spanish Army. Before leaving, he arranged with the *Daily Graphic* to send back letters at a fee of 5 guineas each. They appeared in a series of five articles between 13 December and 13 January 1895.

Next he went to India, on leave from his regiment, as a journalist with General Sir Bindon Blood's expedition to the North West Frontier in 1897. He persuaded his mother, Lady Randolph Churchill, to arrange finances with the *Daily Telegraph*. He wanted £10 and his name on the articles, but she only managed to get £5 per article and the byline was 'by a young officer'. Churchill was furious, calling the *Daily Telegraph* 'stingy pinchers'. However, Lady Randolph made certain that everyone who mattered, from the Prince of Wales downwards, knew the true identity of the 'young officer'. His despatches were excellent, vivid and exciting, but like Russell's from the Crimea, not always appreciated by those in authority.

His next war was in the Sudan (1898) with General Kitchener. He had a difficult time persuading the expedition to take him, as his previous forthright criticism of the Indian Government, and indeed of the Cabinet, had made him numerous enemies. Eventually Kitchener agreed, on the condition that he did not write, which of course Churchill immediately did – ostensibly sending private letters to his friend Oliver Borthwick, who just happened to be the editor of *The Morning*

Post! They were published anonymously, but everyone knew who had written them. Kitchener objected to the criticism they contained and even Churchill's staunchest ally, the Prince of Wales, reprimanded him viz: 'I fear that in matters of discipline in the army I may be considered old fashioned – and I must say that I think an officer serving in a campaign should not write letters for the newspapers or express strong opinions of how operations are carried out . . .'[1] Churchill, who had received £15 for each of his despatches, took the hint and resigned his commission.

On 17 September 1899, a few weeks before the outbreak of the Boer War, Churchill was invited to become the Daily Mail's correspondent in South Africa. He at once contacted *The Morning Post* and offered to write for Oliver Borthwick for 'my expenses – copyright of work and one thousand pounds – for 4 months shore to shore – two hundred a month afterwards'.[2] He also retained freedom of movement and of opinion. Needless to say, his offer was accepted and he thus became the highest paid war correspondent of his day. His despatches rivalled the other two 'greats' – W H Russell, whom we have already covered and G W Stevens, who reported on the Boer War for the *Daily Mail* and died of enteric fever in beleaguered Ladysmith.

In his book *My Early Life*, published in 1930, Churchill recorded that the sales of *The River War* and of his two books of war correspondence from South Africa, together with ten months' salary from *The Morning Post*, had left him in possession of more than £4,000, a tidy sum at any time but a small fortune at the beginning of the century. During the Boer War 'WSC' saw a great deal of action, was a member of the first party to enter beleaguered Ladysmith and was, of course, captured by the Boers and escaped. The last of these events turned him into a hero and the subject of music hall songs such as:

> 'You've heard of Winston Churchill –
> This is all I have to say –
> He's the latest and the greatest
> Correspondent of the day.'

His despatches, like W H Russell's inevitably brought criticism because they praised the enemy as well as praising our own troops and being fervently patriotic.

A GREAT ERA FOR WAR CORRESPONDENTS

The period between the end of the Crimean War in 1856 and the start of WW1, was a great era for war correspondents. Most of the professionals were British or American.

Archibald Forbes (1838-1900) and George W Stevens (1869-1900) were the leading British reporters, whilst Januarius A MacGahan (1844-1878) who reported mainly for London papers, and Richard Harding Davis (1864-1916) were outstanding American reporters.

The more important wars were covered by hundreds of reporters, from all countries, of varying abilities and integrity. During the Great War the best were Sven Anders Hedin, a Swede; Frederick Palmer from the USA, and Englishman Sir Philip Gibbs.

[1] [2] *Young Winston's Wars* edited by Frederick Woods

Early in WW2 it was estimated that there were at least 10,000 reporters, photographers, artists, broadcasters and columnists, field reporters and public relations officers. All those following the armies had to wear uniform. Ernie Pyle and Leyland Stowe were big names in the USA; Alan Moorhead – now an extremely successful military historian, was a WW2 reporter; and a Russian – Ilya Ehrenberg – also made his name.

On the other side of the fence many reporters and photographers worked for Goebbels' Ministry of Propaganda, to produce such magazines as *Signal*. This magazine was the most widely read and had the largest sale of any published in Europe between 1940 and 1945. It owed much of its success to a publicity man called Fritz Solm, who copied the layout of *Life* magazine and was able to get unrestricted funds both to launch the magazine and to continue its publication. Many freelance journalists contributed to *Signal* and nearly 1,000 cameramen were available to the editors from the PK (Propaganda Company) that followed the troops on all battlefronts.

DRAWINGS OF WAR

Whilst there have always been artists who have painted pictures to commemorate particular battles or famous generals, the war illustrator who worked for the pictorial press did a very different job. By means of a quick sketch accompanied by some explanatory notes or perhaps a written report, he endeavoured to portray up to the minute news from the battle zone. His work was then swiftly despatched to the engraver at home, who redrew it onto a block, adding whatever embellishments he saw fit.

This pictorial type of journalism was very popular in the mid-19th century; the first and perhaps most famous British pictorial magazine, *The Illustrated London News*, being founded in 1842. It was not only the public at home who avidly sought these illustrated papers, as Pat Hodgson points out in the introduction to her book *The War Illustrators*: 'There was sometimes unexpected proof of the wide appeal of picture papers. When the British were self-righteously sacking the palace of the "Untutored Savage" Ashanti King at Coomassie in 1874, they found copies of *The Illustrated London News* in the royal library.'

The artist was very much in the hands of the engraver until the 1880s, when it became possible to use photographic methods to place the drawing on the block. Pat Hodgson explains 'This led to bad feeling between artist and engraver, and Rossetti spoke for all artists when he wrote:

> "O woodman spare that block –
> O gash not anyhow!
> It took ten days by clock –
> I'd fain protect it now!"

An engraver worked slowly and a full-page *Illustrated London News* picture might take one man three weeks to complete.'[1] In 1860 Charles Wells invented a speedier method in which the block was split up into its component parts and divided among several engravers – one would do the sky, another the trees, another the figures and so on. *The Illustrated London News*, which cost 6 pence weekly, had 32

Caricature of William (Crimea) Simpson (1823-1899) sketching on the battlefield during the Crimean War

[1] *The War Illustrators* by Pad Hodgson

wood-cuts in its first issue. It reigned supreme in England until 1869 when *The Graphic* was founded. In Europe and America, similar magazines had emerged such as *Illustrierte Zeitung* (1843 – Germany); *Vsemirnaya Illustratziya* (1868 – Russia); *L'Illustration* (1843 – France); Frank Leslie's *Illustrated Newspaper* (1855 – America); and *Harper's Weekly* (1857 – America).

Many artists became war artists, not only for the picture magazines, but also for other publishers who sent them out to the front to produce paintings which could then be reproduced as lithographic prints. One of the most famous of these was William Simpson (1823-1899), popularly known as 'Crimean Simpson', who specialised in lithographs and published two very successful volumes of them on the Crimea. He had been sent to 'The Seat of the War in the East' – as he entitled his series of lithographs – by a London print seller called Colnaghi. He had various letters of introduction to suitable senior officers and, from the start, made a point of keeping on the right side of those in authority.

Accurate and critical war reporting had upset many of the British generals, so Simpson took the precaution of having his drawings cleared by Lord Raglan before they were despatched and by both the War Minister *and* Queen Victoria when they arrived home!

His next expedition for Colnaghi was in 1859 to record the effects of the Indian Mutiny. Unfortunately, most of the lithographic work for which he had been commissioned was never printed as the publishers collapsed. Simpson then joined *The Illustrated London News* and was sent by them to Abyssinia. Unfortunately he did not arrive until the fighting was virtually over and the expedition ready to march home. However, he was able to give the general public some idea of what the conditions in Abyssinia had been like for the soldiers, and to salt away many sketches of the native people and their customs for future use.

After Abyssinia, Simpson spent two years travelling abroad including visits to Jerusalem, the Crimea and to the opening of the Suez Canal. His next assignment was in Europe where France and Germany were at each other's throats. In Metz he was mistaken for a spy by a crowd of angry civilians and mobbed whilst he was drawing the Emperor's carriage. Normally he took the greatest care to disguise the fact that he was an artist. 'A sketch book was a most dangerous article to be found in your possession. . . . At Forbach the idea occurred to me of sketching on a book of cigarette papers. One could do a great deal on a book of that kind, and in the event of being apprehended, could make a cigarette of the sketch and smoke it before the eyes of one's accusers.'[1] He also describes a scoop which he made at the fall of Strasbourg, when, having completed his drawing in the early hours of the day immediately following the fighting, he then walked five miles to General von Werder's headquarters to make certain that the sketch was safely despatched. 'I was up with the first streak of light, and did a sketch of the event of the day before. This I had to take to Mundalsheim to the post. I calculated that if sent off that day, it would reach Mr Jackson, the editor, in time for "next Saturday", which it did.'

Simpson had many more adventures during the Franco-Prussian War, sketching the Battle of Sedan on the back of a piece of wallpaper (the design could still be seen through his finished sketch!). He returned to France in April 1871, and was present during a bombardment in Suresnes. His resulting picture 'A Shell at Suresnes' appeared on the cover of the magazine on Saturday, 29 April 1871. He had several narrow escapes during the 'Bloody Week' of 21-28 May: 'Once he was standing with Dr Austin of *The Times* when a rifle bullet passed between them. Austin paid tribute to Simpson as being "an old campaigner who sketches as coolly under fire as in his own room." '[2]

William Simpson returned to London in June 1871 and for the next few years travelled abroad for his paper, going with the Prince of Wales on his tour of

[1] *Autobiography of William Simpson* by William Simpson
[2] *The War Illustrators* by Pat Hodgson

India. His last campaign as a war artist was the 2nd Afghan War (1878-80), 'where Archibald Forbes recalled seeing him on the day of Ali Musjid, as he stood sketching Sir Sam Browne's advancing brigade, with his back regardlessly to the Afghan fortress and the round shot and shell it was pouring forth (*Graphic* 6 December 1890)'[1]

Simpson continued as an artist covering foreign stories and in 1892 at the age of 69, was an honoured guest at the journal's Jubilee year celebrations.

WAR PHOTOGRAPHERS

Although there are a few examples of war photography very early on in photographic history, such as some daguerreotypes taken during the Mexican War of 1846-48, the first really famous war photographer was Robert Fenton. His classic photographs from the Crimea are still rated among the finest ever taken, despite the fact that all his pictures had to be posed, so none could portray an actual battle in progress.

Fenton had trained as a painter and had been interested in photography for some years before going to the Crimea, founding the Photographic Society of London in 1853. He went out to the war on board the *Hercla* in February 1855 at his own expense, intending to take photographs privately. 'He was fortunate in having influential friends – in particular the Queen and Prince Albert – who smoothed the way for him and made it easier for him to live in reasonable comfort on the campaign.'[2]

Financing the trip was Thomas Agnew, a Manchester publisher, who intended to sell Fenton's photographs commercially. He took with him two assistants, Marcus Sparling, a former corporal of the 4th Light Dragoons, who was to be the driver of Fenton's photographic van, and William, a handyman and cook. The van was an amazing vehicle, converted from a wine merchant's wagon into a portable dark room and caravan for the three of them. It contained as well as all their stores and equipment, 700 glass photographic plates fitted into grooved boxes, each of which contained about 24 plates. The boxes of glass were then packed into more chests to ensure their security. These cumbersome plates were necessary because Fenton used the wet plate collodion process, invented by Frederick Archer in 1851. The camera he used was also large and heavy and was mounted on a solid wood tripod.

The taking of photographs necessitated that the subjects remained absolutely still for at least fifteen seconds, so it is a tribute to Fenton's genius that the pictures look so natural and spontaneous. He took about 360 photographs which included most of the high ranking officers and personalities, during his four months at the front, and on his return to the United Kingdom the best of his work was produced for the public in several portfolios – '50 views of scenery and camps, 60 incidents of camp life, 30 in the Historical Portrait Gallery, plus three panoramas, the whole selling at a slightly reduced price of £53. Expensive though it may have seemed in those days, that investment in contemporary photographs would bring handsome profits today.'[3]

[1] *The War Illustrators* by Pat Hodgson

[2] [3] *Early War Photographs* by Pat Hodgson

Well known war reporter and broadcaster, Frank Gillard making a live Christmas broadcast, 25 December 1944. Sad to say, Corporal Bob Pass of 1/5th Queens, who delivered the message to the 'folks back home' was killed in action in April 1945

It was not until the American Civil War that photography really expanded into a competitive business, mainly through the efforts of Matthew B Brady, a successful pre-war portrait photographer, who founded a team of war photographers on the Union side. He went out himself initially, with a travelling darkroom similar to Roger Fenton's. It was called the 'What-is-it Wagon' by the soldiers of the Army of Potomac. He became famous at the First Battle of Bull Run in July 1861, taking photographs and coming under fire. His wagon was overturned, but he managed to rescue most of his equipment.

Brady soon realised that he could never cover all the war fronts single-handed, as well as continue to manage his lucrative portrait galleries in New York and Washington. So he organised the coverage on mass production lines, sending out teams of photographers into the field. 'I had men in all parts of the Army,' said Brady, 'like a rich newspaper.'

Unfortunately he was not very honest when it came to crediting his photographers with the pictures they had taken, more often than not putting his own name on them. This caused a lot of dissatisfaction among his team and it was not long before one of them, Alexander Gardener – Brady's star photographer – broke away and founded his own gallery. He was very careful to learn from Brady's mistakes and always credited his photographers properly, many of whom were, like himself, ex-employees of Brady's original organisation. In 1869 he tried to get Congress to buy his war photographs, but without success and eventually became a field photographer for the Union Pacific Railroad. Brady also got little financial reward in the end, as public interest in the war waned and the Government refused to buy his negatives for the nation. Eventually he was forced to sell his New York studio and died a pauper on 15 January 1896. The Washington and New York newspapers carried long obituaries of Brady and the *Washington Evening Star* said: 'News of his passing will be received with sincere sorrow by hundreds and hundreds who knew this gentle photographer, whose name is today a household word all over the United States . . .'[1]

REPORTING IN VIETNAM The war in Vietnam attracted more than its fair share of news gatherers – at the height of the Tet offensive, for example, there were nearly 700 correspondents accredited to the Military Assistance Command, Vietnam. The vast majority of these journalists were not in the country long enough to really understand what was going on, never visited units in action and merely wrote down every word that the generals and officials in Saigon told them to write: '. . . The press got all the facts (more or less), it got too many of them. But it never found a way to report meaningfully about death, which it was really all about . . .'[2]

In other words the vast majority produced the stories and the pictures that those in authority felt the general public back home should see – that the war was apparently going well, that the unspeakable VCs were being driven back everywhere, that superior weapons, equipment and American know-how would eventually triumph.

A few correspondents and war photographers told a very different story. These

[1] *Matthew Brady* by James D Horan

[2] *Dispatches* by Michael Herr

wcre the *real* war reporters. And like William Howard Russell before them, officialdom did not take kindly to the way they acted, nor to the things they wrote about and photographed. Some of the best of this new breed of professionals were young photographers Tim Page, Sean (son of Errol) Flynn and Rick Merron, who used to ride in and out of the combat zones on Hondas; reporters like Peter Braestrup of the *Washington Post*, Karsten Prager of *Time* magazine, John Lengle of the Associated Press and freelance writers such as Michael Herr. The latter's frighteningly graphic, but evocative book *Dispatches* has been described as the best personal journal of war that any writer has ever accomplished.

In his book Herr vividly describes the war from a very personal view-point, right in the front-line positions with the 'grunts' as the US Marine Corps marines were called. He also described the strange, guilty feelings that he and other reporters experienced about their profession of living off war: ' . . . There's no way round it, if you photographed a dead Marine and got something for it, you were *some* kind of parasite. But what were you if you pulled the poncho back first to make a better shot and did that in front of his friends? . . .'[1]

The 'grunts' looked upon these reporters with a mixture of awe, coupled with astonishment that anyone would really come to Vietnam without *having* to be there. In some cases this was mixed with a certain amount of hatred. They called them by a wide variety of names – thrill-freaks, death-wishers, wound-seekers, war-lovers, ghouls, seditionists and a lot worse things. Many of the officers were openly offensive: '. . . my Marines are winning this war and you people are losing it for us in your papers . . .'[2] But despite these extreme feelings the majority of the 'grunts' wanted the story of the war to be told and told properly without any frills and coverups, with the full horror and beastliness completely undisguised.

Clearly, Vietnam was a great emotional experience for these young men, and reading Herr's enthralling book one gets the impression that, despite all the horrors, he would not have wanted to have missed one second of it.

[1, 2,] *Dispatches* by Michael Herr

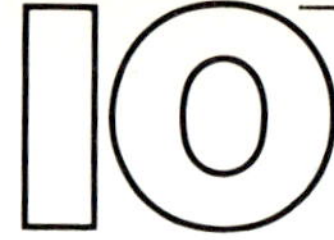

Army Agents

THE COLONEL'S CLERK

The history of Army Agents in the British Army goes back to the middle of the 17th century, when it was the practice for prominent public men to raise regiments of infantry or cavalry under their personal command. Whilst operating under the general authority of the Army's Commander in Chief, each regiment was commanded by its Colonel who was responsible for every aspect of its activities, including the feeding, clothing and paying of the soldiers. He was, of course, later reimbursed for such expenditures from sums voted by Parliament.

The clerical work involved was considerable, even in those days, and soon became too much for the Colonel to deal with personally, so he engaged a civilian clerk to deal with it on his behalf. It was not long before this clerk was recognised as the Regimental Agent. Nearly a hundred years later, a Member of Parliament, giving evidence before the Select Committee set up in 1746 to examine the state of the Army, said: 'The Agent is properly considered the Colonel's Clerk, and keeps his accounts relating to the Regiment.'[1] In return for his labours, the Agent was normally allowed twopence in the pound on the whole pay of the Regiment, and in some cases was also allowed the 'subsistence of a man per Troop or Company', but this latter allowance depended upon the attitude of the particular Colonel concerned.

We may think that monetary matters are complicated in this computerised age, but even in the 1740s money talk could be highly confusing. Take, for example, this explanation of how an Agent got his money which was given by Maynard Guerin, Agent to several regiments, to a Commons Select Committee: 'The Gross Off-reckonings consist of all the Pay of the Non-commissioned Officers and private Men, above the Subsistence; and that the Net Off-reckonings are the Produce of the Gross-Off-reckonings reserved for the Cloathing of the Men, after the Warrant deductions of one shilling in the pound, and the One Day's Pay of the whole Regiment for the Chelsea Hospital, and also, the Deduction of twopence in the Pound for the Agent, are made at the Pay Office: That the Balance of the Pay of the Officers, over and above their Subsistence, after the Warrant Deductions are made, and the Respited pay, if there is any, is charged to the Officer, is called Clearings; which are paid by the Paymaster to the Agent, who pays them to the Officers, and there finds his Twopence.' No doubt they were suitably impressed by that piece of mumbo-jumbo!

Indeed, an anonymous satire: 'Advice to Officers of the British Army', which appeared in 1782, included this advice for the Paymaster: 'Make your accounts as intricate as you can, and, if possible, unintelligible to everyone but yourself . . .

[1] *Reports of the House of Commons* Vol 2, published 1803

Always grumble and make difficulties when officers go to you for money that is due to them . . . Be sure to deduct sixpence in the pound for your friend the agent.'

The appointment of the Agent was a matter entirely for the Colonel himself. Sometimes it was given as a free gift – for example, Maynard Guerin stated that he had given nothing for his agency with the Duke of Montague's Horse. On the other hand he had paid £400 to be appointed Agent to a Regiment of Foot in Minorca, and £800 to a General Evans 'for the Agency to the Regiment now Sir Robert Riches'. Clearly it must have been a highly profitable business being an Agent, in view of these large payments. When a Colonel transferred to a new regiment he usually took his Agent with him.

ADDITIONAL DUTIES

As the complexity of regimental accounting grew, so the Agents took on numerous other duties as well as the funds. They became responsible for the supply of clothing and accoutrements, and for keeping the accounts of the various regimental funds, such as Mess and Band Funds. They conducted the financial business involved with the buying and selling of Commissions, submitted claims for losses on service, and for pensions and wounds. This increase in work did not, however, bring an increase in their remuneration, which remained on the same basis as before and Agents soon found that the only way they could make more money was by developing a general banking business for the soldiers and their families. Some of the accounts which they handled were of a very personal nature, witness this letter from an Agent called Derville to Lord Alvanley of the Coldstream Guards:

7th December 1808

'My Lord,
    Having just been informed that you are going to Spain I take the liberty to send you your account with me owing since four months.
    I trust your generosity to take into consideration my situation on pecuniary account and to be so kind as to let me have the money before your departure, or if you are not in cash, to give me your note for as long a time as your Lordship thinks proper.
    I wish you success and glory and a speedy return.
                    Your Lordships very humble servant,
                    DERVILLE

'To:
  Lord Alvanley
    1st Foot Guards

'Five or six months ago you give me your draft for 25 pounds since that time the same night you sleep in my house and desired me to pay the Lady.

Mr Richard Cox, secretary to Lord Ligonier, is appointed to the 1st Regiment of Foot Guards (now the Grenadier Guards) 1758. From the original painting hanging in the Manager's room at 6, Pall Mall

	£	s
'Lady	5	0
Ditto a country girl	2	2
The same	2	2
One night Mrs Dubois (grande Blonde)	5	5
Few days after at daytime	2	2
11th June. Modest girl	3	3
26th June. Sunday morning	2	2
27th June. By particular appointment	5	5
1st July. An American Lady	10	10
Lately one night with Eliza Farquhar	3	3
30th November	2	2
1st December	3	3
4th December	3	3
11th December. All night Miss N from the Boarding School Chelsea	5	5'

'*Note*: Lord Alvanley was in the Coldstream Guards – not 1st Guards.
Born 20/2/1789
Joined 31/3/1804   789th Officer
Exchanged 50th Foot 16/8/1810
Died (unmarried) 16/11/1849
Was 19 years old at date of letter.
Joined at age of 15'[1]

The Cardwell Reforms of 1872 removed all these additional responsibilities which had been put onto the Agents, leaving them solely responsible for pay, but of course they continued as personal Bankers. Further reforms followed in 1881, when the appointing of an Agent ceased to be the responsibility of the Colonel and was taken over by the Secretary of State for War.

FAMOUS AGENTS

Perhaps the most famous Agents were a Mr Cox, who founded Cox's and King's (now part of Lloyds Bank), and a Mr Kirkland, one of the forebears of Williams and Glyn's Bank. Mr Cox was secretary to Lord Ligonier who, in 1758, was Colonel of the 1st Regiment of Foot Guards (now the Genadier Guards). He appointed Richard Cox as Agent who, with a couple of clerks working at his own house in Albermarle Street, London, began keeping the accounts of that distinguished regiment – a service which proved so valuable to the Guards, that it was soon extended to other regiments.

By 1815, Cox and Company had become bankers and agents to the complete Household Brigade, many cavalry and infantry regiments, the Royal Artillery and the Royal Waggon Train (later to become the Royal Army Service Corps). From then on business continued to expand and customers have included many of the nation's aristocracy as well as army officers. For example, when Cox's cousin, Charles Greenwood, entered the bank as a clerk in 1771, he brought with him the banking account of his friend, the Duke of York, favourite son of George

[1] This letter is published by kind permission of Messrs Lloyds Bank Ltd, Cox's and King's Branch and the RHQs of both the Grenadier and Coldstream Guards

III. It is on record that when the Duke introduced Greenwood to his royal father as 'the gentleman who keeps my money', Greenwood drily corrected: 'I think it is rather his Royal Highness who keeps mine . . .' In those days it was a recognised privilege for a Cox's officer customer, prince or commoner, to keep a small balance on the debit side.

Having outgrown Albermarle Street and moved to Craig's Court, Cox's moved yet again in 1888 to new buildings put up in Charing Cross. It was here that officers on leave from Ypres, Mons and Passchendale cashed their cheques for an evening's forgetfulness at *The Bing Boys*, *Chu Chin Chow* or *The Maid of the Moutains*.

The tradition of Cox's as Army Agents was then, and still is, one of kindliness and friendship, not perhaps normally found in the hard world of banking. The following poem and alleged answer illustrate this well. They first appeared in a trench news sheet called the *BEF Times* on 5 March 1917:

> *'To melt a stone*
> Kindly manager of Cox,
> I am sadly on the rocks,
> For a time my warring ceases,
> My patella is in pieces;
> Though in hospital I lie,
> I am not about to die;
> Therefore let me overdraw
> Just a very little more.
> If you stick to your red tape
> I must go without my grape,
> And my life must sadly fret
> With a cheaper cigarette,
> So pray be not hard upon
> A poor dejected subaltern.
> That is all I have to say,
>   "Impercunious" RFA

> *'Alleged Answer from Cox's*
> Sir, the kindly heart of Cox
> Cannot leave you on the rocks,
> And he could not sleep in bed
> Thinking you were underfed;
> So if you will let us know
> Just how far you want to go,
> Your request will not be vain,
> Written from your bed of pain,
> We will make but one request –
> Keep this locked within your breast,
> For if other know, they'll say,
> "Good old Cox is sure to pay
> Only take him the right way." '

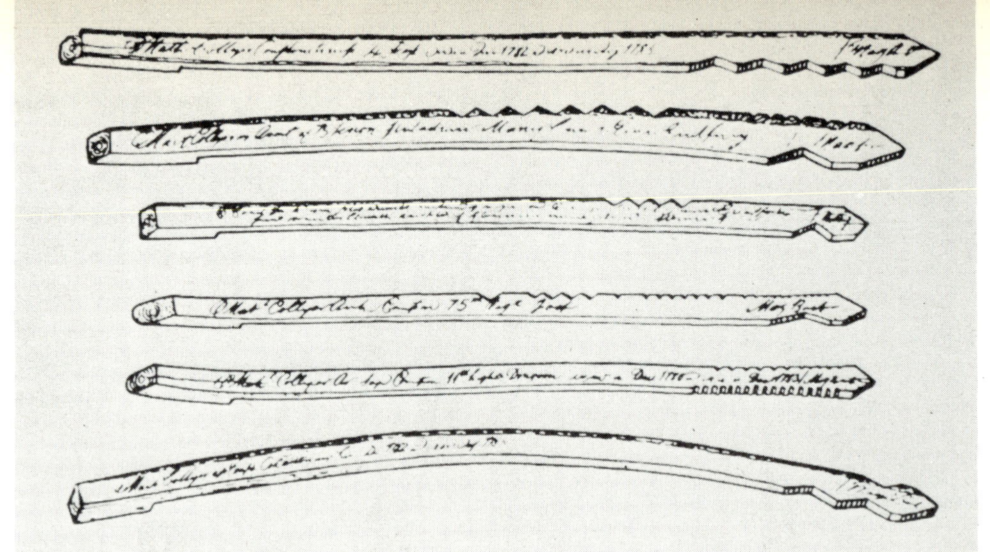

Keeping Tally A collection of 18th century Tally sticks (held by Williams & Glyn's bank at Kirkland House, Whitehall). Such sticks were used by Army Agents to keep records of soldiers' pay and other Regimental accounts. The notching or scoring of the sticks is echoed in the phrase often heard today 'What's the score?'

'Impercunious' RFA, did indeed find his account miraculously transformed from red ink to blue; however, his friends who foolishly tried the same approach got the cold shoulder! 'Thousands of officers must have gone through the same hoops with Cox's as I have,' wrote one officer, 'the first awed visit, newly commissioned, to be presented with a virgin blue cheque book; subsequent visits when "Rocks" might have served for one's telegraphic address, emerging with a reprieve and sometimes good advice as well; and then as one grows older finding Cox's a confidant and a counsellor as well as an Agent.'

In order to trace the story of Holt's as Army Agents we have to go back to the early months of 1794, when a new regiment was formed in Ireland, the 23rd Regiment of Light Dragoons, in which a Mr Nugent Kirkland was appointed as Surgeon. Four years later he became Paymaster and continued as such until 1839, although he was put on half-pay in 1803, presumably due to the regiment being reduced after the Peace of Amiens.

Nugent Kirkland's experience as Paymaster in his own unit was bound to bring him into contact with the civilian agents and he could see that their business was decidedly profitable. This must have been the reason for a Mr William Kirkland starting up as an Army Agent at No 8 Bennett Street, St James's in 1809. What their exact relationship was remains a mystery, but when William's name disappeared from the list of Agents in 1815, he was succeeded by Nugent at the same address. William Kirkland secured his first Agent's appointment in 1811, with the 1st Regiment of Foot, whose Colonel was Edward, Duke of Kent. He retained it until 1820, when there was a change of Colonel. However, in the meantime Kirkland's had been appointed to several other units, including the York Chasseurs.

Nugent left the firm in 1822 to join the East India Company, which he served for twenty years and eventually died at sea off Portsmouth. John Kirkland had taken over in 1821 and was to be the dominating partner of the agency for almost fifty years. During the early years their growth was not as fast as Cox's, they only reached double figures in numbers of regiments served in 1832, reaching a peak of seventeen in 1849. The Cardwell reforms, however, brought expansion which necessitated moving to larger premises – first in Waterloo Place, then Pall Mall and finally in 1859 to No 17 Whitehall Place.

144

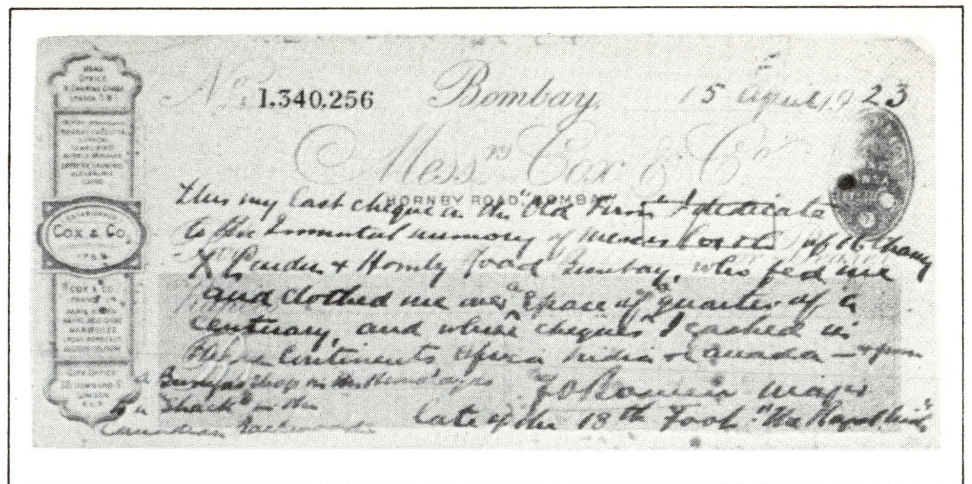

In 1861 John Kirkland was joined in business by Vesey Weston Holt and on the death of Kirkland ten years later, the style of the firm was changed to 'Vesey W Holt & Co'. The First World War saw an enormous increase in work devolving upon Agents; they were now dealing with the pay of over 65,000 officers and had a staff of 850.

CONNECTIONS WITH OTHER SERVICES

When the Royal Air Force was formed in 1918 the Air Ministry offered part of the official pay agency for the RAF to Cox's and part to Holt's, the former getting all the officers whose surnames began with the letters A to R inclusive, the latter S to Z.

Holt's also did some naval business, little of which unfortunately survives today. One record book headed 'Prize Accounts', covering the period 1842-64 and giving details of bounties distributed, capture of pirates and slave traders, does still exist. It gives a fascinating account of the destruction of pirates off the island of Borneo by HMS Dido on 19 August 1844. The bounty granted – for 190 pirates killed and 140 pirates escaped – was £4,500 which, after the deduction of certain legal charges, the Agent's normal five per cent and a similar amount to Greenwich Hospital, left £4,000 to be divided between the captain and his crew of 175. The Captain received £500 and the crew sums ranging from £120 to £4 according to rank.

MODERN TIMES

On Monday 5 February 1923, the various offices of Messrs Cox & Company, Army Agents since 1758, closed their doors for the last time. On the following day they opened for business as branches of Lloyds Bank Limited. It was at the same time as this amalgamation was taking place that Cox's left Charing Cross for a site a few hundred yards further west at 6 Pall Mall, very close to some of London's most famous clubs – the United Services Club being very appropriately directly opposite.

In about August 1969 the Ministry of Defence decided that the payment of army officers via Army Agents should cease with effect from 31 December 1971 and that in future all officers' pay should be handled by the Army Paymaster, using new computerised equipment. They wrote to the Agents explaining this, but ended their letter with the words 'The Board have, however, expressed the hope that the Army will still be able to look to you for advice on banking matters and that you will continue to provide and indeed develop the other valuable non-pay services which you give to Army personnel regiments and corps in the banking and allied field. In recognition of this special relationship the Board consider it appropriate that you retain the title of Agent. The Board have also asked me to express their gratitude for the service you have given to Army officers during your many years as paying agents.'[1]

Cox's and King's Branch of Lloyds Bank, currently employs about 1,100 personnel and despatches well over 6,000 letters each day to their Service customers. Williams and Glyn's Bank recently opened a 'twinned' branch at Farnborough, so that there are now the two Holt's Branches dealing with Services pay in Whitehall and Farnborough. 'Agent' is an honourable and an historic word, it is also a very British institution; certainly the help which these two great firms have given to the officers of the British Army over the years makes them Camp Followers of the highest order.

[1] MOD letter A/48/Misc/4244/F2(AD) of 19 August 1969, quoted here by kind permission of Williams and Glyn's Bank Limited

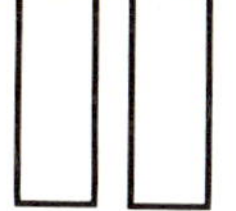

The Tailors

SOLDIERS' DRESS

There are many reasons why soldiers need clothing that is uniform in its appearance, the most obvious being that it must be suitable for battle – although some of the gorgeous gold braided outfits of the 18th and 19th centuries could not have been more impracticable. The need to distinguish friend from foe has always been essential; a uniform has also been a way of promoting a feeling of belonging to any special body of men – such as the bodyguard of a King or a warrior chief. Quantity supplied and mass produced uniforms and equipment were invariably cheaper, as the senators of Rome were quick to discover when equipping their legions. However, it was not until the late 17th century that military dress really became subject to regulations. In England, for example, as in many other countries, various Royal Warrants from the Restoration onwards, specified the various colours of coats and facings to be worn by different units. The more specific and complicated these Warrants, then the more specialised did the task of the tailor become.

We have already seen that when someone raised a regiment, he, as the Colonel, was responsible for providing the soldiers with their uniforms. Cecil Lawson, in his book *A History of the Uniforms of the British Army*, Vol I, gives a good example of this, describing what happened when Farrington's Regiment (later the 29th of Foot and later still the Worcestershire Regiment) was raised in 1694: 'On 30th January of that year a contract was made between Colonel Thomas Farrington and Thomas Plummer, weaver, and James Gutheridge, tailor, for the supply of 754 surtout coats of white kersey faced with yellow for the Private Sentinels and Corporals and as many pairs of breeches of blue kersey to tye below the knee as likewise 39 surtout coats and breeches for the Sergeants and 26 surtout coats of yellow kersey faced with blue bays and as many pairs of breeches for the Drummers.'

The American Civil War soldier had to put up with uniforms made from 'Shoddy', a reclaimed inferior wool which was sold to the government for enormous profits by dishonest manufacturers. 'Shoddy rich' were those who had grown fat from these war contracts.

In the first year of the Civil War the Federal government and various states were all bidding against one another for supplies, and this led to great discomfort for the soldiers, but great fortunes for the unscrupulous. Shoddy clothing, boots with brown paper soles, parched grain sold as sugar and useless foreign weapons, were all supplied to the army. After a year of this kind of malpractice the War Department made strenuous efforts to reform the contract business, but without much success.

The British Army reforms of the 19th century removed the Colonel's responsibility for providing uniforms and, as a contemporary article in the *Navy and Army Illustrated* written by a retired officer of the Royal Army Clothing Department pointed out, the soldier had done very well out of it: 'Since the clothing of the Army has been taken over by the public, the soldier has derived great advantages, for not only has the quality been improved but a greater number of articles are now supplied, many of which under the old system, had to be purchased out of the soldier's own pocket. Thus in the old days when the Colonel supplied the clothing, a cavalry soldier, in two years, obtained only two coats and one pair of overalls; now in the same period he gets from the public three coats and three pairs of overalls, two pairs of boots, two pairs of gloves, two forage caps and a pair of spurs, this represents an increase in pay of £1.10s a year or 1d a day.'

OFFICERS' DRESS

Whilst the other rank was given his uniform free, the British officer still had to buy his from a military tailor, and that could be an extremely expensive business. In the 1800s a subaltern had to pay about £60 to £80, or roughly speaking one year's pay, on his first outfit. If he escaped a frequent recurrence of this expenditure then he was fortunate, for George IV, whether as Regent or as King, was above

Getting ready for parade These camp scenes, published in 1803, show soldiers getting their uniforms, equipment and themselves ready for parade

all things a tailor, and looked upon soldiers as so many dolls to be arrayed according to his whims, in clothing that was as tight as possible, with as much gold and
silver lace as possible, and with headdresses that grew steadily taller with more
and more plumes, all of which were totally unsuitable for the battlefield!

Although uniforms became simpler once khaki was introduced, there were still
dress uniforms, mess kit and so on to keep up the cost of equipping a newly
commissioned subaltern. Over the years, officers' uniform grants have generally
lagged behind these costs, so that in the end the young officer is normally out of
pocket. However, he can certainly not complain about the service he has received
over the years from the small and select band of tailors, who specialise in making
military uniforms. Their addresses are generally in the Savile Row area of London,
but they have branches in the main military towns in England and, in some cases,
abroad as well. Their representatives visit officers' messes regularly, bringing a
selection of their goods into one of the side ante-rooms and taking individual
orders.

At Number One Savile Row, Gieves & Hawkes are at the very heart of men's tailoring – and very close to the heart of London too. For customers in many countries throughout the world, Gieves & Hawkes are 'my tailors' and – just as important – one of the staff cutters is 'my cutter'. When you are ordering a suit which is cut to fit you and you only, and which will last for a sizable part of your life, the whole matter becomes a very personal affair. As the Managing Director says: 'This close relationship with our customers is our greatest asset, just as it has always been during our long history. Our aim is to make a visit to One Savile Row a pleasure for the customer and, in doing so, we are making life much more pleasant for ourselves. While the customer must always be allowed to feel he is right, there is no call for subservience. This just doesn't fit into our sort of shop – or the second half of the 20th century.' Gieves are tailors and outfitters and perhaps the biggest range of Chester Barrie suits to be found anywhere in the world is in their Great Room. Upstairs, in the Adam Room, is the bespoke tailoring department. The elegant, well-proportioned room, with a fine view of Burlington Gardens right down to Old Bond Street, is peaceful and unhurried. Adjoining the Adam Room are the departments for shoes, hats and accessories – as well as the wide range of accoutrements required by officers of HM Armed Forces (over the centuries these have included the Cavalry Shako which Hawkes invented, and the Solar Topee, which they were the first to make).

The firm values its two Royal Warrants: Livery and Military Tailors to HM the Queen; the Naval Tailors and Outfitters to HRH the Duke of Edinburgh. Sometimes to be seen hanging in the shop, are the magnificent gold-embroidered scarlet coats of the State Trumpeters, and the uniforms of the Honourable Company of Gentlemen-at-Arms who take part in all major State functions, such as the Opening of Parliament, the Garter Ceremony at Windsor, or the visit of a foreign Head of State. Before the event, they assemble to dress at Gieves & Hawkes who maintain their splendid uniforms.

The two firms, Gieves and Hawkes, were both started in the 18th century. Gieves, founded in 1785, were Nelson's tailors, and the history of the firm has been closely associated with the Royal Navy. Hawkes, founded in 1771, grew up with the army, and were tailors to the Duke of Wellington. In the days before the Kaiser's war, uniform of great variety and colourful magnificence was looked upon as a matter of the first importance.

Leafing through the ledgers of the 1880s and 1890s, it is quite common to see an Outfit Account of £350 – and in those days a Savile Row civilian suit cost less than 6 guineas. Both firms prospered through the Service connection, despite the fact that in those days it was scarcely done for a gentleman to settle his tailor's bill. In an unpublished memoir, the Head of Hawkes at the turn of the century recalls a dinner at which the Head of Gieves was present. The speaker said: 'Everyone knows how much the Nation owes the Royal Navy, but no-one knows how much the Royal Navy owes to Gieves.' In fact, the Managing Director, looking through old accounts, discovered that in 1938 officers of the Royal Navy had unpaid bills amounting to close on £500,000 – in the money values of those days. 'This would have been enough to have paid for quite a respectable warship', he says. 'Nevertheless, no-one seemed to think this huge bill odd. The Navy was perfectly happy, and we were undoubtedly prosperous.'

An Alkit advertisement which appeared in the first copy of *The Wish Stream* magazine at the Royal Military Academy, Sandhurst, July 1947

Gieves and Hawkes have branches in many parts of the country, including Edinburgh, Portsmouth, Plymouth, Chester, Bath, Leicester and Winchester.[1]

MISS LAWS OF GIEVES & HAWKES

'Violet Laws joined Gieves & Hawkes in 1924, when she was 14. Her first job was putting puggarees on pith helmets; seven yards of material for each, to be meticulously folded and wrapped. Miss Laws works in her own corner of the Gallery above the Big Room at Gieves & Hawkes . . . She is flanked on one hand by a dear old treadle-operated Singer, and on the other by an old electric iron. There is a litter of medal ribbons, medals, gold lace, some item of the uniform of the Gentlemen-at-Arms, and a strip of Cash's name tapes. . . . The greatest monuments to Miss Laws' stitching are the uniforms of the Gentlemen-at-Arms, to many judges of pageantry the most magnificent uniforms in existence. They grace every British State Occasion; their impeccable appearance is due to Miss Laws' care, resource and stitching. Some of these uniforms, and the helmets with their splendid ostrich feather plumes, are fifty or sixty years old. They remain pristine. In 1975 the Gentlemen-at-Arms recognised fifty years of stitching on their behalf with a graceful little private ceremony at which Miss Laws was the focal point, and a presentation was made.

'Perhaps her greatest single job was the creation of Eisenhower's enormous Commander-in-Chief's flag for his advancing headquarters in emancipated Europe. There were seven yards of scarlet bunting, and the five stars of a United States General. . . . A Lieutenant-General in a jeep arrived at the house in Chiswick to collect it. . . . Miss Laws owed her job to her father. He was a Master Tailor in Hawkes from 1898, first as a packer, but in those days a good man was intent on improving himself. When Miss Laws joined she says she knew nothing; she had never been taught to stitch and learned everything by her own trial, error and pricked fingers – "except the cap man who taught me how to put badges and buttons on officers' caps". "I have enjoyed every bit of it" she told me. "I wish I was going to have those fifty years again".'[2]

OVER FIFTY YEARS OF SERVICE

The second army tailor we have chosen is Alkit. Although they have not been in business as long as Gieves & Hawkes, they have been serving the Army for over fifty years and are probably the largest tailors in the United Kingdom giving a regular service to both officers and senior NCOs throughout Great Britain and the British Army of the Rhine. They began with just one branch outside London, which was at Camberley to cater for the officer cadets at Sandhurst. Now they have branches strategically placed all over the United Kingdom.

During the war they dealt not only with newly commissioned officers, but, for example, attended at the reception areas when troops returned from Dunkirk and from prisoner-of-war camps and were highly commended for the service they gave. They have 'followed the flag with the best of 'em', sending out their representatives to visit units abroad. Perhaps the best 'seal of approval' we can give them is this unsolicited testimonial from a clearly satisfied customer:

[1] Taken from a brief kindly provided by Gieves & Hawkes Ltd

[2] From *Miss Laws of Gieves & Hawkes* an Appreciation by P H C Dickens Ltd (Public Relations)

This splendid group of Life Guards NCOs, photographed with Col de Roc shows the wide variety of uniforms to be found in just one regiment in 1873

'Gentlemen,

I have much pleasure in placing at your disposal for a period the Uniform supplied to me by you in 1939, when I proceeded to France.

This is the identical Uniform which I was wearing when embarked on the troopship *Lancastria* June 17th 1940.

As you will recall, the *Lancastria* was sunk by enemy aircraft, with the loss of nearly four thousand British lives; my own Unit lost more than fifty per cent of its strength.

When it became necessary to jump from the rapidly sinking vessel I decided to do so fully dressed, including shoes, but regret to report the loss of my service cap when striking the water.

After swimming for approximately three and a half hours, without a lifebelt, but with some support from a deck chair, I was picked up by the destroyer *Highlander* and later transferred to the troopship *Oronsay*, which vessel eventually reached Plymouth with approximately nine thousand personnel on board. Later this same Uniform accompanied me to the Western Desert, Iraq, Persia, Palestine, North Africa, Salerno Landing, Arromanches and finally to Berlin. As you will see, the Uniform is still in fairly good condition and a credit to your Firm.

Yours very sincerely,
C V Petit (Major)'[1]

[1] Letter kindly provided by Alkit

LOCAL TAILORS

Savile Row tailors could, however, neither cope with the quantity, nor produce suitable garments quickly and cheaply enough for units serving, for example, in India and the tropics. And so local tailors happily supplied the goods. Some of these, have become well known to Servicemen, and have followed the British Army all over the world, providing the tropical uniforms, badges and other necessaries, usually in a matter of hours rather than days. Those who served in Aden will remember Kassim Nazir, who for over 20 years, had exclusive contracts with the Army and the RAF there for the supply of all uniforms for both officers and other ranks.

UNIFORMS WITH A DIFFERENCE

Although the vast majority of US servicemen in WW2 wore issue uniforms and equipment, a few had their own ideas on dress. Because they were usually in fairly exalted positions they were able to get away with uniforms specially made to their own specifications by obliging civilian tailors.

Perhaps the prime example was the late General George S Patton Junior, great commander of the US Third Army, whose troops won spectacular victories throughout North West Europe. His specially tailored 'Ike' jackets, whip-cord riding breeches, hand tooled leather belts and ivory handled six-shooters, were all part of his 'war image'. He deliberately cultivated excesses of dress, always managing to look smarter, more immaculate than anyone else, because he rightly considered that it was good for morale.

In other armies too, such as the British 8th Army in North Africa, many officers adopted items of casual civilian wear – suede desert boots (known to one and all as 'brothel creepers') and coloured neck scarves, became *de rigeur* among those seasoned desert warriors.

And of course even Monty had his own special ideas on dress – his two badged beret must have made those who wrote the dress regulations squirm!

12

Sisters under the skin

A TOAST TO THE LADIES

*'For the Colonel's Lady an' Judy O'Grady
Are sisters under their skins!'*

RUDYARD KIPLING
The Ladies

'In the chapel of Leavenworth, on the monument at Riley, on the walls of Cullum Hall, are names, names of officers dead on the field of honour; bits of marble, slate or bronze commemorating the fact that Lieutenant Willie Jones made the choice and without ostentation or hope of reward, did his duty even unto death. The little plaques tell the story and fame, such as it is, and high honour from us who know, are accorded Willie. But where is Mrs Willie's tablet? Such were the women who year on harrowing year made homes for officers in those bleak western posts; such the women who today uncomplainingly share the luxury of cantonment quarters.

Think of the horror of the slow torture of suspense between the night of Wounded Knee or Chateau Thierry, and the morning at the cemetery. Think of it and thank God for the quick mercy of the bullet. Gentlemen, I reverently pledge you: The Ladies who have shared our lives from the Equator to the Arctic; the Ladies who have condoned our reverses, and inspired, but to applaud, our successes. May we live to make them happy, or, and the Great Day come, so die to make them proud. The Army women God bless them.'[1]

It was General George S Patton Jnr, one of America's greatest soldiers, who made this 'Toast to the Ladies' at a West Point dinner held in Kansas City on 5 April 1924, but it really could have been said by almost any soldier about the army wives of any country and at any time in history. The stories of their tenacity and of the hardships they endured in order to be with their menfolk, have their own special place in military folklore.

ROMAN WIVES For many years the Roman Army did not allow its soldiers to marry Roman women, until Septimus Severus altered the law in AD197. It was a very unfair law anyway, because it was made at a time when civilians were being actively encouraged by the authorities to get married and to have children. Perhaps it was done because the soldiers would be constantly on the move or might become distracted from their task of defending the empire if they had to worry about wives and families.

The law was, for the most part, ignored and remained a theoretical rather than a practical ban on marriage. 'For in the civilian quarters which soon sprang up around their barracks, the legionaries habitually kept women of local origin. Curiously enough, too, the normal forms of marriage with such partners were gone through, evidently with official connivance. Nevertheless this did not mean that the sons born to legionaries by these foreign unions gained Roman citizenship, for they could do so if, like their fathers before them, they joined the legions.

---

[1] *Before the Colours Fade* by Fred Ayer

'Over the garden wall' Love knows no barriers and here an obliging sailor gives this courting couple a chance of a few words. A good example of inter-service co-operation!

And this they frequently did – so that in effect Augustus's measure prohibiting marriages tended to endow legionary service with an hereditary character.'[1]

The law did not extend to senior officers, the legates, auxiliary commanders and tribunes, who were normally given houses of considerable size within the military establishment, whilst the centurions and equivalent rank got quarters large enough for themselves alone, so their families had to live in the villages outside the forts. It was a hard life for any wife, certainly in such places as northern Britain. The tombstones of frontier wives in that area reveal that those who survived the perils of childhood could expect to live only to an average age of 30.

CRUSADING WIVES Ask anyone what happened to the wives of Crusading knights and they will probably tell you that they were left at home in their castles, spinning wool, embroidering tapestries and consoling themselves with young pages, always provided they had a spare key to the 'girdle of chastity' into which they had been incarcerated by their departing husbands! Of course nothing could be further from the truth. The first crusading armies that set out in the spring of 1096, under such leaders as Peter the Hermit, contained nearly as many women as men. The women marched to the Holy Land with their menfolk, braved the same perils along the way, suffered the same dangers and the same miseries of hunger and of thirst during the fighting whilst carrying food and ammunition on the battlefield.

For the second Crusade many ladies, especially in France and Germany, formed themselves into squadrons and regiments of Amazons – the leader of the German Amazons was called 'The Lady of the Golden Legs' on account of her magnificent gilded buckskins and spurs. She enrolled her troop of Amazons under the banner of the Emperor Conrad who started for the Holy Land in 1147. The French Amazons were led by their queen, Eleanor of Aquitaine (afterwards wife of Henry II of England) and formed a squadron of light cavalry.

Many of the barons and knights took their wives with them and, as according to feudal custom, the wife could succeed her husband, some did so, even in the Kingdom of Jerusalem, when their husbands were killed in action. There are also numerous accounts of wives who fought alongside their husbands.

At the siege of Antioch, for example, the women carried water to the soldiers and encouraged them to fight well. At the siege of Acre they worked nonstop to fill in the moats, whilst at all times they nursed the sick and wounded.

As Régine Pernoud explains in her book *The Crusaders*: 'Women's faces look out from every page of the story of the Crusades and the overseas kingdoms, but they have not attracted the attention of modern historians. It would be worth making a study of those peasants and townswomen who worked with ordinary soldiers in the Holy Land and who sometimes stayed on in Syria.

'There they played beside their husbands the humble yet vital role played a great deal later by the wives of the pioneers in the United States to whom the Americans have erected a memorial in Maryland.

'Their presence can be felt, or guessed at, throughout the chronicles, but so little has been written about them that the eye must be content with the portraits of the great ladies, painted in more detail by the scribes.'

[1] *The Army of the Caesars* by Michael Grant

One of these brave women was Margaret of Provence, who accompanied her husband, King Louis, on the first Crusade, in spite of being pregnant.

Their army was defeated and the king taken three days before the birth of her son. Damietta, the town in which she was confined, was in danger of being taken by the Saracens.

The Italian merchants who followed the crusading armies, making fat profits, were about to leave Damietta and all the women, the sick and the elderly who were sheltering there. Margaret called their leaders together and tried to persuade them not to leave. However, it was not until she agreed to requisition all their supplies and to pay for them all herself that she prevailed upon them to stay.

Later Damietta was exchanged in ransom for the king and his men.

Not all the women of the overseas kingdoms were Crusaders. The knights had no racial prejudice and were perfectly happy to marry native girls, provided they were Christians or would accept conversion. In 1180 there were over 5,000 men at arms living in Palestine and the vast majority were married to Armenian or Saracen women.

The barons also married native princesses, particularly when a suitable alliance or a large dowry was in the offing.

Baldron of Boulogne, after the death of his wife Godvere, married an Armenian princess named Arda. He later repudiated the marriage on the grounds of her adultery and then looked around for another rich heiress. He decided upon Adelaid, Countess Regent of Sicily. When she sailed into Acre harbour in August 1113, her galley was plated with gold and silver and her chair stood upon a carpet of gold. Two escorting triremes carried her white robed Arab guards and seven more ships were laden with her treasures. Alas, the marriage did not last long because the Pope made vigorous protests, accusing Baldron of bigamy, as his former wife was still alive and he ordered the couple to separate.

WOMEN WHO FOLLOW AN ARMY

The presence of women with European armies was the custom for many centuries, probably a survival from the time of the migration of peoples from the East. Turner in his *Pallas Armata* says: 'Women who follow an army may be ordered (if they can be ordered) in three ranks, or rather in three classes.

'The first shall be those who are ladies, and are the wives of the general and other principal commanders of the army, who for the most part are carried in coaches, but those coaches must drive according to the quality of them to whom the ladies belong, and as the baggage of their husbands is appointed to march by the wagon master-general.

'The second class is those who ride on horse-back, and they must ride in no other place than where the baggage of the regiment to whom they belong marches, but they are oft extravagant gadding here and there, and therefore in some places they are put in companies and have one or more to command . . .

'The third class is of those who walk afoot, and are the wives of infirm officers and soldiers.

'As woman was created to be a helper to man, so women are great helpers to armies, to their husbands, especially those of the lower conditions, neither should

Jack's Exclusive Privilege No soldier, when walking with his sweetheart, may encircle her waist with his arm in a public thoroughfare, but sailors can! (*Navy & Army Illustrated* 21 October 1899)

A Regimental wedding in India, 1940

they be rashly banisht out of armies; sent away they may be sometimes for weighty considerations: they provide, buy and dress their husband's meat, when their husbands are on duty or newly come from it; they bring in fewel for fire; a soldier's wife may be helpful to others, and gain money to her husband and herself; especially they are useful in camps and leaguers, being permitted (which should not be refused them) to go some miles from the camp to buy victuals and other necessaries.'[1]

WHO WANTS TO MARRY A SOLDIER?

It is interesting to compare the relative advantages and disadvantages of marrying into the army over a period of say, about a hundred years. Here are two differing views on the subject. The first was written by a lady called Cicely McDonnel and appeared in the 1890s in the *Navy and Army Illustrated*, a splendid fortnightly journal. The article was entitled 'The advantages of marrying a soldier' and it gave perhaps a more rosy picture of army life at the turn of the century than was actually the case. In view of the length of the original article we have reproduced it in part only.

In contrast, the modern article was written by Corporal B V J Thompson serving with the Intelligence Section of the 1st Battalion, The Royal Hampshire Regiment, whilst he was on active service in Northern Ireland. It was published in the regiment's monthly news sheet in 1976 and is a tongue in cheek look at the

[1] *The British Soldier* by Col H de Watteville

daily lot of the modern soldier's wife, that will probably bring a wry smile to the faces of all those who have recently 'followed the drum.'

THE ADVANTAGES OF MARRYING A SOLDIER 'To describe the private soldier's wife as a *femme incomprise* would scarcely be an exaggeration; nothing is more difficult to educate than public opinion. From reading Lever and other novelists of years ago, the idea prevails that so soon as any self-willed girl enters the married state with a soldier, her life thereafter consists of a desperate struggle to make both ends meet. Surely nothing could be further from the fact than this notion.

'. . . The advantages, as compared with those of the artisan or married man of any station lower than the middle class, are as follows: Sanitary dwellings, *no rent*, bright and cheerful surroundings, gas, coals, firewood, schooling for children free; the certainty of a fixed daily quantity of wholesome food; the provision of clothing of all kinds (so far as the husband is concerned), without the eternal necessity for painful calculations as to the means of procuring the wherewithal; the opportunity of purchasing everything necessary for housekeeping from the canteen, which is an institution arranged on purely socialistic principles, i.e., the men and women share the profits, which are distributed in kind; the annual change of air and scene; travelling expenses free, and facilities under certain conditions; and a certain, if small, income. Medical attendance and the services of the Army chaplains are always at the disposal of married couples without expense; and in case of the husband being detailed for duty at a distance, a separation allowance is made; that is, in the case of wives who are "on the strength" of the regiment.

'Above all, a soldier's wife is free from the wearing anxiety lest through strikes, business losses, reduction of staff, etc, her husband should lose his berth at short notice, and she should suddenly find herself in the direst straits through complete loss of means.

'Further, a girl who marries either a "trooper" or a "private" realizes that her husband has chances of advancement, distinction and reward, and that, as he rises, her position is improved, and she may become a person of some importance; and again, a private soldier (if he avails himself of them) has opportunities of

Wedding Day, Nanyuki, Kenya 1956

improving himself. From force of circumstances, he is thrown amongst very mixed companionship; but he is also in daily contact with men, such as his officers, who have received the best of education and whose manners he can study, whose bearing he can imitate. Example is better than precept, and the wife sometimes gains vicariously by this association, and, if she is intelligent, adapts herself quickly to the better side of barrack life, and finds the order and discipline regulating her ways too.

'It is well known that married soldiers (as well as single) can add to their pay by taking over various duties, such as orderly clerkships, school-masterships, tailoring, "instruction" etc, while the wives are frequently employed by the officers' families as house-helps, needle-women, dressmakers, and as laundresses.

'When a regiment is ordered for foreign service, the wife has to face the fact that her little home must be broken up and the furniture sold. This, no doubt, seems very hard, but there are compensations in every lot. Women who, if married to clerks and mechanics, would never have a chance of leaving England now experience the pleasures of travel, and those who have been in India long heartily to go there again and enjoy the lazy sunny life.

'The voyage on the troop-ship is a new experience and any discomfort of life on board is amply atoned for by the novelty of the situation. When the vessel touches at a port, permission is given to go on shore for a few hours. In India the non-commissioned officers' wives generally have two native servants, an ayah and a "boy". There also the wife receives an allowance of 4 rupees a month for herself, and 2 rupees 8 annas for each child; this is absolutely her own to spend as she likes. The wives who are not on the strength can only follow the regiment at their own expense.

'When a regiment is ordered for active service the crucial test has to be endured, viz, the separation of husband from wife, child and home. Then the wife goes through a painful struggle between love and duty. The parting may mean parting for ever from the man she loves and may never see again; and she has to muster all her courage to enable her to bear up bravely at the last sad moment. Should he, alas! be killed in action, she receives a gratuity both for herself and orphans, which helps and sustains her at the moment of her heaviest trial.

'Without trying to put a rosy haze on the subject, the foregoing facts show that a woman who marries a soldier has solid comforts that many civilians' wives lack. As regards her happiness in the state, or the comforts she obtains or surrounds herself with, that depends to a great extent on her temperament. A good manager will always make the best of things, a happy disposition finds happiness where others find misery and hardship. Our lives are much as we make them!'

Surely an article like this must have had prospective army brides lining up in droves!

SO YOU ARE GOING TO MARRY A SOLDIER EH? (A WARNING TO WOULD-BE ARMY WIVES!) 'He must seem such a clean living lad to you, with his short hair, smart suit, tales of service overseas and even perhaps a photograph of himself in uniform. However, before you marry your warrior hero, there are a few points which you should bear in mind! The first thing that you ought to know is that when you agree to "have and to hold" – from this day forward – you will only be able to have him and hold him for some of the time. Most of the time he will be on

Christmas Dinner in a soldiers'
married quarter in the late 1890s.
(Did he take off his tunic and medals
once the photographer had
finished?)

Exercise, Operations, On Duty or on Jankers. Occasionally, however, he will be
on leave, and this is when you can have and hold him.

'With any luck at all, you will be given an Army Quarter for which your husband
pays a modest rent. This quarter may be on a civilian housing estate. If it is, then
you will find that your neighbours will complain about the noise that you, your
children or your dog make – theirs are just as bad mind you, but everybody needs
somebody to blame. They will affectionately call your children "Army brats"
and tell their own little darlings not to play with yours . . .

'Make sure you learn how to work a mower, for your husband will usually be
sent away in the summer – just as the grass is growing.

'Things like stoking the boiler, mowing the grass and filling the car with oil
and water in the correct holes will all have to be self taught because your old man
will be far too busy packing his kit before he goes away to let you in on all these
little secrets. Writing to him during his fifth month with the United Nations
Forces in Cyprus to tell him that the car needs a longer dipstick because the one
you have will not reach the oil, will not help your marital bliss!

'The Army is full of initials and your husband will use these to talk to you in
some sort of code. At least try to learn the meaning behind some of them as he
will then think you understand what he has been going on about for the past hour.
The two which are most important are CO (Commanding Officer) and RSM
(Regimental Sergeant Major) – two very important people and you should be
able to recognise these personalities as soon as possible. Your husband's colouring
may assist you in this as he may turn a light red/puce, green or pallid white on
their approach . . .

160

'The names of many of England's Garrison Towns will be familiar to you, and it is in these that you will spend much of your time in between infrequent tours abroad. The names of many of Northern Ireland's towns will be familiar to you from the TV. While *you* are in a Garrison Town it is there in Ballywhatsit that your husband will be spending much of *his* time (returning home for a four day R & R halfway through his four months, most of which will be spent in bed).

'You probably won't have to clean your husband's boots or press his uniforms as he won't trust you to do this. On the subject of uniforms, you will be expected to set aside a complete room of your quarter for kit, packs and webbing. If you can get away with it have all this dumped in the garage or garden shed. Best of all, get him to keep it in camp! If your husband is a senior NCO or Officer he will be the proud possessor of a Mess Kit which he will have paid an absolute fortune for, but will treat like Rugger Kit, expecting you to sort it all out for the next time he needs it. On return from Exercises, invariably during the worst spell of wet weather during the year, he is likely to give you a bundle of dhobi (read "laundry") caked with mud/Camouflage cream/congealing compo soup and expect it to be washed and clean for the following day. His second love after you, and sometimes coming before you, in England, will be his "best boots" which he will lovingly sit and polish for hours on end.

'You will also have heard of the British Army of the Rhine (sometimes called the British Army on the Wine). Should your husband's unit be fortunate enough to be posted abroad, then it is quite likely that he will take you to BAOR – West Germany. If your husband is a driver, you will have to share him in Germany with yet another love – the Armoured Fighting Vehicle 432. If you wake up at 3 in the morning to find he is not beside you, he has probably gone into camp to start up "the wagon" to stop it from freezing up. This is always a good point to bring up in the Divorce Courts.

'You should also learn who the BFO is – the poor man is the Battalion Families Officer (called a UFO in some units in order to confuse the issue, especially as UFO officially stands for Unit Fire Officer). It is to him that you turn with complaints at the slightest annoyance. Chosen for his tact and diplomacy he will allow you, good humour ever evident, to rant and rave to your heart's content. If he can do anything to relieve your distress he will do his utmost to do so. His reward for this is normally to be completely run down to the ground.

'Once your husband reaches the first rung of the promotion ladder he will become a member of a Mess, progressing through the Corporal's Mess to the Sergeant's Mess and possibly even into the Officers' Mess. To enable the Mess to run smoothly he will be forced to attend Mess Meetings which last about three quarters of an hour, from 7pm until 11.30pm. Never be separated voluntarily. The Army will do it for you often enough. Finally, follow the drum where ever it goes or – remember there is still time to change your mind!'

MARRIED QUARTERS

A familiar feature of all garrison towns are the estates of married quarters, so much now the rule that it is difficult to realise that not so long ago the families of soldiers had to live in very different conditions. In the early days of the British

Obeying his Country's Call 'Goodbye Dolly I must leave you, though it breaks my heart to go, something tells me I am needed, at the front to fight the foe. See, the soldier boys are marching, And I can no longer stay – Hark! I hear the bugle calling, Goodbye Dolly Gray!' (From a song that was popular in both the Spanish-American and Boer Wars)

Army, troops were normally billeted in private accommodation and innkeepers and the like were not legally bound to house women.

It was not until the 1790s that the first proper barracks were built and married soldiers were permitted to occupy corners of the barrack rooms with their families. This custom was given official approval in the first Barrack Regulations ever issued, so that from being merely a custom of the service, it became an official rule. As the regulations put it: 'the commanding officer may approve the presence of women in the barrack room for the greater cleanliness and convenience of the soldier.'

There was of course a strict ceiling on the number of wives allowed in barracks – normally six per company. They lived, with their children, behind a thin screen of hanging blankets or canvas, cheek by jowl with the other soldiers. Privacy of any kind was quite impossible, the family had to get on with the normal everyday business of living, eating, sleeping, even having babies, in these abominable conditions.

The soldier and his wife owned only the two single beds allocated to them and virtually nothing else. The rest of the family slept on the floor, although small boys could usually find a bed for the night as there were bound to be soldiers away on duty or absent. But what a life it must have been for teenage daughters.

On the whole, women were treated with rough courtesy and it has been said that the presence of a woman in the barrack room lessened the bad language. Nevertheless, the soldiers and the women, too, for that matter, spent much of their spare time drinking, and it was inevitable that some women and girls would be molested, unless the husband and father was tough enough to defend them with his fists and boots.

In return for being permitted to live in the barrack room, the women cooked, washed and sewed for the occupants, receiving in return a small amount out of the men's pay. One wife would look after about a dozen men.

As Veronica Bamfield explains in her delightful book *On the Strength*, aptly subtitled as 'The story of the British Army Wife': 'Sanitary arrangements were non-existent and typhoid fever and tuberculosis endemic; the last brought about by the lack of facilities for drying clothes when the men came in from sentry duty. The rough communal kitchens bulged with women elbowing each other for space in the greasy smoke-laden atmosphere. Behind some of the barracks, the men dug gardens out of disused ground to grow potatoes and greens, and kept a pig in a sty in the corner. An irritated officer remarked that nobody seemed able to stop them knocking shelves into their barrack corners, and it is evident that from earliest times the army wife showed her genius for snuggling down and making a home for her family whever she happened to be.'

One soldier, Trooper Buck Adams, who enlisted in 1843 said this about his first night in the barrack room: 'I shall never forget my first night in the barrack-room, which was occupied by twenty five single men, not reckoning the married men who had their wives and families. Each family occupied one corner of the room, which was hidden from the rest at night-time only by a sheet fastened across the corner. The scenes I witnessed and the language I heard . . . I have never forgotten.' Truly the barrack room was a very hard life for a wife and one that did not as a rule permit any outward display of true womanly feeling.

'Goodbye' from India to China This picture appeared in the *Navy & Army Illustrated* in July 1900 and serves to illustrate the sad leave taking of soldiers sent from India to deal with the Boxer Rebellion (May 1900)

Widowed 'A simple telegram with a brief but terrible message has filled many a heart with sorrow in the course of this war (The Boer War). We do not penetrate the sacred privacy of such scenes of domestic grief but us the stage delineates the moving passages of life, the camera has here been the agent for bringing before as in faultless character, an episode which will appeal to the imagination and go straight to the heart of all who see it'. (*Navy & Army Illustrated* 5 May 1900)

If these conditions sound bad, then spare a thought for the wives of soldiers married 'off the strength', that is to say without official permission. They could not even find accommodation in the barracks and many commanding officers would do nothing to help them.

A MARRIED QUARTÉR IN THE WILD WEST It was, of course, no better in any other army. For example, the conditions under which the wives of American servicemen had to set up home in the widely dispersed forts in the far distant territories were probably, if anything, worse. A lieutenant's wife described one of the officers' quarters in Fort Lincoln, which she occupied during the Sioux wars, as being so poorly constructed that the wind blew constantly through every crack and crevice. She had to hang old canvas tenting inside to help keep out the cold, whilst the sheet-iron stove in the middle of the room only radiated heat to a distance of 2ft. Furniture was a few campstools, some unpainted chairs and a dining table composed of three planks stretched across two carpenter's horses. The table also doubled as an overnight bed for unexpected visitors. Her dressing table was a packing box turned on its side with shelves nailed in. Upon it stood a tin pitcher, tin basin and a crude mirror. Curtains were unbleached cotton sheeting

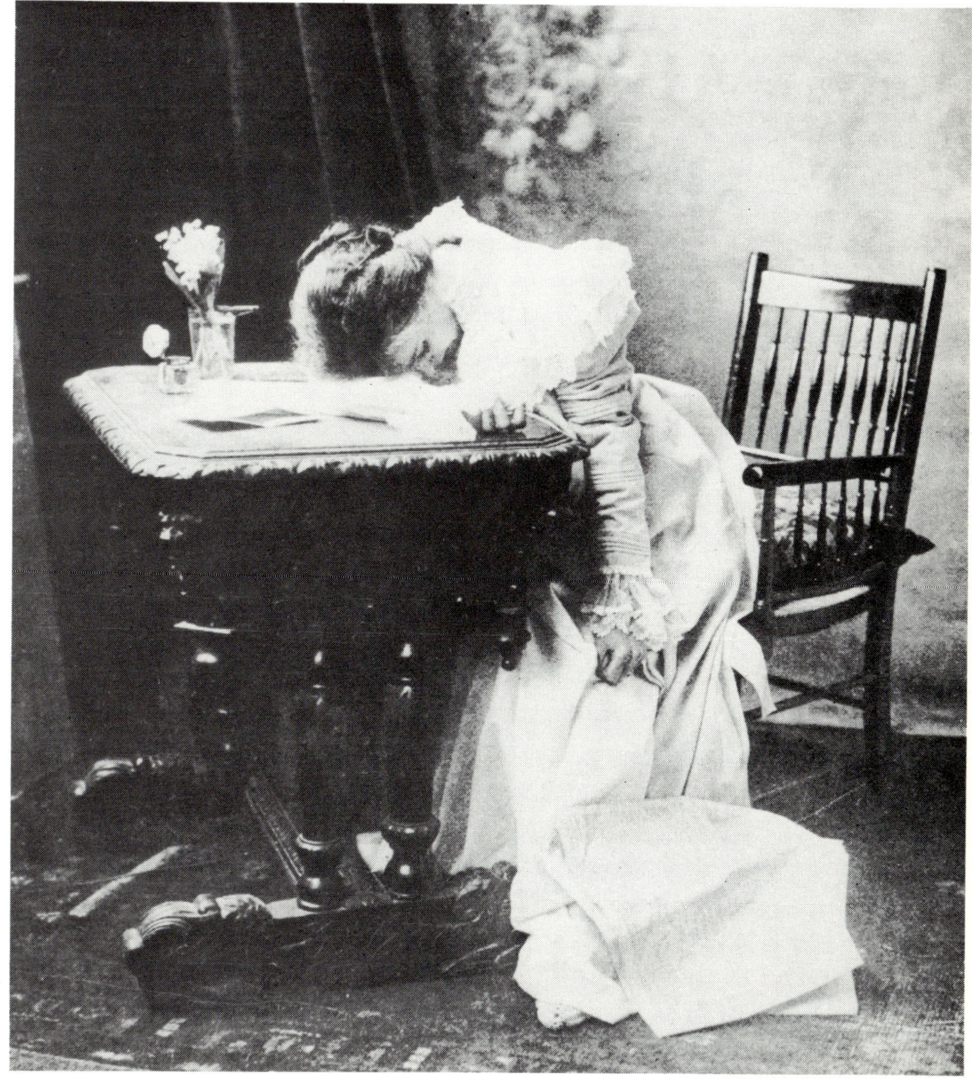

sometimes dyed with beet juice, whilst grey government issue blankets or skins served as floor coverings.

Here is how Elizabeth Bacon Custer, wife of General Custer, described her first army quarter: 'Our railroad journey came to an end about ten miles from Fort Riley. The laborers were laying the tracks from that point . . . We found a wagon waiting for our luggage and an ambulance to carry us the rest of the journey . . . Fort Riley came in sight when we were pretty well tired out. It was my first view of a frontier post.

'I had either been afraid to confess my ignorance, or so assured there was but one variety of fort, and the subject needed no investigation, that Fort Riley came upon me as a great surprise. I supposed, of course, it would be exactly like Fortress Monroe, with stone walls, turrets for sentinels, and a deep moat. As I had heard more and more about Indians since reaching Kansas, a vision of the enclosure where we would eventually live was a great comfort to me. I could scarcely believe that the buildings, a storey and a half high, placed around a parade ground, were all there was of Fort Riley.

'The sutler's store, the quartermaster and commissary storehouse, and the stables for the cavalry horses, were outside the square, near the post, and that was all. No trees, and hardly any signs of vegetation except the buffalo-grass that curled its sweet blades close to the ground, as if to protect the nourishment it held from the blazing sun . . .

'It is a strange sensation to arrive at a place where money is of little use in providing shelter and here we were beyond even the commonest railroad hotel. Mrs Gibbs, who received us, was put to a severe test that night. Already a room in her small house had been prepared for General Sherman, who had arrived earlier in the day, and now there were five of us bearing down upon her . . . She assured me that, having been on the Plains herself before the war, she was quite accustomed to a state of affairs when there was nothing to do but quarter yourself upon strangers; and then gave up her own room for our use . . . I used to try to remember afterward, when for nine years we received and entertained strangers

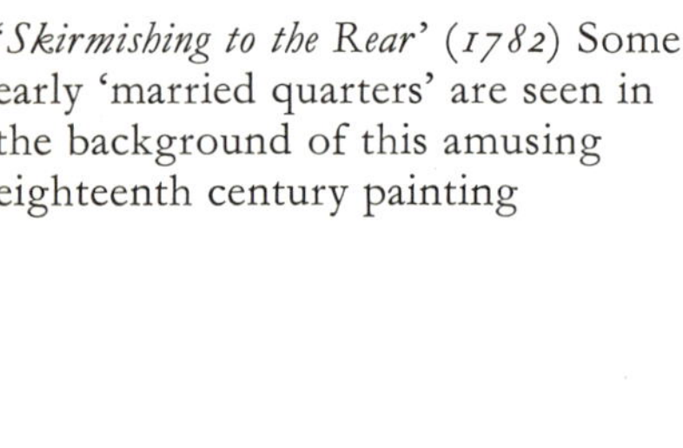

'*Skirmishing to the Rear*' (*1782*) Some early 'married quarters' are seen in the background of this amusing eighteenth century painting

who had nowhere else to go, the example of undisturbed hospitality shown to me by my first friend on the frontier . . .'

Of course there were a lot worse places than Libbie Custer's first posting. George W Grummond and his wife Frances arrived at Fort Phil Kearney whilst it was still under construction. Their temporary quarters consisted of two 'A' tents drawn together, one for trunks, two dilapidated camp-stools and a mess chest; the other for two hospital bunks which filled up nearly all the space. There was just enough room for a small heating stove and a narrow passageway to a tarpaulin covered cook stove where she cooked their meals.

'During their first night in the tents, snow fell, drifting in and covering Frances's face; it was melting and trickling down her cheeks when she awakened. The pillows, bedding and even the stove were also covered with snow. She shook snow out of her stockings and shoes and set about preparing her first breakfast in the wilds of Wyoming. She managed to cook some fair bacon and coffee, but the biscuits were not of the sort she had known in Tennessee. Made from flour, salt and water, they were as hard as stones.'[1]

BUMPING The American army had a very strict code as far as the occupation of officers' married quarters was concerned, which was known by various terms such as 'bumping', 'bricks falling' or 'ranking out'. This meant that an officer's family could be evicted at short notice if an officer of higher rank arrived and demanded the house. The process could be ruthless.

'Mrs Orsemus Boyd, wife of a lieutenant at Fort Clark, was forced by a bachelor captain to move from comfortable quarters into a house with one room and a detached kitchen. Her eviction took place only four weeks after she gave birth to a child; the baby and her other two children were sick with whooping cough and bronchitis at the time. Another woman, given only three hours' notice to turn over her home to a higher-ranking officer, ended up living in a two-room converted chicken house.'[2]

[1] *The Gentle Tamers* by Dee Brown
[2] *The Soldiers* by the Editors of Time Life Books

As one commanding officer explained to a wife who was feeling very remorseful after she and her husband had just forced another family out of their quarters at Fort Russell, Wyoming: 'They'll hate you for doing it, but if you don't do it, they'll not respect you. After you've been turned out once yourself, you will not mind turning others out.'[1]

The system could cause considerable turmoil such as at Fort Clark, Texas, in the 1870s, when at least 50 moves were made by officers' families of the station, because the arrival of one officer would cause the move of some dozen officers junior to him in rank. 'After one series of "bumpings" at Fort Clark, a young lieutenant and his bride, fresh from luxurious eastern homes, found themselves quartered in a hallway between two other families. The wife accepted her lot gracefully, but no sooner had she fixed up the place comfortably than her husband was notified that a superior officer wanted his hall. This was the final blow; the young lieutenant resigned in a huff and left the Army forever.'[2]

'TO GO' OR 'NOT TO GO'

An army wife was always a liability to the authorities, although they did have their uses as washerwomen, nurses or merely as a means of ensuring that their husbands did not desert, so small numbers of wives were normally permitted to accompany regiments travelling overseas. The magic number was usually six per company, although this did vary during certain campaigns.

The actual selection of the lucky wives of who were to be allowed to go was done by the drawing of lots among the married women of the regiment. This gave rise to the most harrowing scenes imaginable, because the poor wives who drew 'Not to go' knew that they would be cast adrift without any means of support. In all probability they would be far from home, ostracised by their families for

1, 2 *The Gentle Tamers* by Dee Brown

166

marrying a soldier, penniless, probably with at least one child and without any real hope of ever seeing their husbands again.

The actual drawing of lots has been described in various contemporary books, but none more vividly than in the following account by Donaldson, when the 71st of Foot were embarking for Portugal from Jersey to fight in the Peninsular War. 'The women assembled in the pay-sergeant's office, husbands crowding round; tickets inscribed "To go" or "Not to go" were placed in a hat.

'Each woman took her turn at the draw, hearts beating, anxiety and suspense on every visage. The first woman, the senior sergeant's wife, drew "Not to go". Nobody cared, for she was no favourite, neither was her husband. A corporal's wife came next – again "Not to go". Not a sound of regret, for she was no more popular than her man.

'The third put in her hand – an outrageous virago, who thought nothing of knocking down her husband and was hated about the barrack-room fire at cooking times. The wishes of the assembly that she should be left was almost audible.

'Boldly she plunged her hand into the hat; triumphantly she waved the scrap inscribed "To go". "Harrah" she shouted, "Old Meg will go yet and live to scold more of you round the fireside." "Hang the old wretch!" came from behind, "she has the devil's own luck and her own!"'

'Then came a modest young woman, wife of the model of the company, beloved of her husband, and esteemed by the roughest of his barrack-mates. Trembling she drew out her ticket. "Not to go" it read, but she could not see for her emotion. "Tell me, for God's sake, what it is! Oh, God help me! Oh, Sandy!" came her cry as she sank fainting on her husband. "Oh, Sandy, you'll no leave me and your poor baby." Her agony touched deeply the hardest of them all . . .

A typical drawing room in an officer's married quarter in India, 1881

'... The next day the regiment sailed. Sandy's wife trudged the weary six miles to the sea and made a last agonized attempt to go with him. All in vain. As the vessel left she gave a shriek never to be forgotten by the men on boardship. Sandy, poor fellow, never returned from the Peninsula, while she was never heard of again.'

TROOPING

Having been among the fortunate few to be allowed on the troop transports, the wives' troubles were far from over. Indeed, the conditions on board were probably far worse than the scruffy corner of the barrack room which they had just left. Below decks there would be little fresh air, no washing facilities except for buckets of salt water, no sanitary arrangements except more buckets, no privacy by day or night no matter what the circumstances – sickness, childbirth or even death. Above all the stench of ammonia from the stables which were normally alongside the troops' accommodation.

Officers' wives had little more in the way of comforts: 'Those who have not been at sea' wrote one Mrs Sherwood, wife of Captain Sherwood, Paymaster of the 52nd Regiment, who travelled to India with her husband in 1805, 'can never conceive the hundredth part of the horrors of a long voyage to a female in a sailing vessel.'[1]

The fear of sinking was of course uppermost in the minds of those early passengers and in time of war there were the additional risks of capture or being fired upon by the enemy, to add to drowning or shipwreck. Perhaps the best known troopship disaster was the wreck of the *Birkenhead*, immortalised by Thomas M Henry's well known painting.

The *Birkenhead* had been modified for use as a troopship and this had included removing a number of her watertight bulkheads. She sailed from Spithead in December 1851, bound for South Africa, with soldiers and their families on board.

[1] *On the Strength* by Veronica Bamfield

'*His horse, his car, his cook, his wife and everything that he hath*' Lt Col and Mrs E B Powell, (CO 1st Battalion The Rifle Brigade) pictured outside their married quarter in Peshawar 1927

Shooting camp in the Kashmir area
1860

On 26 February 1852, she foundered upon a reef whilst approaching Port Elizabeth.

The water flooded in all the faster because of the missing bulkheads and the ship was doomed from the outset.

All the women and children were ordered into the cutters whilst the men fell in on deck. The scene must have been a terrifying one as the women clung to their husbands saying their last goodbyes.

Discipline was impeccable despite the fact that few men could swim and the waiting sharks soon dealt with any of those who did not drown. All the women and children were saved on that occasion.

Conditions improved steadily from those far off days until travelling by troopship became a delightful experience to be savoured by those fortunate enough to sample the good food, shipboard entertainments and fascinating scenery at ports of call such as Port Said, Aden, Columbo, Singapore and Hong Kong.

TROUBLES EN ROUTE

Another of the hazards to be faced by wives whilst 'following the flag' was the threat of being left stranded somewhere en route.

British invalid driving foreign animals from proceeding to the camp. 'You vile pack of vagabonds, what do you mean'. (1780)

Household Removals Chinese Style!
Using a splendid mule-drawn railway, household items belonging to the 1st Battalion The Lancashire Fusiliers who were stationed in Tientsin 1936-1938, are moved to a new station

In 1815, when the British Army sailed to Ostend before the Waterloo campaign, four wives per company were allowed to sail with them. On arrival at Ostend, however, an order was received that only two women would be allowed to proceed further with each company:

'We had now disembarked and boats lay on the canal ready to convey us into the interior of the country; but as we were stepping on board an order was received importing that only two women would be allowed to proceed with each company.

'Those who had gotten on board the boats waiting for our conveyance were turned out and not withstanding their sighs and tears, given in charge to a guard to quarter in a barracks in Ostend. Meanwhile we moved slowly up the canal and left the poor weeping women behind to form their own future plans of proceeding and make arrangements for following the futures of their husbands.'[1]

The regiments then proceeded to Ghent, but they had only been there for two days when the women succeeded in reaching them. They were, however, taken back to Ostend and put under guard. In less than a week they were again up with the troops, having eluded the guards.

Happily the authorities decided to turn a blind eye on this occasion and they were allowed to stay until the battle of Waterloo, when all wives were sent to Brussels to await the outcome of the fighting.

'TENTING ON THE PLAINS'

Overland travel could be just as difficult and dangerous for army wives on their way, for example, to the garrison outposts in the 'Wild West'.

In the early 1800s the journey across America began by train as far as Louisville in Northern Kentucky, then by flat-bottomed boat to New Orleans with the officers, soldiers, wives, children and horses all together in conditions similar to,

[1] *Military Life during the most eventful periods of the late wars* by James Anton

A very striking family group at a
Soldiers' Exhibition, Lucknow,
circa, 1883

if not worse, than the early British troopships which we have already described.
From New Orleans the real journey began by horseback or wagon, fifteen miles a
day when the going permitted, trekking through hostile, often Indian infested,
country.

At this period frontier women could – and did – handle a rifle and drive a team
of horses, so it is not surprising to find many hardy and heroic women. Dr Mary
Walker, Sally Tompkins and Clara Barton, all worked valiantly as nurses, even
under fire, during the Civil War.

Women on both sides were involved in making bandages and clothing, and in
the South especially, many sold their most treasured possessions in aid of the war
effort.

Feminine wiles were put to good use in other directions too – namely espionage.
Belle Boyd, better known as Belle Starr, Pauline Cushman and Mrs Rose Greenhow
all became famous spies, but there were others too and even one or two double
agents.

After the war between the States, when the real western expansion began, the
officers found they could buy condemned Army ambulances at Leavenworth,
Kansas, and fix them up as travelling coaches. In such a coach it took six weeks
to get from Leavenworth to Santa Fe, but it was preferable to train travel. The
trains had no conveniences. The passengers had to get off periodically to eat at
various makeshift places, while the trains took on water. The farther west, the
worse the conditions. Male passengers would shoot game and use the open
windows as latrines!

Travel by coach was not much better. The nightly stops at so called 'inns'
were nightmares of community sleeping, bed bugs and rations of bacon and bread
with an occasional egg. If the ladies wanted toast, they had to learn to ask for
burned bread, because toast, on the frontier meant half a loaf of bread fried in
lard. One lovely lady, following her husband west, brought with her a year's
supply of tea. She stopped at one of these inns and asked the landlady to fix her a
badly needed cup of tea. Half an hour later that worthy came back and said: 'I

done "biled" those greens and I done "biled" 'em an' I done change the water three times, an' they are still too bitter for anyone in this territory to eat.'

Among these travellers was Elizabeth Bacon Custer, wife of the famous General George Armstrong Custer, Civil War hero and Indian fighter. After her husband was killed at the Battle of the Little Big Horn on 25 June 1876, Libbie Custer began to write books – now that she could no longer write letters to her beloved husband.

She wrote about the everyday occurrences in her twelve years of following her husband from post to post as an army wife. Her first book *Boots and Saddles* was published in 1885 and met with great acclaim and financial success, so thereafter whenever she was hard up she again took up her pen. Her Second book *Tenting on the Plains* dealt with the period immediately following the Civil War, when Custer was first stationed in Texas and then on the Kansas frontier. As in all her books she refers to Custer as 'The General' regardless of what rank he was holding at the time.

Here is how she described one of her early journeys: 'The General had an ambulance fitted up as a travelling wagon for me; the seats so arranged that the leather backs could be unstrapped at the sides and laid down to form a bed, if I wished to rest during the march. There was a pocket for my needlework and book, and a box for luncheon, while my travelling bag and shawl were strapped at the side, convenient, but out of the way. It was quite a complete little house of itself. . . .

'My husband had the wagon placed in front of the tent every night when our march was ended, and lifted me in and out of the high bedroom, where I felt that nothing venomous could climb up and sting. . . .

'My life in a wagon became such an old story that I could hardly believe I had ever had a room. It constantly reminded me of my father. He had opposed my marrying in the army, as I suppose most fond fathers do . . . his principal reason, mindful of the deprivations he had seen officers' wives endure in Michigan's early days, was that, after the charm and dazzle of the epaulet had passed, I might travel "in a covered wagon like an emigrant". I told this reason of my father's to my husband, and he often laughed over it. When I was lifted from my rather lofty apartment and set down in the tent in the dark and before dawn in a pine forest it *is* dark – the candle revealed a twinkle in the eye of a man who could joke before breakfast, "I wonder what your father would say now" . . .

'In this expedition I brought the art of dressing in a hurry to so fine a point that I could take my bath and dress entirely in seven minutes. My husband timed me one day, without my knowledge and I had the honour of having this added to a brief list of my attributes as a soldier . . . the General usually said (when introducing Libbie) "Oh, I want you to know my wife; she slept four months in a wagon." '

As well as these light hearted descriptions of the journeys which she endured, Mrs Custer also waxes serious at times, for example when she tells how, years later, she discovered that the escort officer who accompanied her on her many dashes to be with the general, had orders to shoot her if the wagon was attacked by Indians and the odds seemed poor.

8th Cavalry officers and their ladies in camp near Fort Meade, South Dakota, circa 1897

When travelling through hostile country, all the women were instructed to lie on the bottom of the wagons and not to show their faces. The sight of a white woman was sufficient to start a running fight as Indians attached a great deal of importance to capturing one.

At the siege of Fort Phil Kearney, the post commander brought all the women and children into the powder magazine. A trail of gun powder was then laid and he ordered the first sergeant to fire it if the Indians came over the wall. Fortunately this did not happen.

'THE PRAIRIE TRAVELLER' With so many inexperienced travellers heading west it was not long before a handbook was written which contained many helpful

A picnic in the underbrush Army officers and their wives settle down for a picnic near Old Fort Grant, Arizona, 1876. Note the towering desert cacti and the very fetching hats!

Another picnic party from Fort Grant in Arizona Territory. This time the venue is in Reservoir Canyon

hints for the tenderfoot. It was called *The Prairie Traveller*, a handbook for Overland Expeditions, and was written by Captain Randolph Barnes Marcy, US Army, in the mid 1800s.

The preface began: 'The education of our officers at the Military Academy is doubtless well adapted to the art of civilised warfare, but can not familiarise them with the diversified details of border service . . .' Marcy based his book on 'A quarter of a century of frontier life' and it covered the organisation of a column, the equipment needed, types of wagons to use, tentage, food etc and gives details of various routes with the best places to pitch camp.

He also includes useful information like this treatise on snake bites: 'Upon the Southern route to California rattlesnakes are often met with, but it is seldom that any person is bitten by them; yet this is a possible contingency and it can never be amiss to have an antidote at hand.

'Hartshorn (a solution of ammonia in water) applied externally to the wound and drunk in small quantities diluted with water whenever the patient becomes faint or exhausted from the effects of the poison, is one of the most common remedies.

'In the absence of all medicines string or ligature should be bound firmly above the puncture, then scarify deeply with a knife, suck out the poison and spit out the saliva . . .'

And these cures can work as he explains: 'I was present upon one occasion when an Indian child was struck on the fore-finger by a large rattle-snake. His mother, who was near at the time, seized him in her arms and, placing the wounded finger in her mouth, sucked the poison from the punctures for some minutes, repeated spitting out the saliva, after which she chewed and mashed some plantain leaves and applied them to the wound. Over this she sprinkled some finely powdered tobacco and wrapped the finger in a rag . . . The immediate application of the remedies probably saved his life.'

Captain Marcy was not alone on his travels, the intrepid Mrs Marcy going with him and staying as close as possible.

Mrs Ruth Ellen Patton Totten, daughter of the late General George S Patton, Jnr, had this to say about Mrs Marcy: 'In 1840 she was waiting it out in Fort Smith, Arkansas. She had just read Captain Marcy's epitaph in the Fort Smith paper, when he walked through the door. He had been on a mapping party and had become so badly lost that he and his group had to resort to eating their horses, sprinkling gunpowder on the flesh to take the place of salt and pepper, and finally ended up eating rattle-snakes . . .

'He did not remark on what her feelings were at that moment, but gave two vignettes of her dauntless, intrepid character.

'The first account involves several Indian chiefs who were paying him a ceremonial visit. To make small talk (which was difficult with Indians) he brought out some of his wife's embroidery. One of the chiefs was so charmed with her handiwork that he grabbed Mrs Marcy and sent his friend to get one of his squaws to give to Captain Marcy as fair exchange for his wife.

'Marcy related that his "dear wife was completely calm withal, finally demonstrating the impractability of the exchange by removing her false teeth, which the rigors of life on the plains had made a necessity for her some years previous". The chief, upon realizing that Mrs Marcy would not be able to chew his buckskin wearing apparel to the "flexibility and silken smoothness required, relinquished her with many gestures of regret and goodwill".

'Captain Marcy's second anecdote further attests to his wife's fortitude. Mrs Marcy kept the only barnyard turkeys on Fort Smith. She had brought the setting eggs with her from New Orleans. Marcy is very coy in relating how she brought them to camp, mentioning that "the corsage of my dear wife bulged, on arrival, in rather more than a modish way".

'One night, while her husband was off duty, Mrs Marcy heard a commotion in her fowlyard and ran out to find what she thought was a large dog running off with one of her turkeys. She brained the animal with an iron skillet and put the bird back in the pen.

'When Marcy returned that night, he remarked to his wife that he was amazed to find such a well-grown specimen of prairie wolf lying in the yard. He skinned it and made her a little hat and muff.'[1]

LIVING ON THE MARCH

No one has given a better idea of married life 'in the field' in Wellington's Army than Quartermaster Sergeant James Anton of the 42nd Royal Highlanders. He served in the Peninsular War and was accompanied by his wife Mary.

[1] Extract from an article *The Army Wife's Heritage* first published in *Armor* magazine

The Sergeants' Mess of the 14th/20th King's Hussars, New Year's Eve 1923, whilst their regiment was serving in Cologne in the British Army of the Rhine. The Commanding Officer, Lt Col E J Bridges, MC, and Mrs Bridges, are in the centre of the group

Married families of 1st Bn the Rifle
Brigade visit Landi Kotal,
Khyber Pass, NW Frontier, India,
in 1927

In his book *Retrospect of a Military Life*, published in 1841, he gives this sad
tale of one 'married quarter' occupied by another family: 'The sergeant of our
guard, being a married man, considered himself very fortunate in having secured
a small pig-sty near his post for his wife's accommodation and the poor woman
felt happy in the possession, small as it was; for its roof was a shelter from the
wintry blasts, and its contiguity to the guard left no room to fear danger, were she
permitted to keep possession, this was not to be the case.

'Our adjutant's clerk, who had never had occasion to approach the field in time
of danger, had taken up his quarters in one of the adjoining houses, after the action
ceased, but, being dispossessed by some superiors, and every other place preoc-
cupied by soldiers who would not allow his intrusion, he meanly invaded the
miserable shelter selected for the poor woman.

'In vain she remonstrated with him, in vain she requested him with tears to
allow her sole possession of a place so unfit for his accommodation, and which
she had laboured hard to clean out for her own; but to no purpose, she might
remain if she pleased, but he would not depart . . . she therefore bundled up her
few articles and hastening across the road, the only distance by which she had
been separated from her husband, threw herself into his arms and burst into
tears . . .'

Mary Anton spent her first night in the Peninsula in a tent with her husband and
seventeen other men, nineteen pairs of feet towards the centre pole, nineteen
heads against the skirting flap, their bodies piled high with knapsacks and equipment as there was nowhere else to put it –

'Often did my poor wife look up at the canvas that screened her face from the
night and wish for the approaching morn.'

It is little wonder that they resolved to build themselves a little hut the next day
as he explains: 'I now set about erecting a hut for myself and my wife resolving
if possible not to mix blankets with so many bed-fellows again. This I was the
more anxious to do because, at that time, the whole of the men were affected with
an eruption of their skin, similar to the itch and their clothing was in a very filthy
state owing to it being seldom shifted and always kept on during the night . . .

'With the assistance of a few willing hands I finished the hut in the course of a
day, so that it served for a temporary shelter and prevented myself and my wife
from depriving the men of their very limited accommodation in the tent.

'*Grandmother of the Regiment*' The following is an extract from a newspaper report (circa 1929) which appeared about the time this photograph was taken: 'the cries of soldiers wives and daughters at the top of Fort Lahore during the Indian Mutiny, when they looked out and saw through a cloud of dust the mutineers advancing, form the most vivid memory that flashes through the mind of Mrs R Sunmerell of Brixton, who claims to be the only woman now surviving who went through the Mutiny with the 14th Light Dragoons. Mrs Sunmerell, who is 95 years old, was born in India and still proudly calls herself "The Daughter of the Regiment". Once a year she attends the ball at Tidworth given by the 14th Hussars as her regiment is now called, and every one gives her a great reception. She sometimes attends regimental dances where she is hailed as "Grandmother of the Regiment". "My father was Sergeant Major Murray of the 14th Light Dragoons and I was born in India (in 1834), although we were ordered home when I was an infant. The regiment was ordered back to India when I was six years of age. My sister was born as we rounded the Cape of Good Hope. Five years after our arrival in India the

'When I stretched myself down at night in my new habitation my head rested against the one end while my feet touched the other, at which was the entrance; my wife's apron being hung up as a substitute for a door, a couple of pins on each side served for locks and hinges and feeble as this barrier was none of the men entered when that was suspended and we might have left it to its own keeping from morning till night without an article being abstracted; thieving indeed was unknown in the regiment.'

Unfortunately the 42nd received unexpected orders to move so the Antons had to leave their comfortable shelter which they did with great sadness as he explained: 'on leaving the camp that night, many of the married people set fire to their huts, but I left mine with too much regret to become its incendiary; and my poor Mary shed tears as she looked back upon it as a bower of happiness which she was leaving behind.'

ARMY WIVES

The following anecdotes are but a few examples of the wealth of fascinating, amusing and sometimes sad, stories of army wives, which abound in the regimental histories we have studied in the preparation of this book.

AN OFFICER'S WIFE ON THE MARCH A French officer who was at one time a prisoner of war of the British wrote in his diary this delightful account of an English officer's wife on the march in Spain: 'The captain rode first on a very fine horse, warding off the sun with a parasol; then came his wife, very prettily dressed, with a small straw hat, riding on a mule and carrying not only a parasol, but a little black-and-tan dog on her knee, while she led by a cord a goat to supply her with milk.

'Beside madame walked her Irish nurse, carrying in a green silk wrapper a baby, the hope of the family.

'A grenadier, the captain's servant, came behind and occasionally poked up the long-eared steed of his mistress with a staff.

'Last in the procession came a donkey, loaded with miscellaneous luggage, which included a tea-kettle and a cage of canaries; it was guarded by an English servant in livery, mounted on a sturdy cob and carrying a long posting whip with which he occasionally made the donkey mend its pace.'[1]

AN UNFAITHFUL WIFE 'I had finished my evening meal and was sitting drinking a tot of wine with a sergeant of ours named Battersby, who had a few days previously rejoined us from Belem, where he had been some time appointed hospital-sergeant. He brought with him a very pretty-looking English woman that passed for his wife, and who was present with us, and assisted much to keep up the spirit of our conversation.

'We had been seated for some time under the branches of a clump of cork trees, of which, indeed the wood was principally composed, when we were interrupted by some of the men calling for Sergeant Battersby, and in a second or so up marched a tall, fine looking grenadier of the 61st Regiment of Foot, then belonging to the 6th division, which lay encamped some two or three miles in our rear; as he approached, however, he did not notice us, but casting sundry determined

[1] *The British Soldier* by Col H de Watteville

regiment was ordered up country as far as Umballa. Once during the long march I was left in the jungle by natives for some hours while wild beasts roamed close by. We were eventually ordered to Lahore when the Mohammedans were rising. The women and children were confined to one large room in the fort. While we were there we looked out and saw through a cloud of dust the mutineers advancing. We women were ordered to hide ourselves but we did not and later on I can remember seeing Ranjeet Singh being brought in on an elephant as a prisoner. I married shortly afterwards and some of the hardest years I remember followed. Our men were ordered away from us to fight the mutineers somewhere else and we were left at Poonah without their protection. The natives stole everything from us, even our food if it was served in brass dishes. We always slept with a bundle at our side containing a change of clothing in case we had to hurry to the hospital for safety. The Mutiny was over at last. We met our husbands at Bombay and two years after we sailed for home. Our next move was to Newbridge, Ireland. Queen Victoria and Prince Albert came to inspect us there. That was I believe Prince Albert's last public visit. I went to India once, years after when my husband had died, but I found it had changed. There was no place for me there so I had to return home."'

glances about him, more in anguish than ferocity, he drew near the woman, and seated himself on a knapsack near her.

'The latter, from the moment he had first made his appearance, I had perceived, seemed wondrously confused, and changed colour several times.

' "Nelly", said he, fixing a firm and deliberate look on her, his voice at first scarcely articulate with emotion, "Nelly why do you treat me so? How can you stoop" and here he cast an almost contemptuous glance of recognition on Battersby, "how can you stoop to such a disgraceful, so dishonourable a protection". "I am with those" said she, rather snappishly, "who know better how to treat me than you". "That" rejoined the grenadier, "may be your opinion; but why leave the child; it is but three years old, and what can I do with it?"

'To this she made no answer. "Do not think," he again continued, "that I wish you to return to me, that is impossible. But I cannot help my feelings!" This was only replied to by reproaches which I didn't listen to, for as it was no business of mine I turned to converse with my companions. The grenadier, at last, made a move to take his departure, and his wife, for such she evidently was, had agreed to accompany him a little of the way, and they walked together and Battersby and myself followed in their rear.

'They had proceeded a few hundred yards, and were some distance in advance, when she turned to wish him goodnight. The poor fellow paused again, as if in deep thought, fixing her with the same cool, deliberate look that he had exhibited all the evening. "So you are determined Nelly" said he at length, "to continue this way of living?" "Yes" said she. "Well, then" he exclaimed, holding her firmly by the left hand, which she had extended for him to shake, while he drew his bayonet with his right, "take that", and he drove it right through her body.

'The blow was given with such force that it actually tripped him over her, and both fell, the bayonet still sticking in her side.

'The poor woman gave a conclusive scream and in a moment expired . . . he then pulled the bayonet from his dead wife and chased after Battersby but did not catch him before he was able to call out the rearguard.

'He was courtmartialled and sentenced to 3 months' solitary confinement, but after one month was returned to his regiment and killed in action. Battersby was also later killed at Quatre Bras.'[1]

[1] *Military Memoirs* by Edward Costello, edited by Antony Brett-Jones

The problem of Service wives Shopping in Ismailia was very difficult during the troubles in the Canal Zone (circa 1950-51). Here wives queue outside the NAAFI under an armed and watchful guard

AN ARTILLERY MAN'S NATIVE WIFE: CEYLON, 1805 'I fell sinking fast under the fatigue and climate, both of which were aggravated by the diet, which did not agree with me. My confirmed flux, for which I tried every remedy, both native and European, that I could obtain, brought on a weakness in my spine and thighs, so that walking was a burden to me, and I suffered great pain. In this dilemma the old soldiers of the 19th advised me to take a native wife, who would cook for me and purchase better food in the Pettah Bazaar than was used in the barrack-mess. . . . I first set about getting my hut put up, . . . I then began to look for a wife, or rather a nurse – love was out of the question. My affections were elsewhere all engrossed; but I must either take a wife or die.

'My choice fell upon a Cingalese; she was of a clear bronze colour, smooth-skinned, healthy and very cleanly in her person and manner of cooking, which was her chief recommendation. . . . She bore me a son, a fine little boy, who died young. Often have I sat and looked with delight upon his infant gambols. As is the custom here, he smoked cigars as soon as he could walk about. It was strange to see the infant puffing the smoke into the air, and forming circles with it, until weary, then running and placing his head upon his mother's bosom, to quench his thirst from her breast, before finishing his cigar.

'What alone caused me to submit to her humours was that I now began to get stronger and better in my bowels, for my food was cleanly cooked and properly done . . .'

Eventually this married bliss was upset when the regiment moved to a new station: '. . . We parted with some concern, expecting to meet again, but I never saw her more. . . . I continued to send money for a considerable time to her, until I heard from Colombo, by some of our men, that she had got another husband, when I broke off all correspondence with her.'[1]

A GIFT OF GARTERS 'At last, on January 11th, Corunna was reached, Moore having out distanced the enemy, who did not appear in any stength until three days later. This enabled a large body of stragglers to rejoin the army; and a terrible sight many of them presented, as they crawled in on hands and knees, unable to put their lacerated feet to the ground. The various journals of Regimental officers all agree in the descriptions of the countless horrors of the retreat, but they usually contain also some striking episode of which the writer was a witness.

'Captain Diggle, of the 52nd, putting his notes together in after years, thus appreciates the services of a soldier's wife: "Well do I remember," he says, "the kind act of a worthy woman, Sally Macan, the wife of a gallant soldier of my company, who observing me to be falling to the rear from illness and fatigue, whipped off her garters and secured the soles of my boots which were separating from the upper leathers, and set me on my feet again; even then, decorated as I was with the 'Garter', I should have fallen into the hands of the French had not Colonel Barclay sent his horse to the rear for me, being unable from weakness to fetch up my leeway.

A year or so after this, I had the opportunity of requiting the kindness of poor Sally Macan, by giving her a lift on my horse the morning after she had given birth to a child in the bivouac." '[2]

[1] *Rank and File* compiled by T H McGuffie

[2] *Regimental War Tales* by Lt Col A F Mockler-Ferryman

MONEY IS THE ROOT OF ALL EVIL 'Yet another tale of a 52nd woman – Mrs Malony, wife of the Regimental master-tailor – who made her fortune during the retreat, but lost it again, as well as her life, within a few hours.

'As the troops neared Corunna and the enemy's pursuit became more vigorous, the baggage animals broke down, and on reaching a steep mountain a few miles from Nogales, it was found necessary to abandon the military chest. In order that the money (£25,000 in dollars) should not fall into the hands of the enemy, the barrels containing it were rolled over the side of a precipice, where, after bounding from rock to rock, they split in pieces and the dollars were scattered far and wide in the wooded ravines.

'The troops themselves, though witnesses of what had taken place, did not attempt to quit the ranks to gather the money; with the followers, however, it was different, and a rush took place to fill their pockets. The sight of a fortune pouring down the mountain side and to be possessed for the gathering was more than they could withstand and men and women came into Corunna hardly able to walk from the weight of the dollars.

'Mrs Malony, quick of eye and of fingers, had feathered her nest right well, and had a prospect of a comfortable old age. But cruel fate cut short her joy, for on stepping from the boat to the ship to embark for home a few days later, she slipped and fell overboard, the weight of the money distributed about her person causing her to sink like a shotted corpse.'[1]

VICTORIAN HEROINE Fanny (Frances Isabella) Duberly, wife of Captain Henry Duberly Paymaster of the 8th Hussars, was a Victorian heroine par excellence. She was the youngest daughter of a wealthy and influential Wiltshire family. Her childhood was idyllic, with servants attending to her every whim, and ponies to ride. By the time she was eighteen Fanny was a daring, almost reckless rider, with a natural talent on the hunting field where she was greatly admired. In 1850 she married Henry Duberly and became an army wife. She was very popular with Henry's brother officers and after four happy years in various towns in England the 8th Hussars, plus Fanny and her horses, embarked for the Crimea on the *Shooting Star*.

The voyage was a nightmare. Shortly after leaving Devonport a storm broke with tremendous waves and shrieking winds. Both Henry and Fanny were extremely seasick, sailors were injured and horses died – including Fanny's grey.

[1] *Regimental War Tales* by Lt Col A F Mockler-Ferryman

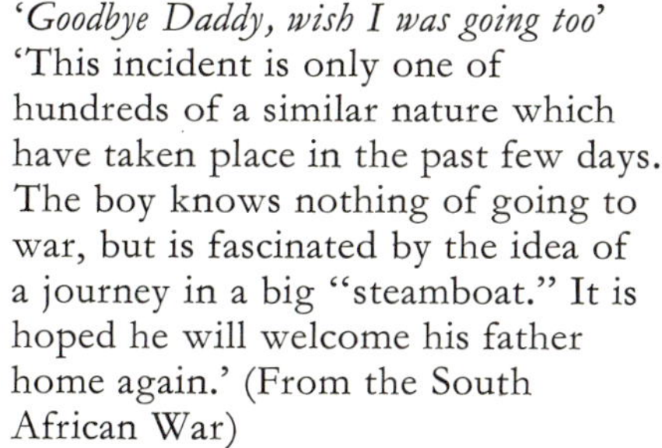

'Goodbye Daddy, wish I was going too'
'This incident is only one of hundreds of a similar nature which have taken place in the past few days. The boy knows nothing of going to war, but is fascinated by the idea of a journey in a big "steamboat." It is hoped he will welcome his father home again.' (From the South African War)

Defenders of the Empire A trooper of
the 1st Madras Lancers at Bellary
with his two small sons. (*Navy &
Army Illustrated*, 20 January 1892)

Attended by an enlisted man
(probably the officer's orderly) an
officer's family takes the air at Fort
Shaw, called 'The Queen of Montana
Forts' because of the shady trees and
well kept lawns

On 1 June the *Shooting Star* dropped anchor in Varna, a small town in Bulgaria. After a short stay in a temporary camp site, the regiment marched to the cavalry camp at Devna. This was Fanny's introduction to a march, in boiling sun and thick dust for eight hours, and when she reached camp she was exhausted. She wrote in her journal: 'Captain Tomkinson made me a bed of his cloak and sheepskin, and drawing my hat over my eyes, I lay down under a bush, close to Bob (her horse) and slept.'

The tented cavalry camp was in a wide green valley, surrounded by hills, with a river running through the middle of it. A few days later Lord Cardigan and his party rode into camp. In spite of being court martialled for cruelty and being dismissed from his regiment – 11th Hussars – he was to command the Light Brigade. The men were outraged, but there was nothing they could do about it. Fanny was very impressed by him, unlike the soldiers who distrusted him as a man and feared him as a commander.

Life was reasonably tranquil for a while, considering that they were waiting to meet the enemy. This tranquility came to an end when a hurricane shrieked its way across the camp, hurling clouds of thick dust in its wake. Every day for a fortnight the hurricane raged through the camp. Barely had they recovered from its effects when a new, even more frightening disaster struck the camp – cholera. Hospital tents were soon filled with men suffering not only from cholera but dysentry, typhoid, and sunstroke as well.

However, the 8th luckily had few casualties and soon were ordered to move to the Crimea. They landed at Calamita Bay – a prophetic name. Fanny realised that she and Henry would have to part for the first time, and she wrote: 'I parted from my dear husband . . . My heart begins to fail me now that I am left alone . . . I have never felt so adrift in my life – but shall get into Sebastopol somehow.'

Fanny lived on board the *Shooting Star* during the battle of the Alma – she listened to the thundering of the guns and then came news that the Allies had won the battle but she had no news of Henry. Later she heard that the cavalry had not been involved.

After many trials and tribulations, and thanks to her many friends and admirers, Fanny managed to get to Balaclava. She was now living on board the *Star of the South* which was moored in the harbour, and making daily visits, on horseback, to the cavalry camp to see Henry.

On 24 October Fanny decided to stay in her cabin for the day, as she was not feeling very well, when a servant appeared with a note from Henry 'The battle of Balaclava has begun, and promises to be a hot one. I send you the horse. Lose no time but come up as quickly as you can; do not wait for breakfast.'

Fanny lost no time at all and had a hair-raising ride to reach the camp. She wrote '. . . Our cavalry were all returning to take up position in rear of our lines when I arrived, looking on the crest to the nearest hill, I saw it covered with running Turks pursued by mounted Cossacks, who were all making straight for where I stood, superintending the striking of our tent and packing of our valuables. . . . Henry flung me on the old horse; and seizing a pair of laden saddle-bags, a great-coat and a few other loose packages, I made the best of my way over a ditch into a vineyard and awaited the event . . . For a moment I lost sight of our pony, Whisker, who was being loaded, but Henry joined me just in time to ride a little to the left, to get clear of the shots, which now began to fly towards us.

'Presently came the Russian cavalry charging over the hillside and across the valley, right against the little line of Highlanders. Charging and surging onwards, what could that little wall of men do against such numbers and such speed? There they stood, Sir Colin did not even form them into a square. They waited until the horsemen were within range, and then poured a volley which hid everything in smoke. The Scots Greys and Inniskillings then left the ranks of our cavalry and charged with all their weight upon them, cutting and hewing right and left . . . A few minutes – moments as it seemed to me – and all that occupied that lately

'Two Extremes' at the Royal Naval
& Military Tournament 1912. (The
wee laddie was a pupil at Queen
Victoria School for sons of Scottish
Servicemen, Dunblaine,
Perthshire)

crowded spot were men and horses, strewn upon the ground. One poor horse galloped up to where we stood: a round shot had taken him in the haunch, and a gaping wound it made. . . .

'Now came the disaster of the day – our fatal charge. So sick of heart am I that I can barely write of it even now. I only know that I saw Captain Nolan galloping; that presently the Light Brigade, leaving their position, advanced in face of the whole Russian force, and under a fire pouring from all sides, as though every bush was a musket, every hillside stone a gun. Faster and faster they rode. How we watched them! They are out of sight, but presently come a few horsemen, straggling, galloping back. What can those skirmishers be doing? See, they form up together again. Good God! it is the Light Brigade . . . I rode up trembling. My nerves began to shatter. Past the scene of the morning we rode slowly; around us were dead and dying horses, numberless. The horses, mostly dead, were all unsaddled . . . Evening was closing in. I was faint and weary, so we turned our horses, and rode slowly back to Balaclava . . . what a night I passed. I slept, but even my closed eyelids were filled with the ruddy glare of blood.'[1]

Fanny witnessed many more horrors during her long campaign in the Crimea and suffered with fortitude all the hardships involved. After a brief spell back in England, the 8th Hussars, and Fanny too, sailed in the new steamship *Great Britain*, for Bombay. The Indian Mutiny had broken out in the spring and the 8th were to join the Rajputana punitive column.

They marched to Booj where their numbers were swelled by some native infantry, then to Deesa where they were joined by other regiments – cavalry, infantry, artillery and native camp followers; then, at last the Rajputana column marched out from Deesa. It must have been an impressive sight – with the red, white and blue uniforms, flashing swords, jingling gun carriages, flying pennants and trotting horses.

Behind them came the camp followers – five times the length of the military section. There were ponies, servants, cooks, water carriers, wives and children on baggage wagons, bullock carts, camels, elephants, dogs, pedlars, shop-keepers, beggars and prostitutes. The noise was tremendous – camel and elephant drivers yelling at their animals, dogs barking, elephants trumpeting, wagons creaking and straining, chattering families and servants and the clatter of horses' hooves – all mixing together.

The heat was indescribable. Their marches took them across scorching, dusty plains, and the rocky precipices of the Cutterbhooj Pass. At Kotah, thanks to a typical misunderstanding, the cavalry was not involved in a battle with the rebels – which was an extremely bloody one – and in consequence the rebels escaped loaded with loot.

They were now travelling by night because it was slightly cooler, and trying to sleep by day, in stifling tents with temperatures reaching 109 degrees. Fanny's journal records: 'The sun blazes and blisters, corrupting everything exposed to its severe heat. I now feel the effects of our severe march. My strength is gone. I look with absolute dread upon the horses, knowing that I am compelled to ride them, however unfit I may be. My mind, overwrought and exhausted, falls back

---

[1] *Mrs Duberly's Campaigns* by E E P Tisdall

In their scarlet tunics, for the first time since WW2, the boys of Queen Victoria School, Dunblaine, march past the saluting base, July 1955. The school was founded in 1906 by public subscription throughout Scotland and among the Services and Scottish Regiments, as a national memorial to Queen Victoria and those who lost their lives in the Boer War

to places long ago left, and to friends many years dead.'[1] The temperature now reached 119 degrees during the day.

With dreadful food, men fainting from heat exhaustion and trying to sleep in a hot airless tent, it was incredible that anyone managed to go on. But go on they did, and in June Fanny wrote: 'Well, I bore up better than Henry till at last I began to break out – not in boils like him – but in a large abscess. It was agony to sit or touch it in any way, but Henry could not put his foot on the ground and was obliged to go in the gharry; so there was nothing for it but to stick to my saddle. I fell off one day, in a dead faint from sheer pain, and the next day, after suffering intense pain, our doctor came and cut me very severely until he was obliged to give me chloroform.'[2]

In fact she later wrote: 'Imagine the pain of riding on a wound nearly three inches deep and two and a half long – with a boil on the other side.' This gives an idea of the sheer guts of the intrepid Fanny. Ill health, bad food and appalling weather still did not make her wish for the comforts of home.

However, after eleven-and-a-half months, 1,800 miles in the saddle, through heat and monsoon, the straw that finally broke Fanny's spirit was an outbreak of cholera in Meerut, and she wrote: 'Everyone was alarmed, my courage, once so strong, has all gone in this enervating climate, and I grow sick and ill with apprehension . . .'[3]

They finally left India in 1864 and after several moves about England the 8th was sent to Dublin and this is where the Duberlys left them.

Ten years after retiring from the army, Henry died aged 69. In their 41 years of marriage they had had more excitement, danger and travel than most couples in our own era, let alone in the narrow confines of the Victorian period. Fanny died in 1903, aged 73.

[1], [2], [3] *Mrs Duberly's Campaigns* by E E P Tisdall

SERVICE CHILDREN AND THEIR EDUCATION

Soldiers' children, living 'behind the curtain' in the corner of a barrack room received little if any formal education. In the early 1800s there were some regimental schools run 'by the zeal, intelligence and liberality of the officers', one of the earliest being in Tangier. Here Richard Reynolds, Fellow of Sidney Sussex College, Cambridge, was employed as schoolmaster in the town – there were about 130 wives and nearly 200 children belonging to the Army in Tangier at the time.

In general the fathers were no better off than the children and in 1858 a report on literacy among soldiers of the British Army showed that 20 per cent could neither read nor write, another 20 per cent could not write and only a bare 5 per cent possessed a 'superior degree of intelligence'.

Within ten years the first two of these statistics had been halved, so what had brought about this educational triumph? The answer lay in the official establishment of a Corps of Army Schoolmasters and of the Queen's Army Schoolmistresses (QAS). The latter were officially established by a Royal Warrant in October 1840 which authorised 'the maintenance of a school mistress in all Regiments of Cavalry and Infantry' although they had been mentioned in Army Regulations as far back as 1805.

Early recruitment was normally from among Army wives, but from 1910 qualified applications from civilian colleges augmented the numbers, including a proportion of graduates. QAS did not wear uniform but were governed by Army Regulations, paid by the Paymaster General (about £30 per annum in 1869), were subject to military discipline and liable to be sent to serve anywhere in the world where there were army children to teach.

Sadly the QAS no longer exists, as recruiting ceased in 1947, when the Services decided to employ teachers seconded from local education authorities. However, they still run their own magazine and hold regular reunions.

The schoolmasters were of course military, and ranked immediately below the

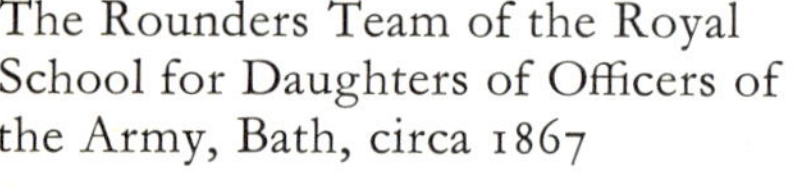

The Rounders Team of the Royal School for Daughters of Officers of the Army, Bath, circa 1867

Centenary celebrations at the Royal School, Bath, July 1965. The photograph shows the finale of the pageant, which was attended by Their Royal Highnesses The Duke and Duchess of Gloucester. The pageant was 'Daughters past and present' and set out to show many of the events and personalities of the School 1865-1965

Regimental Sergeant Major. Their pay was 3 shillings a day, with an increase of 6 pence every two years up to a maximum of 6 shillings and 6 pence after 14 years. After 21 years they were entitled to be retired on 3 shillings and one penny per day.

They wore the blue uniform and chevrons of the Corps of Army Schoolmasters and had to carry swords! In 1869 there were 272 properly trained and certified schoolmasters and 218 trained school mistresses serving with the Army to deal with the education of all the adults and children.

They were assisted by pupil teachers, 'monitoresses' and about 500 assistant teachers. The latter were chosen from the better educated soldiers who were appointed by commanding officers on the recommendation of the Schoolmaster. Normally there were five in each regiment and they received an extra three pence a day in payment for their services. Recruits were required to attend school; however, it was left to the discretion of commanding officers to decide whether to order men to attend or not, and only about 10 per cent went regularly.

A survey in 1867 showed that there were 19,025 soldiers' children under instruction at Army schools. For them from about the age of two or three, attendance was compulsory, but had to be paid for at the rate of two pence per month for a single child and threepence for two or more. Only children of soldiers serving abroad, who were left at home on their fathers' embarkation, were educated free. The girls and infants were normally taught by the regimental schoolmistresses of the QAS.

MILITARY BOARDING SCHOOLS FOR BOYS Occupying the main part of the Royal Military Asylum at Chelsea, was the Duke of York's School which was founded in 1801. It was chiefly designed for the education of the orphan sons of NCOs and private soldiers, born whilst their fathers were serving in the Army. The Asylum Commissioners were responsible for selecting boys to fill the vacancies. These numbered about 80 each year in the 1860s. Applications greatly exceeded vacancies. The establishment varied over the years from about 400 to 500 pupils and the average course lasted from 4½ to 5 years. From 1867 no boy under 7 or over 12 could be admitted.

The school (called The Duke of York's Royal Military School) is now at Dover where it still provides free secondary education, free board and clothing for the sons of soldiers.

Selection of boys for admission rests with Her Majesty's Commissioners.

Preference in general is given to orphans, to those whose fathers have been killed in action or have died while in the Service or after leaving the Service, and to motherless boys whose fathers are serving abroad.

In Phoenix Park, Dublin, there was a similar institution which had been in existence since 1769. Known from 1846 onwards as the Royal Hibernian Military School, its object was to maintain, educate and apprentice 'the orphans and children of soldiers in Ireland'.

'The standard of ex-pupils was very high and demand by COs for boys from the Hibernian was greater than could be met. A large number became regimental bandsmen. In 1870 of the 169 men and boys who had been at the school and who were in the Cavalry, 116 were band members and 6 were boys training as trumpeters.'[1] The School closed in 1922 when the British forces were withdrawn from Ireland.

Scotland also has its military boarding school, the Queen Victoria School at Dunblane. King Edward VII opened the school on 28 September 1908 for the sons of Scottish servicemen. Queen Victoria School is not an orphanage. Boys who have lost their fathers on service do get a high degree of priority for admission to the school, as is proper, but fortunately at the present time there are not many of those, and the proportion of fatherless boys at the school is probably about the same as at any boarding school. Several boys have been admitted recently, however, whose fathers have been killed in Northern Ireland.

SCHOOLS FOR GIRLS The daughters of British Servicemen have not been forgotten and there are two schools, the 'Royal School for Daughters of Officers of the Army' at Bath and the 'Royal Soldiers' Daughters' School' in Hampstead, which both cater for them. The former, instituted in 1864, is open to the daughters of officers who hold and have held permanent commission in the Army or the Royal Marines. Girls are admitted between the ages of 10-14 years and school fees are charged according to circumstances. The latter school was founded in 1855 for the maintenance, clothing and education of the daughters of soldiers, whether serving or ex-Service from the age of 5 up to the school leaving age. The Royal Soldiers' Daughters' School, when originally founded in 1855 after the Crimean War, was the Soldiers' Infants' Home, but at the first Annual General Meeting in May 1855, presided over by the Duke of Wellington, the Duke pointed out that provision was already made for soldiers' sons but not for their daughters. The Meeting agreed, and the school was re-named The Soldiers' Daughters' Home (the minutes of the meeting recorded that it was most numerously and fashionably attended and that the Iron Duke was given a standing ovation when he left).

Girls at the school were given training to fit them for domestic service or, for the most industrious, to be trained as regimental or parochial schoolmistresses. On leaving, each was presented with a small outfit which always included a bible or a prayer book. The school records show that the first girl to be registered was Emily Ann Ward, aged 4 years and 4 months on 4 July 1855. She was the daughter of a Corporal Ward of the 12th Light Dragoons, killed in the Crimea. A payment of £12 was made (there was and still is a sliding scale of fees at the school).

The school punishment book is a fascinating document recording such gems

[1] Extract from *A History of British Cavalry 1816-1919 Volume 2* by the Marquess of Anglesey

as: '*Louisa J Carlo – 10 Nov 08*. Frequent impertinence – solitude 11 and 12 Nov with deprivation of all sweets. Apologised Nov 14 and promised good behaviour', *but* pm 23 November she was disrespectful to the Lady Superintendent and lost her sweets for another 2 days. On 26 Nov Louisa returned twice to the dining hall when ordered not to do so and lost her sweets yet again. On 22 Feb 09 she was impertinent to the laundress and lost her leisure for a week. Between 22 and 28 Feb she was constantly in trouble for talking in the passages and was given 50 lines each time. On 1 March 09 she was impertinent to Matron in the dining hall and was given '24 hours bread and water.'

Clearly poor Louisa did not mend her ways because shortly afterwards she was compulsorily withdrawn from the School by order of the Committee. Before leaving she asked to be forgiven 'but seemed unable to grasp how wrong her conduct had been'.

Other punishments included up to a week of 'solitude'; ordered to wear a white hat on Sundays; slapped on the cheek; no visitors on Boxing Day; put on the 'Slouch Brigade'; made to wear a card 'Thief' for a week. Crimes for which these punishments were awarded included calling matron 'an old beast'; not going to bed at 7pm; impertinent behaviour in Dining Hall, writing clandestinely to a friend and stealing a pinafore belonging to another girl; calling Miss Collins a 'silly looking thing' (that lost one poor mite two days' leisure!).

Despite the punishment book the vast majority of the girls spent a contented and happy time at the School (and no doubt still do!). This is evidenced by the way in which they retained their ties by writing or visiting. As we have explained, originally the majority of girls went into domestic service from the school and, after periods of satisfactory service, were sent cash rewards from the school for their efforts – the amounts do not sound large by today's standards, being £2 and £3 for various periods of good and loyal service, but remembering how little housemaids were paid in those far off days it must have been a windfall not to be missed.

POSTSCRIPT ON A SOLDIER'S WIDOW

A soldier's widow in India in the late 19th century had to get married as quickly as possible, otherwise she would be left destitute in a foreign country. General Sir Neville Lyttleton tells of one especially speedy re-marriage: 'In India,' he wrote, 'burials follow death very rapidly and in one instance at all events, a widow's re-engagement was equally hasty. She attended her husband's funeral the day after he died, and on the same day the Colour Sergeant of the company proposed to her. She burst into tears and the NCO, thinking perhaps that he had been too hasty, said he would come again in 2 or 3 days. 'Oh, it isn't that,' said the bereaved one, 'but on the way back from the cemetery I accepted the Corporal of the firing party, by no means so good a match.'[1]

---

[1] *Eighty Years' Soldiering, Politics, Games* by General Sir Neville Lyttleton

Man's Best Friend

STRAYS AND PETS

It has always been the case that soldiers and their camps have collected stray animals. Perhaps the lack of female companionship and the drabness of their surroundings has led soldiers over the years to transfer a great deal of their affections to members of the animal kingdom. We are dealing here more with private pets, than with official regimental mascots which are, after all, on the regimental establishment and thus not true camp followers.

India was of course an ideal place for a wide variety of exotic private pets, as the pre-war manufacturer of a local brand of cigarettes realised and so included a leaflet entitled *Advice on Pets in Barracks* in each packet of cigarettes he sold, which read: ' "One monkey per regiment is sufficient" said a well known CO, some years ago, when the question of "pets" in barracks arose. "Undoubtedly," he continued "the animal said to be the nearest to man in its mannerisms, makes a fascinating pet, but off its chain it's the devil's own mischief itself."

'India offers an extensive choice of pets to those who love them, and in and around the various barracks (apart from the dignified "mascot" pets which sometimes accompany the band) may be seen strolling leisurely about the troops' bungalows, a young deer, fully grown and long horned "Black Bull", Nilghi (Blue Bull) or perhaps a stately Sarus, a grey long-legged 5ft bird of the stork family, with scarlet head and an 18in beak like a bayonet.

'Tiger cubs and young bears are sometimes seen but as they mature, their ferocious nature asserts itself and the order comes "Get rid of it". Smaller animals such as the Mongoose and Squirrel also make delightful pets if procured young. Parrots, of course, get their share of Government Quarters, and the daily morning screech "Wake up Gunner, make the tea, a cup for you and a cup for me", is as good as any reveille. Fowls and pigeons too, find a place on the pet's roll.

'But last though not least comes our canine pet the dog. There are always a dozen or more dogs of all sizes.'[1]

CUSTER'S DOGS

Dogs have always been firm favourites as soldiers' pets, but can, in large numbers, become a positive menace if not properly controlled. Inevitably in any barracks at home or abroad, the strays go on increasing and increasing until the time comes when they have to be rounded up and shot, a sad but necessary procedure.

As will be seen from the photographs, many officers have kept dogs, and one of the most avid collectors was General George A Custer. Poor Libbie Custer had to put up with a veritable canine army which ran all over the quarters, at the meat in

[1] *Plain Tales from the Raj* edited by Charles Allen

11th Hussar officer, plus bear,
India, circa 1895

the larder and often made it quite impossible to sleep. 'A crescent of dogs always hung about the kitchen door,' she wrote. To feed them she kept ready a huge kettle of mash, boiled with meat bones and grease, 'but they preferred the dainties from the family table.'[1]

Custer on one occasion took some venison to one of his neighbours and during the visit heard a tremendous scuffle from the kitchen. Nine of his dogs had followed him and were busily eating the venison.

One of his female admirers described him as: 'a human island entirely surrounded by his crowding, panting dogs . . . he would halt his dogs with a sweep of his hand, knocking them into a state of complete inertia.'[2] On the march however, the dogs never were really under control and Elizabeth often complained that it was impossible to eat in the field 'without being surrounded by a collection of canines of all ages . . . In order to save the buffalo meat from their tremendous leaps, it had to be strung far up in a tree, and let down by ropes when the meat for dinner was to be cut off.'[3] Even then they had to be beaten away with sticks.

Dogs, of course, were just as popular in the British Army and there are many stories about them, such as the bull terrier called Crib, who served with the Buffs throughout the Peninsular War. He was wounded by a bullet which stuck in his throat for the rest of his life – which was a long one, as he lived to the age of 18 and served in both America and Australia until he died in 1830. Before one of the battles in Spain, Crib fought a duel with a French poodle in 'No man's land', killing his opponent and delighting his regiment who hailed it as a good omen for the forthcoming battle.

[1], [2], [3] *The Gentle Tamers* by Dee Brown

An 11th Hussar officer with a lapful
of leopard, circa 1895

Ypres, Battle of Polygon Wood 27 September 1917. One RFA gunner takes his pup for a walk whilst others fill a shell hole

Another pet was an Irish terrier puppy who joined the 1st Royal Dragoons in 1899, on the quay at Durban, when the regiment was disembarking there to take part in the Boer War. 'Scout', as she was christened, stowed away in one of the railway carriages when the regiment moved up to Pietermaritzburg.

She took to the horses straight away and her habit of keeping just ahead of action at the Battle of Colenso and later, nearly cost her her life crossing the Tugela river. It was said that she also developed the habit of going into enemy trenches and worrying the Boers, but despite this thirst for action, she survived the war and came home to England with the Royals. Their next posting was to India but unfortunately the heat proved too much for Scout and she died in 1905 after having spent only a year there.

FEATHERED FRIENDS

Strangely enough, birds, the feathered variety that is, have also proved to be brave and resourceful pets – like Jacob, the pet goose of the Coldstream Guards, whose head is preserved in a glass case in the Guards Museum. Around its neck is an officer's gorgette (collar) with the inscription 'Jacob, 2nd Battalion Coldstream Guards. Died on duty'. A museum leaflet about him tells how 'this devoted specimen of the feathered tribe, who, having once volunteered to serve the State in the capacity of a sentry, never deserted his post until the great Commander, Death, relieved him from duty'.

In 1838 a rebellion broke out in Canada and two Battalions of the Guards were sent there to assist in quelling it, the 2nd Coldstreams being one of them. Both occupied the Citadel of Quebec, and in turn supplied guards in different parts of the town. Near one of these posts was a farmyard which was pestered by foxes. As the farm in question was suspected of being a rebel meeting place, sentries formed a chain around it. One day the sentry watching the farm entrance heard an unusual noise and looking toward the spot saw a goose fleeing in his direction,

Detail from a gravestone in
Bangalore

closely chased by a fox. His first instinct was to fire at the fox but, as this would have alarmed the guard and probably have got him into trouble for giving a false alarm, he watched the chase in silence until in despair the goose ran between his legs into the safety of the sentry-box evading the fox in the nick of time. Before the fox could escape the sentry speared it with his bayonet.

The goose rubbed its head against the sentry's leg and thereafter never left the post, walking up and down with each successive sentry until the Battalion left Canada to return to England, bringing Jacob with them, as regimental pet.

The most remarkable thing in connection with this story, is that the goose in turn actually saved his preserver's life. Whether it knew that the sentry was the same man or not, must be open to doubt.

Two months after that memorable evening the same sentry was on duty at that same post when there was a surprise attack. It was winter and the moon was obscured by clouds heralding a storm. Unobserved by the less than sharp sentry, men were stealthily approaching his post. Suddenly alerted by a rustling, flinging his musket to his shoulder, he shouted loudly 'Who goes there?' There was no reply.

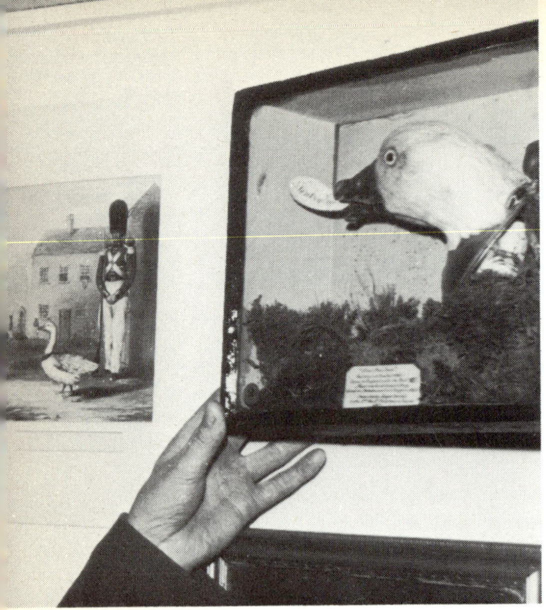

The faithful Jacob, now in the Guards' Museum, Birdcage Walk, London

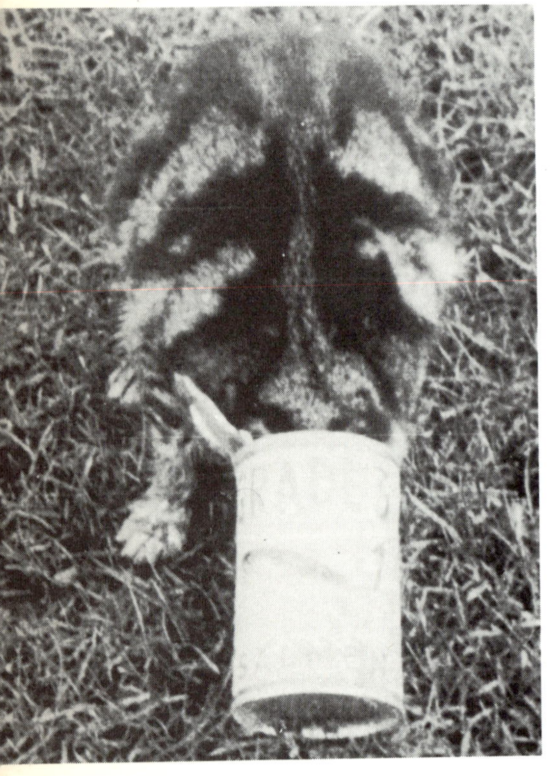

At last someone who likes 'Compo' Grade 3 salmon! Unfortunately she got her head stuck in the can and had to be helped out by her 'protector', 22nd Armoured Brigade Workshops, North West Europe 1944

He continued his marching up and down followed by the devoted goose and then, thinking it was a false alarm, he again stood at ease in front of his box. The thick snow deadened the enemy's footsteps as they crept towards the sentry box and prepared to knife him. Jacob flew into the air and directly at them; the sentry, startled into activity, bayonetted one and shot the other as he was running away. More rebels appeared but Jacob repeated his tactics and enabled the sentry to keep them at bay until the guard, alarmed by the shot, arrived and chased the remaining rebels off.

Jacob was the hero of the Garrison, and the officers bought him a gold collar, which he wore until he died. In London he resumed his sentry duties and seemed to bear a charmed life, but he was run over by a van and suffered a broken leg. Despite all efforts he died, like a true soldier, at his post of duty after a sentry go of no less than 12 years. He was buried with full military honours except his head, which, as we have already said, is in the regimental museum.

Another brave bird was one Fusilier Duck D, whose head and neck hang proudly in the museum of the Royal Regiment of Fusiliers, in the tower of London.

The caption reads: 'Enlisted at Kirkut, Iraq 1942. Took part in the amphibious landings at Salerno and Anzio. Died by drowning at Porta St Georgia, Italy 1944.'

He was the pet of the 8th Battalion, Royal Fusiliers, and was exceptionally astute at giving warning, by day or night, of the approach of unidentified persons.

A GOLDFISH WENT TO WAR

Perhaps the strangest of pets to be carried into the fighting line in WW2, was an American born goldfish. It was brought over to England by a GI inside a whisky bottle, and subsequently travelled throughout the North West European campaign in a steel helmet. It is a good job it never met up with the Grade 3 salmon fancier which we have also featured in this chapter!

KING OF THE BEASTS

Although he was strictly a unit mascot, we would like to round off this short chapter with a word about a very special pet kept by the 19th British Division during WW1. He was a young lion called 'Poilu' and was brought to the division by the Divisional Commander, General Sir Tom Bridges.

He was a great favourite with the soldiers, but scared the local inhabitants stiff whenever they saw him coming, because he followed the general around like a dog. General Bridges recounts one incident in his book *Alarms and Excursions* – when Mr Asquith came to visit the division and met Poilu on his way up to the HQ dugouts at the top of Scherpenberg Hill.

'I may be wrong,' he said, 'but did I see a lion on the path?' – such coolness and aplomb when meeting unexpectedly the king of the beasts! This incident was frowned upon by the authorities and when General Bridges was wounded soon afterwards, he returned to England. Poilu came back with him but had to be put into a private zoo – near Maidstone, where he lived until 1935. He was 19 when he died.

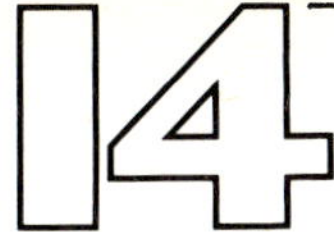

Camp Followers or real soldiers?

In this chapter we are going to deal with two groups of people who are difficult to classify rigidly as camp followers, because they normally wore a form of uniform. However, they are not really and truly soldiers in the accepted sense of the word. The first group are those females who have impersonated men in order to serve in the army for one reason or another. Now that there are official women's military services this stratagem is no longer necessary, and in any case it would be difficult to see anyone being able to get through the modern medical examination without the Medical Officer realising that something was wrong! The second group comprises those specially recruited bodies of individuals who have assisted armies with a special task of some kind, but again are not really soldiers – and this group can vary as widely as between hostile slave labourers and friendly foreign collaborators.

GALLANT SHE-SOLDIERS

Epitaph in a Brighton churchyard

PHOEBE HESSEL

who was born at Stepney, in the Year 1713. She served for many years as a Private Soldier in the Fifth Regiment of Foot in different parts of Europe, and in the year 1745 fought under the command of the Duke of Cumberland, at the Battle of Fontenoy, where she received a Bayonet Wound in her Arm. Her long life, which commenced in the Reign of Queen ANNE, extended to that of King GEORGE IV. By whose munificence she received comfort and support in her latter days. She died at Brighton, where she had long resided, December 12th 1821, aged 108.

First then, the women warriors, who dressed as men and fought alongside them until their sex was discovered. Some have been the subject of poems and songs like, 'Pretty Polly Oliver', 'The Maiden Warrior', 'The Famous Woman Drummer' or the 'Soldier's Delight in the She Volunteer'. Here is one such ballad, called 'The Gallant She-Soldier'; it was written in 1655 and is about a woman who served for some years in the same regiment as her husband under the name of 'Mr Clarke'. Her secret was discovered and her army service terminated, by the birth of a bouncing baby and the ballad concludes with the words: 'All that are

desirous to see the young soldier and his mother let them repair to the sign of the
Blacksmith's Arms in East Smithfield, neere unto Tower Hill in London and
inquire for Mr Clarke, for that was the woman's name.'

'The Gallant She-Soldier

'With musket on her shoulder, her part she acted then,
And every one supposed that she had been a man,
Her bandeleers about her neck, and sword hang'd by her side,
In many brave adventures her valour had been tried.

For Exercising of her armes, good skill indeed had she,
And known to be as active as any one could be,
For firing of a musket, or beating of a drum,
She might compare assuredly with any one that come.

For other manly practices she gain'd the love of all,
For leaping and for running or wrestling for a fall,
For cudgels or for cuffing, if that occasion were
There's hardly one of ten men that might with her compare.

Yet civill in her carriage and modest still was she,
But with her fellow souldiers the oft would merry be;
She would drink and take tobacco and spend her money too,
What as occasion served, that she had nothing else to do.'[1]

[1] *Cromwell's Army* by C H Firth

The women of Sythia attacking a
tower with picks, axes and stones to
avenge the slaughter of their
menfolk. The 'spectacle like' eyes
are a hallmark of the 'Acre' style of
Crusader art. (Taken from L'Histoire
Universelle)

During the 18th century nearly every European army had one or more female soldiers. They sometimes held commissions, but more frequently served as non-commissioned officers or privates. The women who enlisted were generally wives or sweethearts of soldiers whose regiments had been ordered abroad, and the women preferred to put up with the dangers and hardships of a foreign campaign rather than be separated from their lovers. As no personal examination of recruits took place in those days, either in Great Britain or elsewhere, the authorities had no way of finding out their sex until they were wounded.

Mary Ann Talbot was born in 1778 at Worthen, Shropshire, the illegitimate daughter of the Earl of Shewsbury and the Honourable Miss Dyer, (the youngest of his 16 illegitimate children to be exact!). She became a drummer in the 82nd Regiment of Foot, enlisting in 1792 in St Domingo under the name of John

The Gallant 'She-Soldier' The Scots Greys (now Royal Scots Dragoon Guards) number on their old muster rolls the name of Trooper Christopher Welsh. In fact she was Christina Davies, often known as Mother Ross, a famous sutleress, whose exciting life story we have already covered earlier in the book. (Published by kind permission of the Scottish United Services Museum)

Taylor and was trained by Drum Major Richardson. In July 1793, she served at the siege of Valenciennes where she was wounded, getting a rib broken by a musket ball and having her back slashed by a sword-cut from an Austrian cavalryman – an ally who got rather over-excited.

In this battle, her 'captor-lover', Captain Essex Bowen, of the 82nd, was killed in action, so she deserted. It had been Bowen who, having seduced her whilst supposedly her guardian, forced her to disguise herself and serve with him in his regiment. She then went on board a French privateer under a Captain Le Sage, wrongly thinking that the ship was bound for England. She later refused to fight against her own people when they met the flagship *Queen Charlotte* commanded by Admiral Lord Howe. The French ship was captured, but not until Mary Ann had been flogged by the French for refusing to fight. She managed to confide in Howe, telling him that she was a woman and was subsequently discharged.

However, she was unable to settle at home and joined the Royal Navy as a powder monkey on the *Brunswick*. She took part in the battle of the Glorious First of June and during the battle was shot in the thigh and had her ankle smashed. On her return home she received a pension, and a public subscription was taken for her sponsored by the Duke of York. She died in Shropshire at the age of 30 in 1808 having packed more into her short life than most.

This thirst for military adventure was not confined to Englishwomen and there are many accounts of similar she-soldiers in the French Army about the same period.

In a book called *Tales of the Wars*, published in 1838, there is a story about Marshal Massena who, at the battle of Buezenghen, saw a young soldier of the light artillery, whose horse had been wounded by a lance, defending himself desperately against his attackers. 'I immediately despatched an officer, with some men to his assistance,' he recalled, 'but they arrived too late.

'Although this action had taken place on the borders of a wood in front of a bridge, this artilleryman had alone withstood the attack of a small troop of Cossacks and Bavarians, whom the officer and men I had despatched put to flight. His body was covered with wounds, inflicted by shots, lances and swords. There were at least thirty. And do you know what this man was? A woman, yes, a woman, and a handsome woman too, although she was so covered in blood, that it was difficult to judge her beauty. She had followed her lover into the army. The latter was a Captain of Artillery; she never left him; and when he was killed, defended like a lioness the remains of him she had loved. She was a native of Paris, her name was Louise Belletz, and she was the daughter of a fringe-maker, in the Rue de Petit Lion.'

Another example of a brave woman warrior, was a Dutch amazon, who masqueraded under the name of Robert Cornelius, and at the siege of Namur by William III, showed more than ordinary bravery. When the surgeons came to dress her wounds – and she had received several, they were amazed to find that 'Robert Cornelius' was a woman. Because of her bravery on this and other occasions, the event soon came to the ears of the King, who asked to see her. She then told him that she had been born of Dutch parents, who would have lost a small annuity if they had not had a male child, so had decided to christen her as a boy and brought her up as such.

Boer Amazon Mrs Otto Kranz, wife of a hunter, accompanied her husband to Natal and fought at his side at Elandslaagte also in the battles on the Tugela River and in the Free State. She was not by any means the only Boer woman who carried a rifle in the war and used it

Following in the tradition of brave 'She-soldiers' are these Israeli Girl Soldiers. However, like the Women's Services of other modern countries they are not truly 'Camp Followers'. The Israeli Women's Corps is known as the 'Chen' – a Hebrew word meaning charm

She was an adventurous lass and first enlisted as a drummer boy, was soon after made a sergeant and later an ensign. She had been in many actions without her sex being discovered until this occasion. After the Peace of Ryswick, she was given a pension in England and married one of her former comrades, who also presumably knew her secret!

Although no woman has ever been admitted to the Royal Hospital, Chelsea, as an In-Pensioner, two have been placed on the Royal Hospital pension list. One was 'Mother Ross' whom we have met in the chapter on sutlers, the other was a Hannah Snell who was admitted to the pension list in 1750 at 5 pence a day, but in 1785 was allowed one shilling because of her bad health. 'Hannah in briggs behaved so well, that none her gentler sex could tell', so wrote a now forgotten poet of the 18th century in the *Gentlemen's Magazine*.

Hannah was born in 1723, served both as a soldier in Guize's Regiment (later known as the Royal Warwickshire Regiment) and as a marine in Frazers Marines. Whilst serving as a marine aboard the sloop *Swallow*, a unit of Boscawen's squadron, she took part in the siege of Pondicherry and was wounded in twelve places by shell splinters. One of these wounds was in her groin, so her sex was discovered when she was taken to hospital.

She was discharged, became a performer at the Wells-close Theatre in London, dressing as a marine and singing suitably nautical songs. For a while she was a great success, but later retired from the stage and opened a public house in Wapping called 'The Female Warrior'. She applied for and was awarded a military pension and, as we have mentioned, wore the Chelsea hospital uniform. Unfortunately she became insane and was confined in the Bethlehem Hospital, where she died in 1792. She was buried in the graveyard at the Royal Hospital, Chelsea, in an unmarked grave.

When Lord Lake was in India, fighting the Mahrattas, there was a Sergeant of the Artillery who served in nearly all of his major battles. This sergeant had a Hindoo slave, of the lowest class; but through the earnest labours of a Baptist missionary, she was converted to Christianity, and the sergeant made her his wife. She accompanied him on all his campaigns, even following him into battle. When he was tired, she would lend a hand at the guns. In his last action the sergeant was struck by a bullet which passed through his shako and struck his forehead

just above the temple forcing the brass hoop from the shako into his skull. He fell, to all appearances, dead; but his wife, who was determined not to leave his body to the enemy, picked it up, and carried it from the field, amid a rain of bullets.

Perhaps the most successful of all male impersonators was known as Dr James Barry, who pretended to be a man all her life, served for more than 45 years in the army and rose to the rank of major-general. It was not until she died at the age of 71, that it was discovered she was actually a woman! She was gazetted Assistant Surgeon to the Forces in 1815, having received a Diploma as a Doctor of Medicine from Edinburgh University in 1812. Only 5ft in height, she wore 3ins heels and padded jackets to try to give more bulk to her figure. Her first posting was to Capetown, where the natives called her the 'Kapock Doctor', because of her padded shoulders. She was a skilful surgeon and later became a colonial medical inspector, riding on a pony in her plumed cocked hat, immaculate uniform and long sword.

In November 1827 she was promoted to the rank of staff Surgeon to the Forces and served in Mauritius, Jamaica and St Helena, where she became the principal medical officer. After further service in Trinidad and Malta she was promoted Deputy Inspector of Hospitals at Corfu. There she treated 500 wounded from the Crimea with great success and visited the war whilst on leave, staying with her friend Lord Raglan. Whilst she was there she is reputed to have met and snubbed Florence Nightingale.

In 1858, after spending a year in Canada, she was appointed Inspector-General of Army Hospitals, but a year later had to retire from ill-health. She died on 25 July 1865, the death certificate stating that she was a male. However, when the woman who laid out the body reported it was in fact that of a female, the doctor put in writing that the body was of 'a perfect female, who had a child when very

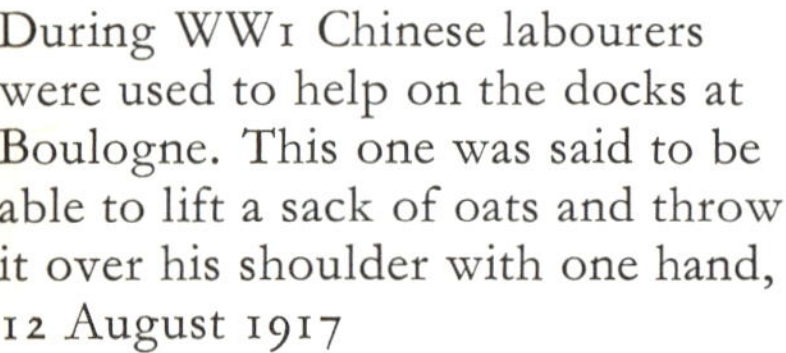

During WW1 Chinese labourers were used to help on the docks at Boulogne. This one was said to be able to lift a sack of oats and throw it over his shoulder with one hand, 12 August 1917

French workgirls in the British Army Boot Repair Shop, Calais, 24 June 1918, putting their heart and 'sole' into their work!

young'. Despite this revelation Dr Barry was still buried as a man in the Kensal Green Cemetery.

AMERICAN SHE-SOLDIERS If we are to judge from the Transatlantic newspapers of the period, the Civil War in America was more productive of female warriors than almost any conflict since the days of the Amazons. The ranks of both the Federals and Confederates were full of women; for example, in the summer of 1864 it was said that over 150 women were known to be serving with the Army of the Potomac. Here is a typical story which appeared in the *Brooklyn Times* in October 1863, just after the battle of Chattanooga: 'About a twelvemonth since, when disaster everywhere overtook the Union arms, and our gallant sons were falling fast under the marvellous sword of rebellion, a young lady, scarce nineteen, from an academy in a sister State, conceived the idea that she was destined by Providence to lead our armies to victory, and our nation through successful war. It was at first thought by her parents – a highly respectable family in Willoughby-street – that her mind was weakened simply by reading continual accounts of reverses to our arms, and they treated her as a sick child. This only had the effect of making her more demonstrative, and her enthusiastic declaration and apparent sincerity gave the family great anxiety. Dr B was consulted, the minister was spoken to, friends advised, family meetings held, interviews with the young lady and her former companions in the academy were frequent, but nothing could shake the feeling which possessed her. It was finally resolved to take her to Michigan. An old maiden aunt accompanied the fair enthusiast, and for weeks Anne Arbour became their home.

'But travel had no effect upon the girl. The stern command of her aunt alone prevented her from making her way to Washington to solicit an interview with the President for the purpose of getting command of the United States Army. Finally it was found necessary to restrain her from seeing any one but her own family, and her private parlour became her prison.

'To a high-spirited girl that would be unendurable at any time, but to a young lady filled with such hallucinations it was worse than death. She resolved to elude

her friends and succeeded – leaving them clandestinely – and although the most distinguished detectives of the east and west were employed to find her whereabouts, it was unavailing. None could conjecture her hiding-place. This was last April. She was mourned as lost, the habiliments of mourning were assumed by her grief-stricken parents, and a suicide's grave assumed to be hers.

'But it was not so. The infatuated girl, finding no sympathy among her friends, resolved to enter the army, disguised as a drummer boy, dreaming, poor girl, that her destiny would be worked out by such a mode. She joined the drum-corps of a Michigan regiment at Detroit, her sex known only to herself, and succeeded in getting with her regiment to the Army of the Cumberland. How the poor girl survived the hardships of the Kentucky campaign, when strong men fell in numbers, must for ever remain a mystery.

'The regiment to which she was attached had a place in the division of the gallant Van Cleve, and, during the bloody battle of last Sunday, the fair girl fell, pierced in the left side with a Minie ball, and when borne to the surgeon's tent, her sex was discovered. She was told by the surgeon that her wound was mortal, and advised to give her name, that her family might be informed of her fate. This she finally, though reluctantly, consented to do, and the colonel of the regiment, suffering himself from a painful wound, became interested in her behalf, and prevailed upon her for him to send a despatch to her father. Here, then, is a short incident of the war, which might read like romance, but to the unhappy family which are now bowed down with grief, romance loses its attraction, and the actual sad, eventful history of poor Emily . . . will be a family record for generations to come.'[1]

A REAL SOLDIER

'In front of us and beyond the trenches, there were two outposts . . . three silent watchers in each, crouching in their hole in 'no-man's land', straining their eyes

[1] *Female Warriors* by Ellen C Clayton

202

without relaxation into the darkness; ready, at the first sign of movement from the enemy, to twitch the cord attached to a bell improvised from a shell-case hanging inside the trench. These outposts were relieved every two hours. It brought an eerie sort of feeling when once one had stepped out of the trench into 'No-man's land' . . .'[1] Those words were written by a soldier in the Great War, but what makes them unique is that the soldier in question was a woman. However, unlike the 'gallant she-soldiers' we have so far discussed in this chapter, whilst she wore a man's uniform, her companions all knew that she was a woman. She was of course Flora Sandes, an Englishwoman who served throughout the hostilities, with the Serbian Army.

She had gone to Serbia in August 1914, just a week after the declaration of war, as a member of Madame Mabel Grouitch's Red Cross ambulance unit. After a spell of nursing under very difficult conditions, whilst the Serbian Army was being slowly driven back by overwhelming numbers – the Germans and Austrians were pressing them from the north, the Bulgarians from the east, the south was blocked by the Greeks, leaving only one avenue of withdrawal through the mountains of

[1] *The Autobiography of a Woman Soldier* by Flora Sandes

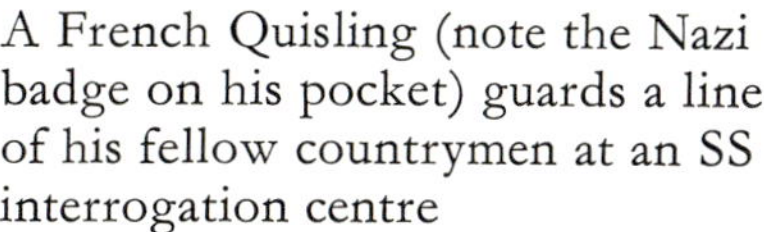

A French Quisling (note the Nazi badge on his pocket) guards a line of his fellow countrymen at an SS interrogation centre

Albania – she eventually took off her Red Cross armband and said that she would join the 2nd Infantry Regiment and fight as a private soldier. As she later recalled in her autobiography: 'When the "commandant" of the regiment, Colonel Militch, laughingly took the little brass figure "2" off his own epaulettes, and fastened them on the shoulder straps of his "new recruit" as he called me, it seemed a *fait accompli*, and official sanction came when we reached Bitol before going into Albania. . . . for me it sounded too good to be true, having fully expected to be ignominiously packed back to Salonique as a female encumbrance . . .'

She saw a great deal of action: 'I did not shoot much last night.' she wrote in a letter home in 1916, 'as we are to advance this afternoon and I am keeping my ammunition, as I can't get any more till I meet one of our mitrailleuses, my carbine using their ammunition and not the same as the rifles. It's shorter and lighter to carry than a rifle, and shoots just as well and very straight and easy to get plenty of ammunition for.'[1]

She was promoted to corporal, then to sergeant, when she was wounded and taken to the First Aid Dressing Station . . . 'by the time we reached it, blood was dripping through the stretcher. I was about at the end of my tether, but they gave me hot drinks, warmed me up and then laid me on the table to probe round and find some of the numerous pieces of bomb . . .'[2]

[1, 2] *The Autobiography of a Woman Soldier* by Flora Sandes

She was then taken by various hair-raising journeys to a base hospital, where she had a surprise visitor. 'When I had been about a week in hospital, King (then Prince Regent) Alexander sent his own aide-de-camp and the aide made quite a little ceremony of it. In the presence of the colonel, doctor, matrons, and many others as could be collected round the bed at short notice, he made a speech, and, to my surprise and delight, pinned on my pyjama-coat the Kara George Star for non-commissioned officers and men – the most coveted decoration in the army, carrying with it promotion to sergeant-major.'[1]

Returning to England for a short spell of leave in late 1917, she met Queen Alexandra – being presented to her in full uniform, appeared at the Alhambra theatre in a gala fund raising performance and even went over to France to lecture to the British troops about the war in Serbia.

She then went back to her regiment, took part in the final advance in August 1918 and was promoted to lieutenant. She remained on active service until 1922, when she married a Russian officer, but continued to live in Serbia.

In 1926 she was promoted captain on the reserve and was in fact called up in 1939 at the age of 63! She remained in Belgrade throughout the war, giving English lessons to maintain herself and her sick husband.

Eventually, after the war, she was flown back to England by the RAF and ended her days in a village near her birthplace in Suffolk. Flora Sandes was certainly not a camp follower. She does, however, serve to bridge the gap between the 'Gallant she-soldier' of the past and the officially recognised womens' services of today.

THOSE WHO SERVE A FOREIGN FLAG

As the photographs which accompany this chapter show, there are many odd organisations which have worked for the armies of other nations, such as the gang of Chinese coolies who were employed on the docks in France in WW1, the slave labourers who were forced to help build the German defences along the Channel coast in WW2; the French collaborators who assisted the occupying Nazi forces against their own countrymen; and even a group of charming young French ladies who mended British soldiers' boots in the Great War! We have tried to make this selection as broad as possible in order to give an idea of the very large numbers of people who could arguably be included as camp followers.

In addition there are groups of exiles who serve, rather like the French Foreign Legion, but not strictly in a fully combatant capacity. Let us look at two such organisations, both of whom work for the British Army.

For over 30 years the Mixed Services Organisation (MSO) has loyally served the British crown, although it is composed entirely of foreigners from all over Europe and the Middle East. It has its origins in a unit, formed in 1946, of ex-Yugoslav soldiers, who were given the task of guarding important and vulnerable installations within the British Zone of Germany. By 1949, the force had grown to 30,000 and included Poles, Ukranians, Latvians, Estonians and Lithuanians. In 1965 large numbers of new refugees who had fled from the communist menace in their homelands, joined the organisation, until there were no fewer than 26

[1] *The Autobiography of a Woman Soldier* by Flora Sandes

countries represented in the MSO. Today their numbers have dwindled to just over 3,000. They serve mainly in defence platoons for brigade and division headquarters, in motor transport, tank transporter and ambulance units and as dog handlers. Two have been awarded the OBE, fourteen the MBE, and four have won the BEM. When they celebrated their thirtieth birthday in 1976 nearly 70 per cent of those serving had been awarded certificates for completing 25 years' service. Anyone who has served in BAOR will remember their distinctive blue battledress, their cheerful efficiency and will echo the hope that this small band of delightful characters will serve on for many years to come.

An even stranger, yet equally charming and efficient 'private army' are a small group of Ukranians, who currently help the Royal Engineers to clear up the unexploded shells and bombs on old wartime training areas and ranges in the UK, before they are handed back to the public. They clear on average about 3,000 acres a year, working in a long staggered line with metal detectors and spades. When the high pitched whine in the earphones of the detector operator indicates a find, the digger steps forward and carefully uncovers it. If it looks as though it is a 'momento of the war', then trained British Army bomb disposal experts are summoned to defuse and blow up the find. As more and more training areas are listed for return to the public, so the men of this strange unit have to clear them. As well as clearing old battle training areas, they also deal with enemy bombs and landmines around the coast, so there is always plenty of work for them to do.

Free Enterprise

THE SMALL TIME TRADERS

'Beyond the men who act as servants, there are a whole tribe of others who make their living by doing a good trade in various articles of commerce', so wrote Captain Claude Bray in the *Navy and Army Illustrated* in 1898. He went on to explain the three most common types amongst these small time Indian traders. First there was the man with dozens of carefully corked bottles in a basket on his head, shuffling along and calling 'Pop good pop!' The bottles contained a species of homemade ginger beer, sometimes palatable, but sometimes quite the reverse. Then there was the egg seller and finally the hawker with milk and butter. They were but three examples of the traders who infested every barracks 'sometimes under due authority, often surreptitiously till they were cast out by the police'. And of course every time the regiment moved the whole motley crew would accompany it.

In *Plain Tales from the Raj*, F S Humphries, who served in India with the Royal Scots between the wars, recalls that there were vendors of all kinds, constantly available to provide sufficient extra food to prevent 'malnutrition' as he put it: 'the egg wallah frying eggs in a large pan, the dud-wallah with his little pats of butter and milk, and the ham-wallah, a fellow with a board with a roll of ham on it which he cut.' The most exotic was however, the sweet-wallah, normally a fat, cheerful looking man who would announce his arrival by chanting: 'Jimmy Kelly good for belly, take and try before you buy. Sweetie! Sweetie!'

All hawkers had to be licensed by the regimental quartermaster, and included such strange specialists as the 'Corn-cuttit wallah', the 'Names-to-put-on-kitbag wallah' or the 'Flying Dhobi'. The first of this fascinating trio would cut corns with a small, horn-shaped tube that he put on the corn to draw it out. If the battalion was warned for a move then the second wallah would arrive, ready to paint names and numbers on kitbags. The flying dhobi would collect the uniforms of soldiers detailed for guard in the morning and produce them beautifully laundered and starched ready to put on that evening before guard mounting. Small time traders have followed armies everywhere, as the photographs show, and there are even now Pakistani char wallahs serving with regiments in Northern Ireland.

THE OLDEST PROFESSION

'Home we bring our bold whoremonger
Romans, lock your wives away!
All the bags of gold you lent him
Went his Gallic tarts to pay.'

So sang the legionaries of the great Julius Caesar as they marched into Rome behind their leader!

Throughout history one of the most faithful of all camp followers has been the whore, both professional and amateur, giving her body in the ultimate act of service to the soldier. Unfortunately she was also wont to give him a good deal more than he bargained for in the shape of the dreaded 'pox'. She has been banned, reviled, tolerated and even, in some cases, given official blessing, but she has always been there and presumably will always remain somewhere in the shadows. It would be wrong therefore if we did not include the 'Oldest Profession' in our survey of camp followers and pretend they didn't exist. Indeed, many people immediately think of prostitutes when one mentions camp followers, but as we have tried to show, they are but one type.

In the ancient world the state rarely undertook to provide the soldiers with women despite the fact that they were not scandalised by the idea. One exception was Pericles, who is said to have done so in BC440-439 at the siege of Samos, when Athenian prostitutes did very good business. Normally the soldiers themselves took the initiative, 'pillage and rape' meaning exactly that!

208

An enterprising Belgian vendor brings his dogcart of goodies to British soldiers resting in a Belgian village, 13 October 1914

Crusader knights were just as randy, James Vitry, Bishop of the Crusader city of Acre wrote: 'And the city is full of brothels, and as the rent of the prostitutes is higher, not only laymen but even clergymen, nay even monks, rent their houses all over the city to public harlots.'

In Wellington's army in the Pennisular things were no better especially when fighting was not actually in progress. For example, when they withdrew to the Lines of Torres Vedra in October 1810, Lisbon became crowded with loose women, who eagerly tried to get both the officers and soldiers to part with their pay. '. . . One young officer in the Royal Dragoons entertained to breakfast six or seven brother officers and four or five very attractive girls, and paid for forty bottles of champagne out of his own pocket. What is more, drunken officers threw half of these out of the window between the laughing, gaping Portuguese street boys.

'As for wanton girls, the prettiest of whom came to Lisbon from Andalusia, the sums they took off the officers in the way of money is almost unbelievable, and the disorder reached such a pitch, especially between common prostitutes and the drunken English soldiery, that Lord Wellington saw himself obliged to take active steps to prevent it. Accordingly he had several shiploads of the most brazen girls sent away.'[1]

Mid-19th century India was just as bad, they tried police regulation and inspection of prostitutes between 1864 and 1883, but the 'do-gooders' stopped it on the grounds that it was no way to improve soldiers' morals. Sensible reformers like Florence Nightingale were of the same opinion, but she believed that the best way to improve the soldiers' morals and to cut down the alarmingly high incidence of venereal diseases – in the 1850s 25 per cent of all sickness cases in the army hospitals in India was accounted for by VD, chiefly syphilis – was to improve their living conditions. 'In civil life you don't expect that every workman who does not marry before he is 30 will become diseased,' she wrote in 1861, 'in military

---

[1] *Life in Wellington's Army* by Antony Brett-James

Two young shoeshine boys somewhere in occupied Germany after WWI

life you do. Why? Because a workman may have occupation and amusement and consort with honest women. . . . Every time you provide a hospital for sick wives and children, means of making marriage respectable, for making the soldier's life comfortable, you are doing something towards prevention.'[1]

In the 1890s the wards of Netley Hospital were full of young soldiers, badly disfigured by VD. Often they were so repulsive that their own relations refused to see them. In an average year about 8,000 VD infected soldiers were discharged and turned loose upon the civil population. 'In Britain the admissions into military hospitals for VD were seven times greater than in the Prussian Army, four and a half times greater than in the French, three times greater than in the Austrian and 90 per cent more than in the Italian Army . . . This was a sorry picture and again it was largely due to supervisory neglect. Soldiers of other nations were as apt to chase women indiscriminately as were British soldiers, but foreign armies enforced health checks on prostitutes.'[2]

When Kitchener was Commander in Chief he more than once addressed commanding officers on the best means of checking VD and he also wrote a memorandum addressed directly to British troops. The primary causes leading to impurity and disease were drink and idleness. A commanding officer, he told them, must encourage his soldiers to lead a good healthy life, mentally and physically. A CO must foster a love of games and keep his men busy, getting them to avoid excess in liquor and to practice self restraint . . . 'every man can, by self-control, restrain the indulgence of these imprudent and reckless impulses that so often lead men astray . . . What would your mothers, your sisters and your friends at home think

[1] *Florence Nightingale* by Cecil Woodham-Smith
[2] *Tommy Atkins* by John Laffin

of you?'[1] At the same time as he was saying this, there were flourishing brothels in Agra and Meerut and probably many other stations, self-supporting through regimental funds, inspected by medical officers and protected by military police from any visitors except British troops.

Little had really changed by the 1920s and 30s, when illicit military brothels existed and some regiments made discreet arrangements with their contractor for the sexual relief of their soldiers. The larger cities had their famous red light districts like 'The Cages' in Bombay and 'The Nadge" in Poona. They were strictly out of bounds: 'if any white soldier be seen in the area whistles were blown by the police, all traffic came to a standstill and the soldier would, of course, get caught. Periodical medical checks, known as "short arm inspections" ensured

[1] *Matter of Honour* by Philip Mason

An 'Onion Wallah' – One anna a bunch – note the vinegar bottle

Indian snake charmers

'Jimmy Kelly, Good for Belly!'. A sweet hawker shows off his wares

A lemonade wallah near Cairo, with his beautiful jugs and highly insanitary lemonade! Western Desert, 1940

that any man who availed himself of the "tree-rats" or "grass bidis" was properly dealt with. He was given a severe ticking off, had his pay stopped and was sent to No 13 Block, which was the dreaded treatment centre. Many turned as a last resort to the "five fingered widow." '[1]

In 'John Company's' time, British officers had kept Indian mistresses, but this was less and less frequent in the 20 years before the Mutiny and by the 1860s it meant social ostracism. A subaltern's life was far too public. To go shooting mountain sheep in Kashmir was a reasonable way to spend one's leave, but no colonel would agree to one of his subalterns spending a couple of months in a hill station like Mussoorie, supposedly frequented by Eurasian girls hoping to make a good match.

'In the 1930s I recall a cavalry officer describing his experiences while showing some Polish officers round India. "And what", they asked him when they had seen the regiment on parade and in stables and on the hockey-field, "do you do about sex?" "I hardly expect you to believe me," he replied, "but we don't do anything about it." They were too polite to say so, but he did not think they believed him. In fact, however, it was true. Yeats-Brown, who joined his regiment in 1905, writes of his early months: "My life was as sexless as any monk's at this time" . . .'[2]

The army tradition was that 'subalterns may not marry, captains may marry, majors should marry, colonel must marry', but few junior officers could afford to marry anyway as the army did not pay marriage allowance until they were 30. In addition, of course, there were but few white women in India for them to marry, even between the wars. John Masters in *Bugles and a Tiger* recounts various amorous tales, such as the Officers' Mess gardener in the 1920s who had three beautiful little daughters who played in and around the mess garden until they grew into three lovely young women. For some years thereafter the girls slept happily and indiscriminately with any subaltern who asked them to. 'For a time the senior officers did not get to hear of it, though there were bitter controversies between the ribald and the righteous groups among the subalterns as to whether what was going on was or was not cricket. In the end all was uncovered. One hot evening a major walked into someone's bedroom without knocking, and disturbed an operation only traditionally military. Then there were banishments and lashings of sensitivities with harsh words. In our time we used to look up the tree and hope a golden dryad would throw leaves at us but one never did.'

He also tells a splendid story about the daughter of a Eurasian lady who wanted her daughter to marry an officer in the Gurkhas and so gave her daughter instructions to offer only the minimum of polite resistance to any advance: 'One warm Wednesday in spring the mother gave a party at her house on the evening of a regimental guest night. One of the subalterns, full of sherry and passion, edged the daughter out of the house into the twilight evening. There didn't seem to be any privacy available. In despair, or perhaps reckoning that life is short and soldiers don't care, he proceeded to the extreme of heterosexual affection on the cement platform of a trophy gun right beside the road.

'Round the corner swung the pipe band on their way to play at the guest night.

[1] *Plain Tales from the Raj* edited by Charles Allen
[2] *A Matter of Honour* by Philip Mason

A Poonah knife grinder gets down to work

A 'Stim Boy' Abdullah was the younger brother of the Arab bearer of one of my troop leaders, stationed at Beihan on the Aden/Yemen border in 1963. He earned pennies by serving in the troop canteen, collecting empty bottles and bringing the soldiers drinks. He is clutching a bottle of Stim, a popular local soft drink bottled by the National Bottling Company Ltd of Aden

The pipe major peered incredulously into the gloom, and having satisfied himself that he really saw what he thought he saw, gave the command "Eyes right!" The rows of Gurkha faces went by without a shadow of a smile or a titter. Here and there one may have held a glint of respect, but no more. The officer returned the salute, and so in due course became a major-general.'

TWENTIETH CENTURY WARS In Europe during WW1 the number of brothels grew, particularly in the Communications Zones of the combatants and around the supply areas with their supporting garrisons. A speciality of this war was the motorised field service brothel, the vehicles for officers and men being carefully marked with a blue lamp for the former and a red one for the latter! The rush of customers was so great that many prostitutes withdrew from 'front line service' having made enough money after only a few weeks.

Ernst Jirgal wrote of one such brothel in the Belgian Communications Zone: 'Only the brutish side of love, no, less than that remained. The female acted as a fast and automatic deflector of lusts. Consequently all family feeling was destroyed, both its germ in the younger men and its flowering in their seniors. Neither well intentioned "Mother's Days" nor strict marriage laws were of any avail against this hidden plague-spot. For the strange thing is that evil once learned is never forgotten.'[1]

'BROTHEL PRICE LIST[1]

A *Beverages*

Champagne Henkell Dry, per bottle	18 marks
Bordeaux Chateau Lafitte	6 marks
Hungarian wine	8 marks
Beer, large bottle	1.50 marks
Coffee per cup	1 mark
Coffee per small jug containing 6 cups	6 marks
Coffee per large jug containing 12 cups	12 marks
Tea, per glass	.60 marks
Sodawater, small bottle	.30 marks

B *Intercourse*

All night	30 marks
Two to three hours evening or night	20 marks
One hour	10 marks
Any period between 9am and 6pm	10 marks

Lodz, March 1917   Social Discipline Police'

Brothels and prostitution were also used for espionage purposes. Two famous cases of female spies prepared to 'give their all' were Mata Hari (born Margarette Zelle of mixed Dutch and Indonesian blood) who was executed as a German spy in 1917, and the legendary 'Fraulein Doktor' (Annemarie Lesser, a Jewess) who after WW1 renounced all further service in this line. A less well known, but terrible case, was Gertrud von Oppeln, Countess of Nys, who was once a friend of the Kaiser. She sank to the status of a Communications Zone harlot in order to

---

[1] Taken from *The Oldest Profession* by Lujo Bassermann

[1] *The Oldest Profession* by Lujo Bassermann

spy for her country. By the time her husband found her and put an end to her life, she had become riddled with syphilis and a drug addict in the bargain. He is said to have put her corpse in to the bed of her chief in the German Secret Service in retaliation for the dreadful way she had been treated by the country she loved.

AMERICAN SOLDIERS The GI has long been the target for 'mankind's oldest business'; George Washington constantly had to warn his officers against vice and immorality. Prostitutes followed the columns in the early American army. George Washington ordered that, in war, only a limited number of these 'wives' would be permitted and a figure of 6 per 100 men in camp was finally fixed as the 'norm'. They were able to draw rations on condition that they behaved themselves and did the washing and cooking for the soldiers.

These women were also followers in the Revolutionary War, the British army having more than the American because of its better pay and rations. Washington had to issue orders forbidding them to ride on the wagons when the army was on the march and when marching through Philadelphia in August 1777, he ordered that: 'not a woman belonging to the Army is to be seen with the troops on their march through the city.' Consequently, the women were herded through the back streets and joined up with the army again on the outskirts.

In the American Army, before 1812 rumour had it that 'many officers kept stables of prostitutes available to their men and even that General Anthony Wayne took a mistress with him on campaigns. Near frontier posts there were many Indian women who could be purchased for a mere trifle.'[1]

The American frontier army found similar problems, when, in 1881, it was decided to prohibit the sale of liquor on the posts, large numbers of 'hog ranches' sprang up outside. Here, in addition to whisky and beer, the soldiers could sample

[1] *The American Fighting Man* by Victor Hicken

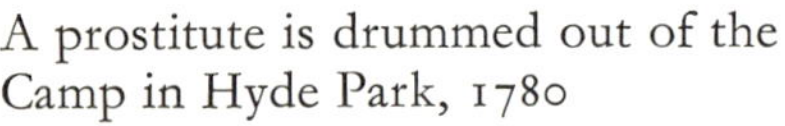

A prostitute is drummed out of the Camp in Hyde Park, 1780

'the ladies of joy', with the inevitable results that, just as in India, troops became infected with VD – about 8 per cent of the American Army in the 1880s were infected. Some commanders permitted prostitutes to live on the post, whilst some of the unmarried laundresses tried their hand at the amateur game. General Tasker Bliss once quoted a common army belief that post doctors had 'nothing to do but to confine laundresses and treat the clap'.

During the Civil War women became such a problem to the Army authorities that in Memphis for example, prostitutes were shipped out of the town en masse. Every large Army camp thereafter had a 'red-light' district close by and, in Mexico, during the campaign against Pancho Villa in 1916, the soldiers stood in line outside filthy native shacks: 'One Mexican woman admitted to having served as many as sixty American soldiers on one night, forty on the next, with fifty customers being the normal nightly business.'[1]

The doughboys of the Great War found the French mademoiselles both cheap and plentiful, disease and booze leading to a loss of over 6 million man-hours recovering from VD and drunkenness – which represents 18,000 men out of action daily. In WW2 the figure had dropped to 606, or 221,184 man-hours lost to VD. A more detailed study however, showed four cases of VD per thousand sexual contacts.

Although many said that the GIs had 'wrecked the moral code' of Europe by being too sexually motivated, there is plenty of evidence to show that professional 'houses' existed for use by the Wehrmacht; witness this diary entry written by a German in Milan: 'Milan's female beauties are considered more forthcoming

[1] *The American Fighting Man* by Victor Hicken

than the girls of Sicily, who refused to associate themselves with Kuderna's men. An amicable agreement has been reached regarding the brothels. Our divisional medical officer has declared the supervision by the Italian authorities to be excellent, and praises the business-like organisation of these houses of professional leisure which enables them to arrange a fortnightly alternative of girls.'[1]

During the Korean war and the American occupation of Japan there was a tremendous growth of prostitution in both countries. In Korea the army authorities encouraged the medical inspection and control of prostitutes, whilst in Japan the problem was out of all proportion – for example the town of Chitose had over 8,400 prostitutes. In 1946 a large munitions plant, closed because of the end of the war, was soon re-opened as a brothel for American and allied troops. 'Called "Willow Run" by the troops, it was partitioned into fifty cubicles and was operated

Inside the Freudenhaus, the girls get the customers 'in the mood' with a few drinks

twenty four hours each day. The 250 girls working there had all previously worked on the munitions assembly line. Now, in eight hour shifts, they were expected to handle fifteen GIs each during the daily working time.'[2]

It was the same old story in Vietnam, where prostitution, long encouraged under the French, underwent a boom in 1963. 'Such places as the Josephine, Sporting, Capitol and Tu Do are famous bordellos which cater for Americans in Saigon. In Danang there is an equally famous whorehouse which bears the probably appropriate name 'Forget me Not'. Prostitutes have sometimes followed the troops into the rural areas. In the cemetery of a Catholic church there was a sin tent called 'The Graveyard'; a somewhat analogous historical coincidence with one called 'The Holy Ground' during the American Revolution.'[3]

[1, 2, 3] All quotes from *The American Fighting Man* by Victor Hicken

Epilogue

HOME IS WHERE THE HEART IS

As we said at the beginning of this book, it has been deliberately designed as an anthology, being a collection of pictures and anecdotes which we have put together, in order to shed a little light on the people who were camp followers, rather than as an exhaustive encylopedia on the subject.

We hope that the reader will now more fully appreciate the wide variety of fascinating people who have followed armies over the centuries. On the one hand they have been a continual source of comfort, help and even inspiration: on the other a cause of pain and suffering too.

Some have taken an active part in the combat such as the intrepid Crusading wives and the Indian porters and water carriers. Others have deliberately made as much profit, at the expense of the ill-used soldier, for as little effort as possible; and yet others have stood on the sidelines in order to report and assess objectively and to try to see that the soldier was treated fairly.

Although the cynics will conclude that camp followers were a necessary evil which now have been dispensed with thus enabling the soldier to concentrate on his real job – that of fighting his country's battles – there will be those who will mourn the passing of these colourful characters.

Good and bad alike have added their small fragments to the patchwork that is the history of the world's armies.

We looked for a suitable quotation with which to end our anthology, and decided that the following passage, written by an American army wife, accurately sums up those difficult-to-express feelings that soldier and camp follower alike have about their chosen profession and the love hate relationship they wage with it. Rudyard Kipling achieved the right words for the soldier in his Barrack-Room Ballad 'Back to the Army again'. Martha Summerhayes does a similar service for the camp follower:

'It all seemed good to me. I was happy to see the soldiers again, the drivers and teamsters, and even the sleek government mules. The old blue uniforms made my heart glad. Every sound was familiar, even the rattling of the harness with its ivory rings and the harsh sound of the heavy brakes reinforced with old leather soles. . . . I was back again in the army. I had cast my lot with a soldier, and where he was, was home to me.'[1]

[1] *Recollections of My Army Life* by Martha Summerhayes, as quoted by Dee Brown in his book *The Gentle Tamers*

Bibliography

BOOKS

ALLEN, CHARLES, EDITOR: *Plain Tales of the Raj* (Andre Deutsch) 1975

ANGLESEY, MARQUESS OF, FSA: *The History of British Cavalry* (Leo Cooper) 1975

ANTON, JAMES: *Military life during the most eventful periods of the late wars*

ANTON, JAMES: *Retrospect on Military Life* (W H Lizars) 1841

AYER, FRED: *Before the Colours fade* (Cassell & Co Ltd)

BAMFIELD, VERONICA: *On the Strength* (Charles Knight & Co Ltd) 1974

BARBER, D H: *The Church Army in World War Two* (Church Army) 1948

BASSERMAN LUJO: *The Oldest Profession* (Arthur Barker Ltd) 1967, translated from the German by James Clough

BELL, SIR GEORGE: *Rough Notes by an Old Soldier* (G Bell & Sons Ltd) 1867

BIRLEY, ROBIN, MA, FSA: *Civilians on the Roman Frontier* (Frank Graham) 1973

BRETT-JAMES, ANTONY: *Life in Wellington's Army* (George Allen & Unwin Ltd) 1973

BRIDGES, GENERAL SIR TOM: *Alarms and Excursions*

BROWN, DEE: *The Gentle Tamers* (Barrie & Jenkins Ltd) 1973

BRYANT, ARTHUR: *Jackets of Green* (Collins) 1972

BURN A R: *Persia and the Greeks* (Edward Arnold Ltd) 1962

CARRINGTON, CHARLES, EDITOR: *The Complete Barrack-Room Ballads of Rudyard Kipling* (Methuen) 1973

COLLIER, RICHARD: *The Indian Mutiny* (Fontana) 1966

COMPTON, PIERS: *Colonel's Lady and Camp Follower* (Hale) 1970

CLAYTON, ELLEN C: *Female Warriors* (Tinsley Brothers) 1879

CLAYTON, P B, CH, MC: *Tales of Talbot House* (Toc H) 1919

COSTELLO EDWARD: *Military Memoirs* (Colburn & Co) 1852 and (Longmans Green & Co Ltd) 1967

CUSTER, ELIZABETH BACON: *Tenting on the Plains* (Charles L Webster & Co) 1893 and (University of Oklahoma Press) 1971

DEAN C G T, CAPT, MBE: *The Royal Hospital* (Hutchinson & Co Ltd) 1950

DICKINSON, LT COL R J: *Officers' Mess – Life and Customs in the Regiments* (Midas) 1973

DUNLOP J, MD: *Mooltan* 1849

EDWARDS, MAJOR J T: *Mascots of the Services* (Gale & Polden) 1953

EWING, ELIZABETH: *Women in Uniform* (B T Batsford Ltd) 1975

FARMBOROUGH, FLORENCE: *Nurse at the Russian Front* (Constable) 1974

FIRTH, SIR CHARLES H: *Cromwell's Army* (Methuen) 1962

FITZMAURICE, MRS: *Recollections of a Rifleman's Wife* (Hope & Co) 1851

FORTESCUE, JOHN, LLD, D LITT: *Canteens in the British Army* (Cambridge University Press) 1928

GIBBS, PETER: *Crimean Blunder* (Frederick Muller Ltd) 1960

GRANT, MICHAEL: *The Army of the Caesars* (Weidenfeld & Nicholson) 1974

GRAVES, CHARLES: *Women in Green* (William Heinemann Ltd) 1948

HERR, MICHAEL: *Dispatches* (Alfred A Knopf Inc) 1977 & (Pan Books Ltd) 1978

HICKEN, VICTOR: *The American Fighting Man* (Macmillan) 1969

HODGSON, PAT: *Early War Photographs* (Osprey) 1974 & *The War Illustrators*
    (Osprey) 1977

HORAN, JAMES D: *Matthew Brady, Historian with a Camera* (Crown) 1955

HOWARD, MAJ GEN SIR FRANCIS: *Reminiscences 1848-1890* (John Murray) 1924

INSIGHT-TEAM OF THE SUNDAY TIMES: *The Yom Kippur War*
    (Andre Deutsch) 1975

JEFFREY, HELEN M: *The Trumpet Call Obey* (Marshall, Morgan & Scott) 1968

LAFFIN, JOHN: *Tommy Atkins* (Cassell) 1968

LAWSON, C C P: *History of Uniforms of the British Army* Vol I
    (Norman Pubs) 1961

LYTTLETON, GEN SIR NEVILLE: *Eight Years Soldiering, Politics, Games,* 1927

MARCY, CAPT RANDOLPH BARNES: *The Prairie Traveller* 1859

MARWICK, ARTHUR: *Women at War 1914-18* (Fontana) 1977

MASON, PHILIP: *A Matter of Honour* (Jonathan Cape Ltd) 1974

MASTERS, JOHN: *Bugles and a Tiger* (M Joseph) 1956

MCGUFFIE T H, COMPILER: *Rank and File* (Hutchinson & Co) 1964

MILLER HARRY: *Service to the Services* (Newman Neame) 1971

MOCKLER-FERRYMAN, LT COL A F: *Regimental War Tales*
    (Slatter & Rose Ltd) 1915

OSBORNE, HONOR & MANISTY PEGGY: *A History of the Royal School for Daughters
    of Officers of the Army 1964-1965* (Hodder & Stoughton) 1966

PEDRICK, GALE: *Battledress Broadcasters* (BFBS) 1964

PERNOUD, RÉGINE: *The Crusaders* (Oliver & Boyd Ltd) translated from the
    French by Enid Grant

POTTER, ELLA, AND MATHESON, WINIFRED: *Elise Sandes & Theodora
    Schofield* (Marshall, Morgan & Scott Ltd) circa 1936

LORD ROBERTS OF KANDAHAR, VC: *Forty One years in India*
    (Macmillan & Son Ltd) 1898

ROBERTSON, PATRICK: *The Shell Book of Firsts* (Ebury Press
    & Michael Joseph Ltd) 1974

ROGERS, COL H C B: *Napoleon's Army* (Ian Allan Ltd) 1974

ROGERS, COL H C B: *Troopships and their history* (Seeley Service & Co Ltd) 1963

ROWAN, EDGAR: *Wilson Carlile and the Church Army*

RUSSELL W H: *My Indian Mutiny Diary* edited by Michael Edwards
    (Cassell & Co Ltd) 1957

SALWAY, PETER: *The Frontier People of Roman Britain* (Cambridge
    University Press) 1965

SANDES, FLORA: *Autobiography of a Woman Soldier* (H F & G Witherby) 1927

SHEPPARD, E W: *Red Coat* (Batchworth Press) 1952

SIMPSON WILLIAM: *Autobiography of William Simpson* edited by George Eyre-
    Todd (T Fisher Unwin) 1903

SOYER, ALEXIS: *A Culinary Campaign* 1857

STANFORD J K: *Ladies in the Sun* (Galley Press) 1962
TIME-LIFE BOOKS, EDITORS: *The Soldiers* (Time Life Books) 1973
TISDALL, E E P: *Mrs Duberly's Campaigns* (Jarrolds) 1963
TOC H: *In Flanders Fields* (Toc H) 1954
UTLEY, ROBERT M: *Bluecoats and Redskins* (Cassell) 1975
WATTEVILLE COL H DE: *The British Soldier* (J M Dent & Sons Ltd) 1954
WEBSTER, GRAHAM: *The Roman Army* (Grosvenor Museum, Chester) 1973
WOODS, FREDERICK, EDITOR: *Young Winston's Wars* (Leo Cooper Ltd) 1972
WOODHAM-SMITH, CECIL: *Florence Nightingale* (Constable) 1953

MAGAZINES, PAPERS AND PAMPHLETS

Armor Magazine, (Nov/Dec 1973 issue, Jan/Feb 1975 issue)
BEF Times dated 5 March 1917
British Red Cross Centenary Souvenir, *The Ceaseless Challenge*
British Red Cross Society, *The Proudest Badge*, 1972
The County Times of 17 March 1923
The Church Army Blue Book for 1916-17
Eighth Army News of 4 April 1944
Eleventh Hussar Journal, January 1922
House of Commons Report Vol 2 pub 1803
Lloyds Bank Ltd: *The Story of an Old Association*
The Listener: *Women at War, the two heroines of Pervyse*
Navy & Army Illustrated, Issues of September 1898 and 1899
Rifle Brigade Chronicle for 1897
An Introduction to SSAFA Work, SSAFA 1976
SSAFA News and Reports
The Story of NAAFI (P R Branch Handout) 1944
USO Historical Highlights 25th Anniversary Souvenir 1966
The Times newspaper 14 November 1854
Tiger Rag newssheet of 1 Royal Hants, November 1976 issue
Vista, the first fifty years of Toc H compiled by Geoffrey Martin, 1965
WRVS Information Sheets
YMCA Fact Sheets